THEY SAW IT HAPPEN
IN
CLASSICAL TIMES

THEY
SAW IT HAPPEN
IN
CLASSICAL TIMES

An Anthology
of Eye-witnesses' Accounts of
Events in the Histories of Greece and Rome
1400 B.C.-A.D. 540

Compiled by
B. K. WORKMAN
Senior Classics Master, Repton School

Maps by
C. W. JUDGE

BASIL BLACKWELL
OXFORD

First printed 1964
Reprinted 1965
"   1970
"   1973
0 631 05250 X

Printed in Great Britain for Basil Blackwell & Mott, Ltd
by Alden & Mowbray Ltd at the Alden Press, Oxford
and bound at Kemp Hall Bindery

CONTENTS

INTRODUCTION

The compilation of this collection of eye-witnesses' accounts of events in Classical Times has presented certain problems, some of which were not experienced by other editors in this series.

The most fundamental difficulty has been to counter, if possible, the accident of survival. No doubt some of the ordinary Greeks and Romans left their personal impressions of the times in which they lived. But with the exception of private epitaphs, some graffiti on the walls of Pompeii and the collections of Papyri from Egypt, all the extant classical writings are the work of literary figures. Even the letters of such men as Cicero and Pliny were written with a view to their publication. Some degree of spontaneity is therefore lacking, perhaps especially in the Greek extracts because of the inherent failing in the ancient Athenian character for theorising. The matter of survival has also robbed us of many contemporary accounts from well-known authors, such as the Greek histories of Hellanicus or the books by Tacitus on his own later years. All this leaves obvious gaps.

In addition to the survival of ancient authors, there is also the history of ancient literature itself to consider. Herodotus (fl. *c.* 445 B.C.) is the earliest extant Greek prose writer, and Cato the Censor (fl. *c.* 180 B.C.) the earliest Roman. Poets had preceded them, it is true, but in the case of Rome even these are only surviving in fragments. So we have virtually no contemporary records of Rome before Cato, although the city was traditionally founded nearly 600 years earlier. If the date of the first Olympiad is taken as the start of Greek history, then 300 years are not covered by prose writers. Some poetic excerpts have been included in this collection, but they have obvious drawbacks.

The unevenness of coverage inside the well-documented periods is a natural hazard and is reflected in the dates of the extracts. Cicero and Pliny wrote enough interesting letters to fill a volume by themselves, and yet there are no real first-hand accounts of the Battle of Marathon, Alexander, the Hannibalian Wars or the murder of Julius Caesar.

Some of the passages in this selection need a special word. With only one exception they were written by men alive during the events they purport to describe, and, in the vast majority of cases, by actual eye-witnesses. The one exception is the death of Alexander (p. 60), but I have indicated the reliability of that extract as giving an eye-witness account. A few of the extracts do not really describe events, public or private. Two of them require a separate mention—the Funeral Speech of Pericles (p. 16) and the 'Memoirs' of Augustus (p. 125). Both are rightly famous, the former for giving utterance to all that is considered most noble in the 'Glory that was Greece', and the latter for being a unique testimony from the leading world-figure of his time. Both are long, but it seemed wrong to cut them short.

With two exceptions (pp. 1, 88) I have translated all the passages myself. The only reason I can give is that I enjoyed doing so, in spite of the knowledge that many excellent translations are now coming onto the market. Apologies are needed for the piece of doggerel on page 167, but it can only be said that much more of the pith of the poem would be lost in a prose translation. In no case have I tried to write a 'crib'. Though always striving for accuracy, I have not hesitated to take certain liberties if English idiom did not permit a literal translation.

Technical terms, especially those of finance, are notoriously difficult, and I have followed an inconsistent line. Where the sense and understanding were not impaired, the ancient terms, like Council, Centurion or Denarius, have been retained. But there are instances where the whole interpretation depends on a knowledge of these terms, and in these I have given modern equivalents. The Greek Talent can be assessed at anything between £250 and £2 million by various methods. The safest guide that can be given is that the pay for a Greek soldier in 350 B.C. was a drachma a day, and for the Roman soldier in A.D. 14 was a denarius. The actual tables of value were:

Greek: 6 obols = 1 drachma, 100 drachmas = 1 mna, 60 mnas = 1 talent.

Roman: 4 asses = 1 sesterce, 4 sesterces = 1 denarius.

Personal names are another ever-recurring problem. I have followed a usual but inconsistent policy in transliterating the majority, while printing an anglicized version of some which are better known. I hope that professional historians will accept these solecisms.

On pages 213 and 214 will be found two very simplified charts of the main events and periods in the histories of Greece and Rome. I hope they may prove useful to those unacquainted with the outline history behind the extracts. They do not pretend to give any details, which can be found from the histories given below.

A last word. It was difficult to know quite when to bring Classical Times to an end. The usual date given for the end of the Western Empire is A.D. 476, though Alaric's sack of Rome in 410 is another very suitable terminus. I have continued to the time of Justinian. His name in jurisprudence, the fact that he was the last Latin-speaking Emperor and the closing sentence of the Procopius's extract all seemed to make it a fitting climax to the Decline and Fall of Rome.

FURTHER READING

In the separate lists under extracts I have usually omitted references to certain standard works. In almost every case they may be consulted with advantage. Some of these are:

General History: *A History of Greece* by J. Bury (rev. R. Meiggs)
A History of Greece by N. G. L. Hammond
A History of Rome by M. Cary

Shorter Histories: *The Greeks* by H. D. F. Kitto
The Romans by R. H. Barrow
The Ancient World by T. R. Glover

Companions, etc.: *A Companion to Greek Studies* (ed. L. Whibley)
A Companion to Latin Studies (ed. J. E. Sandys)
Smith's Dictionary of Classical Biography
Smith's Dictionary of Classical Antiquities
The Oxford Classical Dictionary
The Legacy of Greece

Companions, etc.   *The Legacy of Rome*
(*contd.*):   *The Greeks* (ed. Hugh Lloyd-Jones)
               The Civilization of Rome by P. Grimal (trans.
               W. S. Maguinness)

and in a lighter vein:

    Greeks ⎱ both by Michael Grant, wittily illustrated
    Romans ⎰ by D. Pottinger

In other cases I have tried to mention only books, in English, which are reasonably accessible in paper-back editions or most libraries. I have usually referred to chapters in the *Cambridge Ancient History* (*C.A.H.* throughout) and in the later pieces to Gibbon's *Decline and Fall of the Roman Empire*, which deserves to be widely read.

ACKNOWLEDGEMENTS

I have used the text in the Oxford Classical Texts for all possible authors. In the absence of an Oxford text, I have translated that printed in the Loeb series. My thanks are due to the Oxford University Press and to Heinemann & Sons for this permission. In particular I have leaned heavily on the text and interpretation of various Papyri in the two volumes of *Select Papyri* in the Loeb series, which were edited and translated by A. S. Hunt and C. C. Edgar. I am also grateful to the Syndics of the Cambridge University Press and to Mr. John Chadwick for permission to quote from *Documents in Mycenaean Greek*, and to William Heinemann and E. H. Warmington to quote from *Remains of Old Latin*, Vol. IV.

LIFE AT PYLOS
c. 1400 B.C.

The excavations by Sir Arthur Evans at Cnossus in Crete in 1900 revealed the presence of tablets with three different styles of writing on them. Further tablets with the latest of these scripts (the so-called Linear B) were found on the Greek Mainland, especially at Pylos, the home of the Homeric Nestor. Linear B was deciphered by Michael Ventris in 1953 and shown beyond reasonable doubt to be an early form of Greek. The tablets are non-literary, and mostly contain lists of personnel, crops, etc. But much can be gathered of the social life of the times from them. The three quoted here show something of the organization of labour, a possible naval operation, and the dues paid to a god. The sum of the tablets does much to supplement the poems of Homer.

Source: Documents in Mycenaean Greek, by Michael Ventris and John Chadwick (C.U.P.), nos. 52, 53 and 171.

Further Reading: The above book contains introductions and a translation of 300 tablets. Chadwick has also written *The Decipherment of Linear B* (now in a Pelican edition). Many books are now being written on the subject, perhaps the most important being by L. R. Palmer, *Mycenaeans and Minoans* and *The Interpretation of Mycenaean Greek Texts*. Books which link up the tablets with Homer include D. L. Page's *History and the Homeric Iliad*, and *From Mycenae to Homer* by T. B. L. Webster. Translations of Homer are numerous, the most accessible being in the Penguin Classics by E. V. Rieu.

1. [A list of tradesmen. Each group has an adjective describing their origin, which is omitted here. Some of the trades are not certain.]

Cutlers	2 Men
Binders	2 Men
Potters	2 Men
Temple-servants	12 Men
Wine-pourers	10 Men
Goldsmiths	4 Men
Bow-makers	5 Men
Tailors	? Men
Tailors	? Men

Tailors	? Men
Tailors	? Men
Tailors	20 Men

2. [A possible naval expedition and recruitment of sailors. Most of the places are uncertain and are here printed in a non-Greek form.]

Rowers to go to Pleuron: eight from Roowa, five from Rhion, four from Pora, six from Tetarane, seven from Aponewe.

3. [Ritual offerings to Poseidon.]

The ?lands to Poseidon, its contribution.

As far as one can see, Ekhelawon will give so much as a contribution: 480 litres wheat, 108 litres wine, one bull, ten cheeses, one sheepskin, 6 litres honey.

And similarly the village will give: 240 litres wheat, 72 litres wine, two rams, five cheeses, 4 litres fat, one sheepskin.

And the military leader will give so much: two rams, 72 litres flour, 24 litres wine.

And similarly the estate of the cult association will give: 72 litres wheat, 11 litres wine, five cheeses, 14 litres honey.

THE PERILS OF THE SEA
c. 700 B.C.

Not much is known about Hesiod and his brother, Perses, apart from what we gather here. Even his dates are very uncertain. He lived in Boeotia, which was later the butt of other Greeks as producing slow-witted farmers. The essential agricultural nature of the Boeotians' livelihood may have had something to do with Hesiod's fear of the sea. But this, and the extract from the Acts of the Apostles (page 148), underlines the perilous nature of ancient navigation.

Source: Hesiod, *Works and Days*, ll. 618 ff.

Further Reading: Loeb translation by H. G. E. White. For sailing, see L. Casson, *The Ancient Mariners.* For Hesiod's times, *Cambridge Ancient History* Vol. III, chs. xxiv and xxv by M. Cary and J. L. Myres. For Hesiod in Literature, see the chapters in Gilbert Murray's *The Literature of Ancient Greece* and H. J. Rose's *Handbook of Greek Literature*; also *C.A.H.* vol. IV, ch. xiv, by J. R. Bury.

If you are afflicted with the desire for uncomfortable travelling over the sea, then remember that the blasts of all the winds rage when the Pleiades flee before the mighty strength of Orion and set in the misty deep. At such a time, keep your boats no longer in the wine-dark sea, but be mindful to work the soil as I bid you. Drag up your boat on the land, and pack it tightly around with stones to withstand the damp force of the gusting winds, taking out the plug so that the rain of heaven may not rot it. Put all the fitted tackle in your home, folding carefully the sails of the ship that travels the deep. Hang the well-made tiller above the smoke of the fire.

You yourself wait for a journey till the proper season comes. Then pull your swift boat down to the water, and load in it a fitting cargo, that you may bring home profit, just as my father and yours, foolish Perses, did, as he sailed far over the sea in his dark ship, leaving Cume in Aeolis. He fled not from abundance, riches and wealth, but from the evil poverty which Zeus gives to men. He came to live near Helicon in a dreadful village, Ascra, which is harsh in winter and stifling in summer, never good.

And you, Perses, remember the proper season for all work, especially that concerned with sea-faring. Give your praises to small boats, but put your goods in a large one. The cargo is greater and the gain will be greater too, if the winds keep their evil blasts away. Whenever you turn your senseless heart to merchandising and wish to escape debts and joyless poverty, I, though not very skilled in sea-faring or in ships, will show you the measures of the loud-resounding sea. I have never sailed on the broad sea in a boat except to Euboea from Aulis, where once the Achaeans waited for the storm when they raised a mighty host from holy Greece against Troy, fair in women. I was crossing over to Chalcis to the games of great-hearted Amphidamas. . . .

The right season for mortals to sail is fifty days after the solstice, when the burdensome days of summer come to an end. At that time you will not wreck your ship, nor will the sea destroy the men, unless the Earth-Shaker Poseidon desires it or Zeus, king of the immortals, wishes to destroy them. For in the gods is the end of good and bad alike. The winds then are easy to judge and the sea is free from blame. In those days entrust your swift ship to the winds without worry, drag it into the sea, and, putting all your cargo on it, hasten to come back home again quickly. But do not wait for the time of the new wine and the harvest showers, the coming of winter and the terrible blasts of the North Wind which accompany the heavy autumnal rain of Zeus, stirring up the sea and making it difficult.

Spring is another time for mortals to sail. When the fig-leaf first appears on the branch as big as the mark that a crow makes in the ground, then the sea can be crossed. This is the spring time for sailing. But I do not praise it and it is not pleasant to my heart, for it is a time which is stolen. Hardly would you escape evil. But men do even this in the senselessness of their hearts, for money is dear to wretched men. It is horrible to die in the waves. I bid you take thought of all these things in your heart. Do not put all your livelihood in hollow ships, but leave more behind, putting less on board. Dreadful it is to meet misfortune in the waves of the sea; dreadful, too, if you put an over-heavy weight on your wagon, break your axle, and spoil your load. Keep to moderation. The right time is the best time.

PATRIOTISM
c. 650 B.C.

About 660 B.C. the Spartans launched the Second Messenian War against their Western neighbours. They needed the rich plain of Messenia, and also Messenian slaves who formed in later years a large percentage of their Helot population. No contemporary account remains of the actual fighting, but the Spartan poet Tyrtaeus has left us this clarion call to arms, with its hints of conscientious objectors and displaced persons.

Source: Tyrtaeus, in *Oxford Book of Greek Verse*, poem 97.

Further Reading: A History of Greece by N. G. L. Hammond gives a general account. Specialist books on Sparta are by W. den Boer, G. L. Huxley and K. M. T. Grimes. For the constitution of Sparta see Xenophon's *Constitution*, translated by E. C. Marchant, in the Loeb series. H. T. Wade-Gery wrote the chapter in *C.A.H.* vol. III, ch. xxii.

Glorious it is for a good man to die fighting for his country in the front rank of battle. But for a man to desert his city and rich lands and to play the beggar is of all things most accursed, if he wanders abroad with his old father and mother, his little children and young wife. A burden will he be to those to whom he comes, a victim to beggary and harsh poverty. He brings shame on his family and disgraces his fair reputation. Dishonour and utter ruin follow. If, then, no help comes to such a wanderer, no memory thereafter of his family, let us in good spirit fight for this land, let us fight for our children, sparing not our souls.

Young men, stand by each other and fight. Set no example of flight or fear, which bring shame, but make the hearts in your breasts strong and courageous, taking no thought of your lives as you fight with men. Do not flee and leave behind the veterans, men older than you, whose limbs are no longer supple. Disgraceful it is for an older man, with white head and grey beard, to fall and lie dead in front of a younger man, breathing out his valiant spirit in the dust, clutching his bloody stomach in his hands, with his flesh bared. Shameful it is for the eye and dreadful to see. But all this is fair enough for a young man, while he has the possession of the glorious flower of his lovely youth. Men wonder to behold him, and women love him while he lives, and his death as he falls in the front rank is noble. But let a man press on and suffer hardship with both feet firmly planted on the ground, biting his lips to stifle the pain.

ATHENS
594 B.C.

Solon was the founder of Athenian democracy, as well as being a poet. He was called upon to bring order into the chaos caused by the break-up of the old feudal state.

Source: Solon, poem quoted by Demosthenes in *On the Embassy*, 255.

Further Reading: Aristotle's *Athenian Constitution* is translated in the Loeb series by H. Rackham. *The History of the Athenian Constitution* by

C. Hignett is the fullest commentary on Solon and the future changes. It is slightly partisan. *C.A.H.* vol. IV, ch. ii, is by F. E. Adcock, and A. R. Burn devotes some space in *The Lyric Age of Greece*.

In accordance with the fate ordained by Zeus and the will of the blessed immortal gods, our city will never be destroyed. For Pallas Athene, daughter of a mighty father, keeps her hands over it as a keen and loyal watch. It is the citizens themselves who want to destroy it in their foolishness, corrupted as they are by money. The minds of the leaders of the people are lawless; they are ready that the people should suffer great grief from their sinful conduct. For they do not understand how to be satisfied with what is enough, nor how to keep their present sense of decorum in quiet enjoyment. Yet they grow rich in the lawlessness of their actions. They spare no sacred or public possessions, but steal and seize from each other. Nor do they abide by the holy ordinances of Justice, who sits in silence with the knowledge of past and present alike and has always come in time to bring punishment on the guilty.

This is now the incurable wound that has afflicted the whole city, and she has quickly come into evil slavery. It has woken up tribal dissension and war, once asleep, that has destroyed many men in their lovely prime. For the charming city is wasted away by her enemies in conspiracies dear only to wicked men. These are the public wrongs that are happening. Many of the poor have gone to foreign lands, sold and bound to shameless masters. This public evil has come into each man's home. The walls can no longer hold it out, but it leaps over the high fence and finds man out everywhere, even if he flees to hide in the innermost nook of his room.

My heart bids me tell the Athenians this, that lawlessness provides hosts of misfortunes for the city, but good laws make everything pleasant and wholesome to see. They put chains on the wicked, smooth down the rough, put an end to excess, cast arrogance to oblivion. They dry up the flourishing flowers of ruin, make straight the crooked paths of justice, temper overweening actions. Lastly, they make an end of the works of discord and the anger that comes from bitter strife. Everything under the rule of good laws becomes whole and clean.

LETTER OF DARIUS
c. 510 B.C.

Darius was King of Persia from 521 to 486 B.C. On the Behistun inscription there is a rather impersonal record of some of his achievements. This letter, if genuine, gives a more intimate picture of his relationships with one of his satraps or district governors. The precise date is unknown.

Source: Tod, *Greek Historical Inscriptions,* 10.

Further Reading: For the reign of Darius, see *Persia and the West* by A. R. Burn and also *C.A.H.* vol. IV, ch. vii, by G. B. Gray and M. Cary.

Darius, son of Hystaspes, King of Kings, to his servant Gadatas:

I hear that you are not obeying my instructions in all respects. In so far as you are cultivating my lands and planting fruit-trees to the west of the Euphrates in Asia Minor, I praise you for your attention, and you will receive great thanks in the royal palace. But in so far as you are disregarding my ordinance about the gods, I will grant you experience of my wrath when wronged, unless you amend your ways. For you have exacted tribute from the sacred gardeners of Apollo and have ordered them to dig profane ground, disobeying the intention of my forebears towards the gods.

THE BATTLE OF SALAMIS
480 B.C.

Xerxes' invasion of Greece was briefly checked at Thermopylae, but the first main engagement was fought at Salamis. Aeschylus is thought to have taken part in the battle, and eight years later he wrote a play, *Persae*, in which news of the disaster is brought to the Persian Court. The following is a messenger's speech to the Queen Mother.

Source: Aeschylus, *Persae*, ll. 353 ff.

Further Reading: Loeb translation by H. Weir Smyth, Penguin translation by P. Vellacott. Different interpretations of the battle are found in J. L. Myres's *Herodotus, Father of History,* A. R. Burn's *Persia and the West* and C. Hignett's *Xerxes' Invasion of Greece.* The *C.A.H.*

account is by J. A. R. Munro in vol. IV, ch. ix. On Aeschylus, read
Gilbert Murray's *Aeschylus: The Creator of Tragedy* and other histories
of literature.

Your Majesty, it was at the appearance of some avenging
fury or evil spirit that the whole tragedy began. A Greek came
from the Athenian fleet to tell your son, Xerxes, that the Greeks
would not remain when the shades of darkest night came on, but,
sitting on the benches of their ships, would each try indepen-
dently to save his life in secret flight. Xerxes did not realize that
the Greek was tricking him nor that the gods were planning his
destruction. So immediately he heard the news, he gave orders
to all his captains. When the sun's rays stopped lighting up the
earth and darkness stole over the empire of the sky, they must
draw up their massed ships in three squadrons. Some must
encircle Ajax's isle (Salamis) to guard the exit and the sea-beaten
straits. In this way, if the Greeks tried to escape their fate, finding
some means of flight in secret on their ships, it was sure that all
power of doing so would be denied them. These were his orders
in the confidence of his heart, for he did not understand the
future that the gods held in store. His sailors obeyed his orders
and prepared their evening meal in good discipline, while all the
shipwrights fitted the blades in the shaped rowlocks.

When the light of the sun vanished and night came on, each
man, master of his oar, went on board, and each marine as well.
Rank called to rank among the ships of the line as they sailed
on their appointed course. All night long the captains kept the
whole fleet moving. But when night drew to its close, nowhere
had the Greeks attempted stealthily to break away. Indeed, when
the white horses of day bathed all the earth in light and made
things clear to see, then the strains of a hymn rang tunefully from
the Greeks, and the answering echo came straight back from the
island cliffs. Fear came upon all the Persian fleet when they
realized that they were mistaken, for the sacred hymn which the
Greeks were singing did not suggest flight, but betokened men
about to rush into battle with emboldened hearts. A trumpet
with its bray enflamed the Greeks where they lay at anchor, and
dipping at once their oars in the surf, they struck the deep brine
of the sea in time. All were soon easy to see, the right wing

leading the van in good order, followed by the rest who came out after them in line astern. We could hear a great shout arise: 'Come, sons of Greece, free your country, free your children, your wives, the altars of your ancestral gods, free the tombs of your fathers. Our fight is now for very life itself.' An answering burst of sound in the Persian tongue broke from us. Passed now was the hour for holding back.

Straightway ship struck ship with brazen beak. The attack was started by a Greek ship which sheared off the whole prow of her Phoenician foe, and others aimed their onslaught on different opponents. At first the flood-tide of the Persian fleet held its own. But when the ships became jammed and crushed in one place, they could bring no help to each other. Ships began to strike their own friends with their bronze-jawed rams, and to shatter the whole bank of oars. The Greek ships, in careful plan, pressed round on us in a circle, and ships' hulls gave in. You could no longer see the water, so full was it of wrecked vessels and dead men, while the beaches and rocks were thick with corpses. Each Persian ship now rowed in chaos for flight, every one of the whole invading force. The Greeks attacked and caught them up like tunny or some other fish in a net, tangled with broken oars and pieces of wreckage. A piteous cry covered the sea, until sight was removed by blackest night. I could not recount in detail the whole mass of our misfortunes, no, not if I were to speak for ten whole days on end. But this you may know, that never has one day seen the death of half so many men. . . .

Those most naturally brave among the Persians, most courageous and most noble of birth, and most loyal to their lord, they died most horribly in a fate that is painful to tell. . . . There is an islet near Salamis, rugged and without anchorage for ships. Here Pan walks on the sea-shore, the god who delights in the country dance. Xerxes sent his bravest there to kill at their ease any members of the Greek fleet who had lost their ships and swum to land to safety. They could also save their friends from the paths of the waters. But he judged the future ill. For, when the Greeks received from god the glorious victory in the naval fight, they clad their bodies in good bronze armour and leapt on shore, surrounding the islet so that our men had nowhere to turn. Many were killed by stones hurled by hand, and arrows from the twanging bowstring fell fast on others, dealing death. Finally the enemy rushed forward in one surge, hacking and killing all the luckless men. There was a cry from Xerxes as he saw the depth of this calamity from the spot where he was sitting, on a high cliff at the sea's edge, visible to all the fleet. Tearing his clothes, he screamed out shrilly, bidding the land forces retreat, then fled in panicked flight himself. For this second disaster, not just the first, your tears are called.

EGYPTIAN EMBALMING
c. 450 B.C.

Herodotus, the 'Father of History', was an inveterate traveller. In his search for the causes of the Persian Wars, he visited most of the districts of the Persian Empire, and carefully noted down the customs and past history of the places. As a historian he was quite ready to give alternative interpretations of events, but did not always show good judgement in his final choice. It is unfortunate that he was a poor military historian, for that was clearly the central part of his story. But he had not been present at any of the battles (he was born in 484 B.C., six years after Marathon and four years before Salamis), and his value lies in his passionate interest in antiquities.

Source: Herodotus, II, 86.

Further Reading: Loeb translation by A. D. Godley, Penguin translation by A. de Selincourt. There are pictures and descriptions in *A Picture History of Archaeology* by C. W. Ceram. R. W. Macan writes on Herodotus in *C.A.H.* vol. V, ch. xiv.

The embalmers, when a corpse is brought to them, show the relatives wooden models of dead bodies, as accurate as a painting. They say that the most perfect of these images belongs to a god whose name I consider it sacrilege to mention in this connection. They also show a second, slightly inferior to the first and less expensive, and a third as well, the cheapest of the lot. After the demonstration, they ask the relatives in which style they want the corpse prepared. The latter agree on a price and go off home, but the embalmers stay in their workshops and use the following method for the most expensive style.

First, they remove the brain through the nostrils with a curved iron implement, getting some of it out like this and the rest by pouring in solvents. Then they cut open the side of the corpse with a sharp Ethiopian stone, remove the intestines, and wash out the belly, cleaning it with palm wine and again with pounded aromatics. They fill up the body with pure crushed myrrh, cassia and other herbs (except frankincense) and sow it up again. After this, they pickle the body in natrum, hiding it away for seventy days, the longest time possible. After the seventy days, they wash the body and wrap it up completely in cut bandages of linen muslin, smearing it with gum which the Egyptians use instead of glue. The relatives then get the body back and make a man-sized wooden image, into which they insert the mummy and then store it away in a burial chamber, standing it upright against the wall.

That is the most expensive way. The method for those wanting the middle way, to escape great expense, is as follows. They pack syringes with cedar-oil and fill the stomach of the corpse with the oil, not cutting it open and taking out the intestines, but inserting the oil through the anus and stopping it flowing out. Then they soak the body in spices for the prescribed number of days, on the last of which they remove from the belly the cedar-oil which they put in before. This has such strength that it brings out with it all the dissolved stomach and intestines. The natrum dissolves the flesh and only the skin and bones are left. When this is over, they return the body, their job completed.

The third method of embalming is the one used by the poorer classes. They just wash out the inside with a solvent, then pickle it for seventy days and return it to the relatives.

EGYPTIAN CROCODILES
c. 450 B.C.

Herodotus describes all aspects of Egyptian life, sometimes, as in the case of the Pyramids, with annoying obscurity. He notices many details of Egyptian religion which must have mystified the Greek with his anthropomorphic gods. Mummified crocodiles have survived, together with mummies of cats and other animals.

Source: Herodotus, II, 68.

Further Reading: Loeb translation by A. D. Godley, Penguin translation by A. de Selincourt. *A Picture History of Archaeology* shows illustrations of mummified animals.

The crocodile is a four-footed land and marsh creature which
eats nothing for the four winter months. It lays its eggs on the
bank, where it leaves them, spends most of the day on dry-land
and the whole of the night in the river, for the water is warmer
than the clear open sky and the dew. We know of no animal
which starts so small and grows so large. The eggs it lays are
not much bigger than those of a goose, and the young crocodile
is proportionate in size to the egg, but it grows to a length of
twenty-seven feet or more. It has pig-like eyes, and large tusk-
like teeth to match its body. It is the only animal to have no
tongue. It does not move its lower jaw, but is again the only
animal to bring its upper jaw down on to the lower. It has strong
claws and a scaly skin, unpierceable over its back. It is blind in
the water, but very sharp-sighted out of it. As it spends so much
time in the water, its mouth is quite full of leeches. All birds and
animals avoid it, except the sandpiper which makes itself useful
and so has a covenant with it. When the crocodile climbs out of
the water and lies with its mouth wide open (which it normally
does facing the west), then the bird hops into its mouth and eats
up the leeches. The crocodile is pleased with this assistance and
does the bird no harm.

Some of the Egyptians hold the crocodile as sacred, but others
do not, and hunt it as an enemy. Those that live in the neighbourhood of Thebes and the lake of Moeris consider it to be extremely
sacred. Each community rears one crocodile which is trained to
come to hand; they put glass and gold ornaments on its ears and
bracelets on its front feet, giving it special food and divine
offerings, and treating it extremely well as long as it lives. On its
death it is embalmed and placed in sacred coffins. But the inhabitants of the city of Elephantine do not think of them as sacred,
and even eat them. . . .

There are all sorts of methods of hunting them. I will just
describe the one that seems to me to be the cleverest. They bait
a hook with a pig's chine and float it in the middle of the river.

Then they hold a live pig on the bank and beat it. The crocodile hears the pig's squeals and makes for the sound. Coming across the chine, it gobbles it down; whereupon the hunters drag it ashore. When it has been brought to land, they first of all smear its eyes with mud. You can easily despatch a crocodile if you do that first, but only with considerable difficulty if you do not.

ATHENIAN IMPERIALISM
445 B.C.

After the Persian wars a confederacy was founded based on Delos, to further the war against Persia. But with the withdrawal of Sparta and the decrease in the Persian threat, Athens quickly dominated the League, and it rapidly became her Empire. This inscription, one of several on the same topic, regulates relations with Chalcis in Euboea after a revolt had been put down in the previous year.

Source: Tod, *Greek Historical Inscriptions*, 42.

Further Reading: A. E. Zimmern's *The Greek Commonwealth* is still the best book on fifth-century Athens. A short, readable history of the times is by A. R. Burn in *Pericles and Athens*. Chapters in *C.A.H.* are in vol. V, chs. i–iv and vii, by M. N. Tod, E. M. Walker and F. E. Adcock.

Decree of the Council and People
(Duty-tribe, Antiochis; President, Dracontides; Proposer, Diognetos)

Moved:

1. That the Council and Jury Panels of the Athenians should take the following oath:

'I will not exile any Chalcidians from Chalcis, nor upset their internal management. I will not declare any private individual outlawed, I will not punish him with banishment, nor arrest him, nor execute him, nor sequester his property, without fair trial and without the approval of the Athenian People. I will support no measure against their community at large, or any member of it, unless they are represented.

I promise to bring before the Council and People any deputation that comes from Chalcis during my term of office, within
ten days if possible. This I guarantee to the Chalcidians
subject to their loyalty to the Athenian People.'

2. That the Athenians should make a deputation from Chalcis
take an oath in front of the proper officials, and that a list
should be made of those who have taken the oath. The generals
are to be responsible that all take the oath. The Chalcidians
must bind themselves as follows:

'I will not defect from the Athenian People by trick or guile,
in word or in deed, nor will I side with anyone who does
defect. And if anyone does revolt, I will inform the Athenians.
I will pay to the Athenians the tribute that is agreed between
us, and I will, to the best of my ability, be a good and loyal
ally. I will assist and defend the Athenian People if anyone
injures the Athenian People and, I will obey the Athenian
People.'

All adult Chalcidians must take this oath. Anyone refusing
to do so is to be declared outlaw, his property is to be confiscated, and 10% of the value to be dedicated to Zeus Olympios.

3. That an Athenian deputation should go to Chalcis, and in
front of the proper officials there in Chalcis should list all the
Chalcidians who take the oath.

[There follows a rider moved by Anticles which tables several
additional points.]

Rider by Archestratos: That Anticles' proposal should stand.
But with regard to court cases for the Chalcidians, they should
have the power of trying their own cases as have the Athenians
in Athens, except in trials involving exile, death or outlawry. In
these cases there should be appeal to Athens to the Court of the
Thesmothetae in accordance with the decree of the People. Also
the generals must make such provisions as they can for the
defence of Euboea in the best interests of the Athenian People.

BUILDING ACCOUNTS AT ATHENS
440–433 B.C.

One of the original aims of the Delian League had been to rebuild the temples destroyed by the Persians in 480 B.C. From 448 B.C. vast sums of money were spent on the Acropolis towards the Parthenon, Propylaia and the chryselephantine statue of Athene.

The total spent on the statue was probably in excess of 700 talents. The inscription here shows income and expenditure for one year, and shows the relative values of gold and silver as being 14 : 1.

The account for the Parthenon is for the year 434–433 B.C., just before it was completed. So the sums seem very small. The total cost is unknown, but the figure of 2,000 talents is mentioned by one historian. It is impossible to be certain of some of the figures in this inscription. Those printed here with dots in front of them are absolute minimums.

Source: Tod, *Greek Historical Inscriptions,* 47 and 52.

Further Reading: The best books on Architecture and Sculpture are *Greek Architecture* by A. W. Lawrence and *Greek Sculpture* by R. Lullies and M. Hirmer. On Greek Art in general, see J. D. Beazley in *C.A.H.* vol. V, ch. xv, and for economic conditions in Athens, see Zimmern's *Greek Commonwealth* and Tod's chapter in *C.A.H.* vol. V.

(a) *Statue of Athene, c.* 440 B.C.

Kichesippos was Secretary to the Council. Myrrhinousios was Superintendent of the Statue. Received from the Stewards, of whom Demostratos was Secretary—100 talents. The Stewards were Ctesion, Strosias, Antiphates, Menandros, Thymochares, Smokordos, Pheideleides.

(*Weight*)	(*Cost, in silver*)
Gold bought: 6 talents 1618 drachmas 3 obols	87 tal. 4652 drr. 5 obb.
Ivory bought: (approx. 23 talents)	2 tal. 743 drr.

(b) *The Parthenon,* 434–3 B.C.

Crates was Archon at Athens; the fourteenth year of construction, in which Metagenes was the first Secretary to the Council.

Accounts presented by the Superintendents (of whom Anticles was Secretary) for the current year, as follows:

Receipts:

Brought forward from pre-	
vious year	1470 drachmas
	70 Gold Lampsacene Staters
	27 1/6th Gold Cyzicene Staters
Received from the Stewards	
of the Goddess (Secretary—	
Crates)	25,000 drachmas
from gold sold	
(weight: 98 drachmas)	1,372 drachmas
from ivory sold	
(weight: 2 talents 60	
drachmas)	2,305 drachmas 4 obols

Expenses:

Purchases:	...404 drachmas 1 obol
Wages:	
— to quarriers and transpor-	
ters of stone at Mt. Pen-	
telicus	...2,426 drachmas 2 obols
— to sculptors, year's pay	16,392 drachmas
— to monthly salaries	1,800 drachmas
Carried forward from this year:	... drachmas
	70 Gold Lampsacene Staters
	27 1/6th Gold Cyzicene Staters

FUNERAL AT ATHENS
431 B.C.

The Peloponnesian War, fought between Athens and Sparta, started in the Spring of 431 B.C. Tension had been mounting for years, and the increasing power and arrogance of Athens was bound to lead to war. Thucydides must have been present at the scene which he describes here. The speech which he puts into the mouth of Pericles is the noblest expression of what Athenians of the Golden Age thought of their city. It is all the more poignant because these high ideals were destined to be abandoned even before Sparta emerged victorious in 404 B.C.

Source: Thucydides, II, 34.

Further Reading: Loeb translation by C. F. Smith, Penguin translation by Rex Warner. Of a host of books on Periclean Athens, A. R. Burn's *Pericles and Athens* is short and precise, Zimmern's *Greek Commonwealth* full and interesting, and A. Bonnard's *Greek Civilization* provocative. Other general books include A. H. M. Jones's *Athenian Democracy* to contrast with H. Michell's *Sparta,* and C. M. Bowra's *The Greek Experience.*

During the same winter, the Athenians followed their time-honoured custom in giving a public funeral for the first casualties of the war. The bones of the dead are laid out for three days under a canopy, and offerings are brought by relatives if they so desire. When the day of interment comes, ten coffins, made of cypress wood, one for each tribe, are taken out on carriages. Every man's bones are in the coffin of his tribe. There is one empty bier, covered in a shroud, for the missing whose bodies could not be found and brought home. Anyone, citizen or foreigner alike, may accompany the procession, and the women-folk related to the dead stand by the grave in mourning. The bones are buried in the public cemetery in the most beautiful suburb of the city. All war victims are buried there with the exception of the heroes of Marathon, whose valour was con-sidered quite unique and who were buried on the field of battle. At the end of the interment, a man of wisdom and high reputation is chosen by the community to speak a fitting eulogy over the dead. This brings the funeral to an end. This was their custom, and they followed it throughout the war whenever the occasion demanded it.

On this first day, the man chosen to speak was Pericles, the son of Xanthippus. When the moment came, he stepped forward onto a specially prepared rostrum, so that his voice would carry as far as possible, and said:

'Most of the previous speakers on this occasion have praised the man who first thought of the idea of this speech, saying how right it was for it to be delivered at the funeral of those killed in war. But it seems to me that sufficent honour is paid to men who have proved themselves valiant in action by our actions to-day, in the public preparations for this funeral which you now see. I feel, too, that it is wrong to risk the virtues of many in the words of one single man, who may speak well or badly. It is hard to talk adequately of things in which it is difficult to achieve clear demonstration of the truth. Those of my audience who know the facts and are well-disposed towards the dead will perhaps think that my remarks fall somewhat short of what they know and what they wish to hear, while the ignorant, in their jealousy, will feel that certain things have been exaggerated, if they hear anything beyond their own ability. The praise accorded to others is bearable just so far as a man can believe that he too is capable of doing what he hears being praised. Anything more than this arouses jealousy and disbelief. But, since those of old decided that this was a good custom, I must obey the law, and try, as best I may, to meet the desire and true opinions of you all.

I will start first with our ancestors, for it is right and fitting at the present time to pay them this honour of remembering them. For they were always independent and received this land from their forebears, handing it down, by their courage, in all its freedom to the present day. Praise is due to them, and even more to your fathers who, in addition to what they inherited, increased with great efforts the extent of the empire we now own, and left it to us who are alive to-day. Those of us of full years who are still here increased its size and made the city sufficiently well provided in everything, for peace or war. I will omit the exploits of valour which won for us each of our possessions, and the times when we or our fathers eagerly repelled the attacks of Greek or barbarian; for I do not want to dwell at length on matters known to you all. My first aim will be to show the sort of training which has enabled us to reach our present state, the type of constitution and customs that have made us great; only then will I proceed to the praise of these men. For I do not think it inappropriate at the present time for these things to be recalled, and it seems beneficial for the whole crowd of citizens and aliens alike to hear of them.

The constitution we employ does not try to copy the laws of our neighbours. We do not imitate them, but serve rather as an example to them. Because arrangements are not in the hands of the few but of the many, its name is Democracy. In private differences, each man has an equal status in law, but in his public reputation he is preferred according to his ability, with consideration paid not to his class but to his individual merit. In terms of wealth and poverty, if a man can do some service to the state, he is not debarred by obscurity of position. Our public life is regulated with freedom, and in the mutual suspicion of our day to day dealings we are not angry with our neighbour if pleasure is his guide, nor do we inflict on him gloomy looks, which are so unpleasant to see even if they do no actual injury. Our private relationships are thus free from offence, and in our public conduct we abide by the laws mainly from respect, in obedience to those in power at the time and to the laws themselves, especially those of them which were passed to help the wronged and the unwritten laws which bring that dishonour on which we all agree.

We have fashioned for our minds many relaxations from work, in the establishment of games and festivals throughout the year, and also by the beauty of our private homes. Our daily pleasure in them drives care away. Because of the size of the city, products are imported from all over the world; goods produced at home fill us with an enjoyment no more personal than those of other men.

We differ from our opponents in our training for war. We have an open city, and there has never been a time when we have excluded anyone by alien acts from learning or seeing anything which might benefit one of our enemies if it were not concealed. We trust to our own valour in action rather than to preparation and acts of deceit. Our opponents acquire bravery through education and a wearisome discipline from an early age; but we, who live less restricted lives, can face comparable dangers with a spirit equal to theirs. The Spartans invade our land not by themselves but with all their allies, but we are alone when we attack the land of our neighbours. Yet, though we are fighting against men who are defending their own homes, we usually win with ease. No enemy has ever yet met our whole combined power, because of our attention to the sea and the number of our land expeditions. So they encounter just a part of our forces; if they defeat them, they boast that they have worsted us all, while if they suffer defeat, they claim to have been worsted by us all. We wish to meet dangers by ease of life rather than by training and discipline, with bravery established not by law but by custom. So we have the advantage of not worrying about future events, and when we meet them, of appearing just as bold as those perpetually in training. This is one of many respects in which our city deserves to be regarded.

We love beauty without luxury and wisdom without softness. We employ our wealth more as an aid to action than as a subject for boasting. We do not think it disgraceful for anyone to be poor; much more disgrace is attached to those who do not try to escape poverty by hard work. It is possible for the same men to care for public and private duties, and in spite of varying occupations to be fully acquainted with politics. We are the only people who consider a man who takes no share of public duties not as lazy but as useless, and the self-same citizens also form judgements and sound opinions about what should be done. We do not consider argument a hindrance to action, which seems rather to be impeded by no previous discussion. We, too, are unique in both doing the acts of daring and in closely considering what we will attempt; in others ignorance brings boldness, and deliberation fear. Men are rightly held to be greatest of soul who know most soundly the boundaries of pleasure and pain, and for that reason do not shrink from danger. As regards humanity, we are again different from most, for we gain our friends by conferring benefits, not by receiving them. The man who acts thus is more sure to keep alive the gratitude, as if the one on whom he had conferred the benefit owed him a debt of kindness. But the man who should be grateful is the duller friend, knowing that he will be returning the benefit, not as a favour but in settlement of a debt. We do not reckon up our personal advantages in conferring these benefits, but have a fearless trust in our freedom.

In short I say that the whole city is the school of Greece. With us, each particular person can with ease show himself self-sufficient in most aspects of life and with the most graces. The power which we have won for the city by these manners reveals that this is no verbal boast used for immediate effect, but the actual truth. For Athens alone of all present-day cities exceeds her reputation in any enterprise she undertakes; she alone causes a belligerent enemy no irritation when he reflects by whom he is defeated, and arouses no resentment in her subjects that she is not fit to rule them. Our power is proved by many sure signs and an abundance of witnesses; it is an object of wonder to the present day and will be in the future. We need no Homer to sing our praises, no man who gives immediate pleasure by his words, but whose interpretation is harmed by the actual truth. But we have compelled every sea and every land to allow passage to our daring, and so have everywhere left eternal memorials to our successes and the harm we have done to our enemies. This was the city for which these men fought and fell, men who nobly thought it right that she should not be deprived of these blessings; and it is right for each one of us still alive to be prepared to toil on her behalf.

I have spent some time on the nature of the city, wanting to show you that we are fighting for a very different prize from that of men who do not possess any of these benefits, and wishing to prove unquestionably the truth of the eulogy I am now delivering on these men. Most of this has now been spoken, for the glories of the city, of which I have told you, were achieved by the valour of these and others like them. In very few of the Greeks would reputation and truth march so hand-in-hand. Death seems to me to have declared their valour, perhaps revealing it for the first time, perhaps setting the final seal on its existence. Those who fell short in other respects must gain the credit of this devotion to their country against her enemies; for they have obliterated evil with good, and their public services have been greater than their private faults. Not one of them was enfeebled by preferring the enjoyment of wealth; not one of them shirked danger in the hope poor men have, that they will grow rich if they can only escape. They preferred the punishment of their foes to such things, they were willing, whatever the danger, to avenge themselves on their enemies, to them the finest danger of all, and to give up everything

else, they entrusted to hope the uncertainty of success, they felt
it to be their duty to stake their own lives in each immediate
physical risk. They thought that resistance and suffering were
fairer than surrender and life, they shunned the disgrace of poor
report but endured the action with their lives; and so, in an
instant, at the crisis of their fate, they gained release not from
their fear but from their glory.

These men acted full worthily of their city. For the survivors,
we may pray for a spirit against our foes which brings less danger
but which must not be less bold. We must appreciate, not in
words alone, the advantages and benefits there are in resisting
the enemy, on which I, like you, with knowledge of the facts might
dwell at length. We must, rather, protect the city's power by our
actions. We must become its lovers, and when we think of its
greatness, we must remember that men achieved this by daring
and by a true sense of duty and honour in the hour of need.
When they failed in any enterprise, they did not think it right to
deprive the city of their valour, but sacrificed their noblest
possession for it. By this public gift of their lives, they have won
in private an undying praise and the finest sepulchre of all, not
that in which they now lie, but that in which their glory shall
endure, eternally remembered, at any time of deed or word. For
the whole world is the grave of famous men. It is not merely a
few words on a stone in their own land that recalls them, but there
lives on, even in countries not their own, an unwritten memorial
in each man's heart. Do you, now, try to emulate them. Consider
happiness to mean freedom, and freedom to need courage. Do
not think of the dangers of war. For it is not those who fare badly
and have no hope of improvement who are most justified in
hazarding their lives, but rather those for whom a change of
circumstances is attended with most risk, and for whom there is
the biggest difference if they meet with misfortune. It is more
bitter for a spirited man to be disgraced through cowardice than
to win a death which is unperceived when it comes at the moment
of his strength and of the faith which he shares with all.

So I do not weep for you parents of these men, but I try to
comfort you. You know, you have lived through many forms of
adversity. Real good fortune is to acquire, as these have now,

the finest end, or, like you, the noblest grief; it is achieved by those who have found in their happiness and their death the same standard in their lives. I know that it will be difficult to persuade you of this, for you will often be reminded of them by the good fortunes of others, in which you, too, once rejoiced. Grief is not felt for the good things you lose which you have never enjoyed, but for the things to which you have been accustomed and of which you are now deprived. Those of you still of an age to bear children must be strong in the hope of further sons. They will for you personally be a way to forget those who are no more, and the city will gain double benefit, from the help that numbers give and in the additional safety that this will bring. Those who do not run the same risks of hazarding their children cannot deliberate fairly and justly. To those of you past the age of child-bearing, I say this. You must think that the happiness in which you have spent the majority of your lives is what you have gained; the rest will be short, so comfort yourselves in your children's fame. Love of honour never dies, and in the weak, useless period of life, it is honour which brings more pleasure, not profit as some say.

For the sons and brothers of the fallen I see a mighty struggle ahead, for everyone is wont to praise a man no longer alive, and it will be difficult for you, because of their supreme valour, to be judged, I will not say their equals, but just a little their inferiors. For the living are rivals and have envy of each other, but those no longer with us are honoured with a will quite free from rivalry.

If I must speak of the virtue of women, for those among you who are now widows, I can sum up all in a few words of advice. Your greatest glory is to be no different from your natural selves and to be least on the lips of men, in words of praise or reproach.

I have, in accordance with the law, spoken such fitting words as I could, and these who are being buried have now received their due measure of honour. Their children will be maintained by the city at public expense from this day until they reach manhood; which will bestow on them and the survivors a proper crown for their achievements. Where the prizes of valour are greatest, there the most valiant men are found. So, when each has made lament for his own relatives, I bid you return to the city.'

PLAGUE IN ATHENS
430 B.C.

Shortly after the start of the Peloponnesian War, plague broke out in Athens. Thucydides, who was about twenty-five years old at the time, gives us this description of the plague.

Source: Thucydides, II, 47.

Further Reading: Loeb translation by C. F. Smith, Penguin translation by Rex Warner. A. W. Gomme considers the plague in his Thucydides II, p. 150. Two articles in *Classical Quarterly* by D. L. Page in iii (1953) and by W. P. MacArthur iv (1954) give interpretations of the plague in terms of measles and typhus. *C.A.H.* vol. V, ch. viii, is by F. E. Adcock.

The Peloponnesian forces had only been a few days in Attica when the plague made its first attack on the Athenians. Reports indicated that it had affected many other places prior to this, especially in the neighbourhood of Lemnos, but nowhere else was there record of a comparable virulence or of such destruction of human life. In the early days the doctors were unable to help because of their ignorance of the disease, and the more they visited the sick the faster they died. Human skill of any description was quite unavailing, and any recourse that men had to religion or divine prophecies or similar agencies was all useless. Indeed, in the end they stopped making the effort, and gave in to the disaster.

The plague was said to have started in Egypt above the cataracts. From there it spread into Egypt proper, to Libya and most of the Persian Empire. Its onset in Athens was very sudden. It first attacked men in the Peiraeus, which made the inhabitants spread the rumour that the Peloponnesians had thrown poison into the water-cisterns (there were no wells there at the time). It then spread to the city itself, and the death rate increased considerably. I expect that everyone, doctor and layman alike, will give his personal views about its likely origin and the reasons which he thinks explain why it became virulent enough to cause such a catastrophe. I will merely describe its symptoms, adding such points as will help anyone to a knowledge of the disease in the event of any future occurrence. I can do this as an actual victim of the plague, and as a witness of other people's suffering.

It is generally agreed that this year was completely free from other complaints; and even if anyone caught some other disease, it always ended up in this. It struck the healthy without warning, starting with high fever in the head, and a reddening and inflammation of the eyes. Internally, the throat and tongue became immediately inflamed, and the breath was laboured and foul. Sneezing and sore throats followed, and soon the trouble descended to the chest, causing a severe cough. On entering the stomach it produced acute indigestion and every type of purging of bile that is known to medical science. Pain was acute, for most were affected by a hollow retching accompanied by violent spasms which lasted for different times in different cases. The outside of the body was not excessively hot to the touch nor pallid, but rather reddish and blotchy, breaking out into small pustules and sores. But internally the fever was so intense that men could not stand even the lightest clothes of muslin being thrown on them. They much preferred to lie quite naked, and would with pleasure have thrown themselves into cold water. Indeed, many of those unattended were afflicted with an unquenchable thirst and did actually hurl themselves into wells. But it made no difference whether they drank little or much; sufferers were all quite unable to lie still or get any sleep. There was no wasting of the body while the disease was at its height, but it seemed to resist the complaint in an astonishing fashion. Most, then, died from the internal fever on the seventh or ninth day with their bodily strength unimpaired. Those who survived past that found the disease entering their intestines, where severe ulcerations and acute diarrhoea meant that weakness was the most likely cause of death for those who still survived.

The disease started in the head and spread downwards through the whole body. If anyone survived the first attacks he still was marked by the loss of his extremities, for it attacked the genitals and the tips of the hands and feet. Many lost these, or even their eyes, and lived. An immediate and total amnesia affected those who recovered. They even forgot who they were, and failed to recognize close relations. The nature of the disease really beggars description and was far too severe for the human frame to stand. Its difference from the normal types of sickness was most marked. The birds and animals which scavenge around corpses never went near the many dead bodies lying about unburied, or if they did so and touched the body, they died. As evidence may be cited the obvious absence of such birds, not one of which was seen near a corpse or anywhere else, while dogs provided a clear proof of the consequences because of their domesticity.

This, then, to omit individual peculiarities, was the general nature of the plague. As said above, none of the normal diseases occurred while the plague lasted, or if they did they ended up in this. Men died whether receiving every attention or left uncared for. There was virtually no remedy which could be applied to do any good, for what assisted one sufferer harmed another. No physique seemed strong enough to withstand the attack which removed even those who received every attention. The very worst thing about the calamity was the despair which anyone felt if he thought that he was sickening. Thrown into utter dejection, he let himself go and stopped trying to resist the disease. Some caught it from nursing others and they died like sheep. This, indeed, caused the highest death role. For if men shrank from visiting others, they died by themselves, and many households were wiped out through lack of attention. If they did pay visits the result was just the same, and this particularly affected those who made any pretensions to virtue. When the very relations of the dead were quite overcome by the disaster and had even stopped bewailing their loss, good men went to their help out of a sense of shame, and were unsparing of their own lives. Survivors showed the most pity for the sick and dying because of their personal knowledge of the pain. They also felt very confident, for the disease never attacked the same man twice, at least not fatally. They also received the congratulations of others, and in their immediate joy even entertained the vain hope that they would never be killed by any other disease in the future.

The evacuation from the countryside into the town greatly increased the trouble, especially for the evacuees who had no houses to go to, and lived in stifling hovels at the hottest time of the year. Death came upon them without warning. Corpses lay where they died on top of each other, and the dying lurched around the streets and wells in their crying need for water. The sacred places, also, where they squatted, were filled with the corpses of those who died there. For as the disease gained strength men had no idea what would become of them, and the natural reaction was to belittle all sacred and holy things. Their previous observances about burial were disregarded, and they buried the dead as best they might. Many were buried in unhallowed ground, as most of their relatives had already been destroyed. Some men took corpses to a pyre which was meant for another, threw them on and set light to it, while some even hurled their load onto a pyre that was already burning and ran off. In addition to its other effects, the plague caused a great increase in lawlessness.

SOCRATES THE SOLDIER
429 B.C.

The normal picture that we get of Socrates finds him in a portico in Athens conversing with young men about the meaning of various moral terms. His questions to them and his refusal to give answers himself are often maddening. Aristophanes used one aspect of this picture, the ability to twist words to suit his own convenience, to considerable comic effect in *The Clouds*, which was first performed in 423 B.C. But there was another side. It was Socrates who tried to take a stand against the legality of the trial of six admirals after the successful battle near the Arginusae Islands in 406 B.C.

This extract also shows that even such a man as Socrates was expected to play his part in the ordinary duties of a citizen. Plato's *Symposium* is an account of a drinking party, at which each member was required to give his definition of Love. Alcibiades (for whom see pages 34–9) takes the opportunity to give us this unexpected glimpse into the character of his friend. Everything in Plato suggests that the party actually took place, and there is no reason to doubt the two stories. Potidaea was besieged from 432 to 429 B.C., and the expedition to Delion was made in 424 B.C.

Source: Plato, *Symposium,* 219e

Further Reading: Loeb translation by W. R. M. Lamb; Penguin translation by W. Hamilton. The Clouds is translated by B. B. Rogers

in the Loeb series. The story of the two campaigns can be found in
Thucydides (Penguin by Rex Warner), and in general histories. See
also under the extract on page 49.

Later we both served on the expedition to Potidaea and shared
the same mess. Socrates proved himself equal to anyone in his
ability to endure hardships, not just better than me. For instance,
we might be cut off, as happens on active service, and forced
to go hungry; but when it came to doing without food, the rest
were nowhere. And if there was plenty to eat, he was the only
man truly able to enjoy himself. Though he was not an habitual
drinker, he drank everyone under the table when forced to,
and—most remarkable, this—no one ever saw Socrates drunk.
I fancy that we shall have proof of this by and by.

His endurance of the rigours of winter, and winters there are
pretty severe, was equally notable. Once there was a particularly
sharp frost when no one willingly went out of doors at all,
or if he had to, he took extraordinary care to wrap himself up
and cover his feet in a binding of felt or sheepskin boots. But
Socrates used to go out in these conditions wearing the same
clothes as usual, and walked barefoot through the snow just as
easily as others did fully shod. The soldiers thought that he was
deliberately showing them up. . . .

Once a problem occurred to him early in the morning, and
he stood there thinking it over. When the answer would not
come, he did not give up, but stayed searching for it. Midday
came and men pointed out in amazement and astonishment to
each other that Socrates had been standing wrapped in thought
since daybreak. When evening finally arrived and they had had
their dinner, some of the Ionians spread some blankets outside
to sleep on (it was summer then), while keeping half an eye open
to see if he would stand there all night. Stand there he did till
dawn came and the sun rose. Then after a prayer to the sun he
moved away at last.

Socrates was also a good sight when the army was in retreat
from Delion. He and I happened to be there too, I serving in the
cavalry and he as a hoplite. The rest of the army was in confusion
when I fell in with Socrates and Laches who were walking along
together. On seeing them I encouraged them to be of good

heart, for I would not desert them. I, you will remember, was on horseback and so had less to fear, and I got a clearer view of how Socrates behaved then than I had at Potidaea. He was far more under control than Laches, and if I may borrow your expression, Aristophanes, he seemed to be walking along as he does here in Athens, 'strutting along with his head in the air, with many a glance to the side'. He quietly observed friend and foe, making it quite clear for all to see that he would defend himself stoutly if anyone molested him. He and Laches got safely away, for it is usually true that people who behave like this are not troubled; the pursuit is directed against men in headlong flight.

CIVIL UNREST IN GREECE
426 B.C.

Thucydides here describes an endemic failing of all Greek states. Athens herself had been comparatively free from trouble for eighty years, but in 411 and 404 party clashes were to happen there too, as a later extract shows. It is interesting to note that Solon made neutrality in times of civil conflict a crime punishable by loss of citizen-rights.

Source: Thucydides, III, 82.

Further Reading: Loeb translation by C. F. Smith, Penguin translation by Rex Warner. The nature of the City State is described in W. Warde Fowler's *The City State of the Greeks and Romans,* and V. Ehrenberg's *The Greek State.* The Oligarchic Revolutions in 411 B.C. and 404 B.C. in Athens afford a parallel. They are described in Thucydides, Book VIII, and Xenophon, *Hellenica,* Book II, and are analysed in C. Hignett's *A History of the Athenian Constitution. C.A.H.* vol. V, ch. viii, by F. E. Adcock. G. B. Grundy has an interesting chapter on the Philosophy of History in *Thucydides—A History of his Age.*

So the civil war continued on its violent way, seeming all the more violent since it broke out first in Corcyra. Later, virtually all Greece was affected, the differences in each city causing the popular party to espouse the cause of Athens, while the oligarchs favoured Sparta. During time of peace the parties had no real excuse or urge to call in support, but in wartime, when alliances had been formed with the hope that they would be able both to harm their enemies and at the same time gain some advantage for themselves, encouragement to call in help was given to either party if they wished to revolt. The usual multiple and serious effects of party strife affected the cities, as they always will as long as Man's nature remains the same, though the type varied in violence and form according to the different circumstances in which the trouble took place.

In times of peace and prosperity, cities and individuals retain a better set of values, for they do not suffer from sudden calamities. But War is a hard master, and removes the comfort of daily life, making the characters of men as grim as the events through which they live.

Civil war started in various cities, and the later seditions, on receipt of the news of what had happened elsewhere, brought about an increasing novelty of design in both the skill of attack and the enormity of the reprisals taken. Ordinary words changed their meaning to suit the times. 'Irrational daring' was called 'courageous loyalty to one's party', 'intelligent hesitation' became 'specious cowardice', 'prudence' took over the mantle of 'effeminacy', while 'complete understanding' became synonymous with 'complete inactivity'. Sharpness of an undisciplined kind was added to the conception of courage, and plans formed for personal safety were considered a fair-seeming excuse for inaction. Trouble-makers were always trusted, just as their opponents were automatically suspect. Anyone who hatched plots was considered clever, but a man who suspected them even cleverer. Men who took thought that neither of these was needed, were held to be a danger to the party, and frightened of their opponents. In short, a man who harmed others before they could harm him won approval, as did anyone who persuaded another not so inclined to follow his example. Loyalty to party became stronger than that to family from the increased readiness of party members for unconsidered recklessness. Such confederacies were not based on mutual help within the constitution, but for selfish ends in opposition to any such laws. Even their pledges to each other were kept not from any feeling that this was right, but simply to enable them to break the law in concert. Their reception of any of their opponents' just claims amounted to actions to forestall them, rather than an honest welcome. Revenge for suffering was valued more highly than prevention of suffering. Any oaths of agreement were given merely for the immediate present in view of the difficulties of the moment, and lasted as long as the parties had no other safeguards. In the moment of action a man who was able to steal a march if he saw an unguarded spot felt that his revenge was all the sweeter, because of the previous trust between the two, than it would have been if taken quite openly. He not only considered the greater safety of so doing, but also laid claim to greater intelligence in that he had survived by cunning. Most people were called clever if bad men, stupid if good men: they were ashamed of the latter, but proud of the former.

The cause of all this was power pursued for greed or ambition. There followed a readiness to quarrel once the trouble had started. The leading members of the parties had fair-sounding manifestos, championing civil equality for all or a reasonable limited aristocracy. But while paying lip-service to this public aim, they laid claim to the prizes, striving to outdo each other by appalling deeds of daring, and resorting to greater and greater measures of revenge, with no limit set by justice or the benefit of the city at large. Individual pleasure, power gained by false condemnation, or force enabling them to satisfy their immediate love of victory, these were their targets. So neither side considered acting honestly, for reputation depended on who could gain their horrible ends with the best and most specious pleas. The moderate citizens were wiped out by both parties, either because they would not join in, or in anger at their possible survival.

This was the general picture of the misfortunes which beset the Greek world through civil war. Simplicity of conduct, so much a part of real nobility of character, was laughed out of court and vanished, while mutual distrust and opposition steadily gained ground. No pledge was strong enough and no oath fearsome enough to bring it to an end. As factions grew the stronger in their calculation of the unlikelihood of security, they took steps to avoid suffering and found it impossible to trust anyone. Those with weaker intellects were the most likely survivors, for they feared their own shortcomings and their opponents' intelligence. So, in case they were worsted in argument or suffered from plots hatched by their enemies' subtle minds, they went boldly to work on violent measures. This meant that people who presumed contemptuously that they would spot trouble, and thought that physical action should only be taken as a last resort when intelligence had failed, were mostly caught off their guard and destroyed.

AN OLIGARCH'S VIEW OF ATHENS
c. 425 B.C.

It is always of advantage to see both sides of a question. In Pericles' Funeral Speech the democratic view was put forward. Among the works attributed to Xenophon is the Constitution of Athens, which has a very strong oligarchic bias. It is almost certain that this was not written by Xenophon, but by someone rather earlier, possibly at the time of the supremacy of the demagogue, Cleon. The later Athenian attitude to democracy was almost universally hostile, largely because democratic government was blamed for the failure in the Peloponnesian War. Plato put Democracy next to Anarchy in his Rake's Progress of constitutions.

Source: Pseudo-Xenophon, *Constitution of Athens*, I, 10.

Further Reading: Full text in Oxford Classical Texts: edition by K. M. T. Grimes. For other books, see those mentioned under the Funeral Speech (page 17).

Insolent conduct of slaves and resident aliens is everywhere rife in Athens. You cannot strike a slave there, and he will not get out of your way in the street. There is a good reason for this being the local custom. If the law allowed a free-born citizen to strike a slave, an alien, or a freedman, then you would often strike an Athenian citizen in the mistaken impression that he was a slave. For the common people dress as poorly as slaves or aliens and their general appearance is no better. If this causes surprise, that some slaves are allowed to live above their station and to act arrogantly, then the reason might be as follows. Where a state is based on naval power, free men must be excused for service in the fleet, and so it is necessary in financial matters to be servant to your slaves, to get profit from their work. Where slaves become rich, it is of no advantage for my slave to live in fear of you, whereas in Sparta my slave does fear you. And if your slave fears me, then he will be likely to pay me protection-money. This is the reason why we allow freedom of speech to slaves when talking to us, and indeed to aliens when speaking to citizens, because the city needs aliens for the numerous industries and for the fleet. That makes freedom of speech for aliens perfectly reasonable.

The common people take no supervisory interest in athletic or aesthetic shows, feeling that it is not right for them, since they know that they have not the ability to become expert at them. When it is necessary to provide men to put on stage-shows or games or to finance and build triremes, they know that impresarios come from the rich, the actors and chorus from the people. In the same way, organizers and ship-masters are the rich, while the common people take a subordinate part in the games and act as oarsmen for the triremes. But they do at least think it right to receive pay for singing or running or dancing or rowing in the fleet, to level up the incomes of rich and poor. The same holds good for the law-courts as well; they are more interested in what profit they can make than in the true ends of justice. . . .

Because of their overseas possessions, Athenians almost automatically learn to row, as do their slaves. Both have repeatedly to sail or row somewhere, and to learn the names of ships' terms. Helmsmen become skilful from experience and practice of commanding simple boats, merchant ships, or triremes. The mass of the people are able to row without practice immediately on boarding, for all their life has been devoted to it. This accounts for the low esteem in which the Athenians hold the hoplite body, who seem to consider themselves inferior to their opponents. Their only land-empire is over their tributary allies, and the hoplite force is held to be sufficient if it is superior to them. There is also a natural reason for this. Land powers can unite small cities and fight in combination, but sea-empires, with most of their members being islanders, cannot bring these citizens together. The sea intervenes, and the supremacy rests with those who command the sea. Even if by some accident all the islanders could be brought together onto one island, they would die of hunger.

Of the mainland cities in the Athenian Empire, the large ones are governed by fear, the small ones by want. For all states must import and export, and this they cannot do unless they remain subject to the mistress of the seas. Secondly, sea-powers can do what land powers cannot—ravage a superior enemy's country. For they can sail where few or no enemy troops are stationed, and, if some enemies do arrive, they can embark and sail somewhere else. This causes fewer difficulties than military assistance by land. A third advantage is that naval-powers can sail from their own lands in any direction they choose, but journeys of several days cannot be made by land-powers, for the travelling is slow and marching men cannot get provisions for any length of time. Furthermore a land-force must either march through friendly country or be prepared to overcome opponents in battle. But a sea-power can land where it has superiority, and lie off where it has not, or rather sail on until it comes to a friendly coast or to a people weaker than itself. A last point is that natural diseases to crops are a sore burden to land-powers but not to sea-powers. Since the whole world does not suffer from such diseases at the same time, crops from healthy districts can be brought to the cities of those who command the sea.

THE MUTILATION OF THE HERMAE
415 B.C.

Just before the Athenian expedition set sail for Sicily, all the busts of Hermes, which were found on every street corner in Athens, were disfigured during the night. The Athenians were keyed up to a high state of expectancy, and treated this as a fearful omen for the success of the expedition. Immediate inquiries seemed to implicate Alcibiades, one of the generals in charge of the force, but though he demanded an investigation, the fleet sailed. Later, further evidence led the Athenians to recall him. This, as much as anything, ruined the chances in Sicily. The story that Andocides tells is clear enough, however fabricated it may have been. It formed part of a speech on his return from exile after 404 B.C., when he was charged with profaning the Mysteries.

Source: Andocides, *About the Mysteries,* 38.

Further Reading: Loeb translation by K. J. Maidment. Grote's *History of Greece* has a full description of the incident, which is reported by Thucydides in Book VI. *C.A.H.* vol. V, ch. ix, by W. S. Ferguson.

The story that Diocleides told was as follows. He owned a slave at Laurium, and he had to go to collect the proceeds of his work. Making a mistake about the time, he got up rather early and set off. It was full moon. When he came to the entrance gateway to the Lenaion, he saw a large group of men going down from the Odeion onto the dance-floor of the theatre. In fright, he went and sat in the shadows between a pillar and the column with the bronze statue of a general on it. He could see about three hundred men standing in a circle in groups of fifteen or twenty. Their faces were clearly visible in the moonlight, and he recognized most of them. (He invented this appalling tale to enable him to include or exclude any Athenian he wished.) He claims that after this he went on his way to Laurium, and heard on the following day that the Hermae had been mutilated. He immediately realized that this was the work of the men whom he had seen. Returning to Athens, he found inquiry agents already appointed, and rewards of £10,000 offered for information received. . . .

He gave in the names of the men he claimed to have recognized, forty-two in all. Peisander immediately suggested that the Decree of Scamandrias should be suspended, and that those indicted should be put to the torture to make sure that not a minute was lost in discovering the rest of the culprits. The Council gave him a rousing acclaim. Two of the men he had mentioned, both Councillors, took their seat at the sacred hearth, begging not to be put on the rack, and asking for bail and a proper trial. This was reluctantly conceded, and they managed to find men to go surety for them. Whereupon they immediately took to horse, and went and deserted to the Spartans, leaving in the lurch their guarantors, who were liable at law to the same constraints as those for whom they had gone bail.

The Council, after a secret session, had us seized and put in irons. Then they summoned the generals and ordered them to get the citizens of Athens to collect their arms and assemble in the Agora, those on the Long Walls at the Theseion and those in the Peiraeus at the Hippodameian Agora. The cavalry were to be summoned by night to the Anakeion, and the Council was to go to the Acropolis and sleep there, while the duty-members were to sleep in the Guard-House. For the Boeotians had news of the trouble and were encamped on the frontier. Diocleides, the man responsible for all this panic, was garlanded and taken on a carriage to the Presidency as a public saviour, and there he had dinner.

We were all chained up in one prison. Before night fell and the prison was shut, men were visited by their mothers, sisters, wives and children. There were pitiful cries of people weeping and bemoaning their plight. Then Charmides, a cousin of mine of about my own age who had lived with us from childhood, said to me, 'Andocides, if you know anything about this, do speak up. You will be saving yourself, your father who especially deserves your love, the man who married your only sister, and all these other relatives and acquaintances. Last of all, you will be saving me, who have never done you any injury in your whole life, but have always been most ready to assist you and your affairs in any circumstances.' The words of Charmides were reinforced by the prayers and individual entreaties of the others, and I took stock of the position. . . .

On reflection, I realized that the least that I could do in the present trouble was to say what had happened with all speed, to prove that Diocleides had lied, and to bring justice down on the head of the man who was wickedly trying to ruin us and deceive the city, gaining for this the reputation as a benefactor, not to mention a large sum of money. So I informed the Council that I knew the culprits, and gave my definite proof.

While some of us were having a drink, I said that Euphiletus had proposed the crime, but that I steadfastly refused to have anything to do with it, and prevented any action for the moment. Later on, I had gone to a shop of mine in the suburbs, where I fell, breaking my collar-bone and cutting my head open. I was put on a stretcher and carried home. Euphiletus saw my condition, and told the others that I had agreed to take part in the affair and had undertaken the mutilation of the Herm by the Pharbanteum. (This was totally untrue, but it did mean that the only

Herm not mutilated that night in Athens was the one you can see near my father's house, originally set up by the Aegeis deme. You see, I was meant to deal with that one, as Euphiletus told them.)

When the rest of the gang discovered that I knew everything about the plot but had done nothing, they were furious. Two of them, Miletus and Euphiletus, came to visit me the next day. 'We have done what we said we would, Andocides. If you are prepared to keep quiet and say nothing, then you will find us as good friends as ever we were. But if you talk, then our enmity will be much more effective than any friendship you may gain by betraying us.' I replied that I thought that Euphiletus had committed a monstrous crime, and that any danger which threatened them would not come from my knowledge of it, but simply because the outrage had been perpetrated.

I then handed over my slave to undergo examination under torture to prove the truth of my contention that I was ill and had not got up from my bed. The Presidents of the Council also questioned some maidservants from the house used as a base for the operation. The Council and investigation committee checked the truth of all this, and when they supported my statement and everything was clear, they summoned Diocleides. Not many words were needed. He soon confessed that he had lied, begging for mercy if he revealed the names of the people who had paid him to tell the tale. These were Alcibiades from Phegae and Amiantos from Aegina, who had both fled in panic. On this admission, Diocleides was handed over for trial and executed. The prisoners, who were in immediate fear for their lives, were released, and, by my agency, my kinsmen who had fled were welcomed back. Then all you Athenians took up arms to fight and went on your way, freed from this wicked, dangerous crime.

CONFISCATED PROPERTY
414-413 B.C.

The investigations into the Mutilation of the Hermae led to many arrests and executions. The property of the condemned men was confiscated and sold by the State. The first inscription is part of a general list, and is interesting for the number of slaves owned by one man. The names are known elsewhere as implicated in the plot. The second inscription is almost certainly part of the sale-list for the effects of Alcibiades himself.

Source: Tod, *Greek Historical Inscriptions*, 79 and 80.

Further Reading: See the books under the previous extract. M. I. Finley's collection entitled *Slavery in Classical Antiquity* and a chapter in Zimmern's *Greek Commonwealth* consider the position of slaves.

(*a*)	*Tax*	*Purchase Price (drachmas)*	*Goods, etc.*

The property of Polystratos from Ankyle

2 drr. 1 obol	202	A slave—Pistos
1 dr.	42	Crops at Ankyle

Total with taxes—247 drachmas 1 obol

The property of Cephisodoros, an alien resident in Peiraeus

2 drr.	165	A Thracian slave-woman
1 dr. 3 obb.	135	A Thracian slave-woman
2 drr.	170	A Thracian slave
2 drr. 3 obb.	240	A Syrian slave
1 dr. 3 obb.	105	A Carian slave
2 drr.	161	An Illyrian slave
2 drr. 3 obb.	220	A Thracian slave-woman
1 dr. 3 obb.	115	A Thracian slave
1 dr. 3 obb.	144	A Scythian slave
1 dr. 3 obb.	121	An Illyrian slave
2 drr.	153	A Colchian slave
2 drr.	174	A Carian boy
1 dr.	72	A Carian child
3 drt. 1 ob.	301	A Syrian slave
2 drr.	106	A Melitan slave
2 drr.	170	A Lydian slave-woman

(*b*)	*Number*	*Item*	*Price (drachmas)*
	1	Two-doored chest	
	1	Four-doored chest	
	11	Milesian beds	90
	4	Tables	16

Number	Item	Price (drachmas)
1	Single-ended couch	17
1	Linen curtain	11
1	Double-ended couch (Milesian)	
6	Perfume jars	
5	Chairs	
1	Bench	1 1/6th
2	Wicker Baskets	
1	Reed Mat	
2	Garments	
1	Linen chest	
1	Amount yellow wool	
1	Linen chest	
2	Horse harness	
1	Small flat box	
3	Small boxes	
2	Stuffed pillows	
16	Blankets	

ATHENIAN TRAGEDIANS
406 B.C.

Aristophanes was a younger contemporary of Sophocles and Euripides, and was born about the year that Aeschylus died. He must have seen plays by all three. This satiric account of an event in the Underworld contains much pertinent criticism of a specialist kind. From it can be seen the common faults that were found in the realist and rationalist plays of Euripides.

Source: Aristophanes, *Frogs,* ll. 757 ff.

Further Reading: Loeb translation by B. B. Rogers; also translated by Dudley Fitts. For the Greek tragedians, see the histories of Greek Literature by G. Murray, J. H. Rose or C. M. Bowra. For Aristophanes, see the above and K. Lever's *The Art of Greek Comedy.* T. B. L. Webster has revised A. W. Pickard-Cambridge's *Dithyramb, tragedy and comedy. C.A.H.* vol. V, ch. v, also deals with Athenian drama. A similar contest between Homer and Hesiod is translated in the Loeb edition of Hesiod by H. G. Evelyn-White and dates from *c.* 400 B.C.

[The scene is set in Hell, where an Athenian meets one of the judges of the Underworld, Aiakos. Dionysus is the god of drama.]

XANTHIAS: What on earth is all that uproar and shocking din?

AIAKOS: A squabble between Aeschylus and Euripides.

XANTHIAS: I see.

XIAKOS: It's a very, very big thing among the dead, a great row.

XANTHIAS: Why is that?

AIAKOS: There is a law established here that in all the important fine arts the best artist has his board free at the Prytaneion and his Chair from Pluto. . . .

XANTHIAS: I understand.

AIAKOS: Until someone better at the art turns up. Then he has to give place.

XANTHIAS: What has upset Aeschylus?

AIAKOS: He held the Chair of Tragic Poetry, as supreme in his art.

XANTHIAS: Who does now?

AIAKOS: When Euripides came down here, he showed himself off to all his fan-club of robbers, cutpurses, father-beaters and burglars (and there are masses of them in Hell). They listened to his arguments, logicalities and word-play, went dotty and thought him marvellous. Encouraged by this, he grabbed the Chair where Aeschylus was sitting.

XANTHIAS: Wasn't he thrown out?

AIAKOS: There was a cry from the crowd that there must be a trial to decide which was better at his art.

XANTHIAS: What? The crowd of ruffians?

AIAKOS: Yes, the whole damn lot of them.

XANTHIAS: Didn't Aeschylus have any supporters?

AIAKOS: It's the same here as up top—good men are hard to find.

XANTHIAS: Then what did Pluto decide to do?

AIAKOS: Oh, he proclaimed a contest, trial and proof of their skill.

XANTHIAS: Then why didn't Sophocles claim the Chair?

AIAKOS: You don't imagine *he* would. When he came down he gave Aeschylus a kiss, shook hands and left him the Chair. But now, according to my information, he is going to stand by. If Aeschylus wins, he'll go and live in the country. If not, then he says he'll have a go against Euripides for the title.

XANTHIAS: Then there will be a to-do.

AIAKOS: Yes, any moment now. You will see strange things happening. Poetry is going to be measured by the ounce.

XANTHIAS: What? Are they going to bring Tragedy as low as this?

AIAKOS: They'll bring rulers and word-measurers and folding scales.

XANTHIAS: Are they going to build a house?

AIAKOS: We'll have circles, diameters and set-squares. For Euripides says that he is going to measure Tragedy by the word.

XANTHIAS: I should say that Aeschylus is pretty annoyed.

AIAKOS: You're right. He scowled and looked as mad as a bull.

XANTHIAS: Who will be judge?

AIAKOS: Ah, that was difficult. They found a distinct shortage of educated people here. Aeschylus didn't get on with Athenians.

XANTHIAS: Perhaps he thought too many of them were burglars?

AIAKOS: They thought it a waste of time to know about the nature of poetry. So they turned to your master, because he was pretty experienced. Let's go in. When our betters are ready and waiting, we'll be for it if we don't hurry.

. . . . .

EURIPIDES: I won't resign the Chair: don't try to persuade me. I claim that I am a better artist than he is.

DIONYSUS: Why don't you say something, Aeschylus? You must understand what he says.

EURIPIDES: He's thinking up some pompous remark, like the marvels he always poured forth in all his tragedies.

DIONYSUS: Don't be arrogant, fool.

EURIPIDES: I know this man and have done so for some time. He's a crude poet, brash of speech with a tongue unbridled, uncontrolled, unguarded and chattering, that would make pomposity out of a simple yes.

AESCHYLUS: Is this right, child of the goddess of the earth? So you call me this, do you, you snivelling dung-collector, pauper-panderer, rag-and-bone merchant. But you'll pay for saying it.

DIONYSUS: Stop, Aeschylus. Let not your heart be warmed to wrath and ire.

[After many attacks and counter-attacks on each other's plays, Aeschylus is awarded the prize and sent back to earth to educate the Athenians, degenerated by Euripides.]

AESCHYLUS: I'll go and do it. Give Sophocles my Chair to guard and save if I come back here. For I judge him second in skill. And mind that this shocking liar, this vandal, never sits on my seat, even by mistake.

THE ATHENIAN SURRENDER
404 B.C.

The battle of Aegospotami was the real end of the Peloponnesian War, though it theoretically dragged on into 404 B.C., with a Spartan force besieging Athens while peace terms were negotiated. Lysias was clearly present in Athens at the time, as the next extract shows. This one comes from a speech he made in c. 399 B.C.

Source: Lysias, *For Agoratus*, 5.

Further Reading: Loeb translation by W. R. M. Lamb. Xenophon describes the events in *Hellenica*, Book II (Loeb translation by Brownson and Todd). W. S. Ferguson wrote *C.A.H.* vol. V, ch. xii.

Shortly after the destruction of your fleet, when things in the city were desperate, the Spartan ships arrived at the Peiraeus and peace negotiations were started with them. Thereupon those with revolutionary ideas in Athens began their scheming, for they felt that they had a marvellous opportunity to arrange matters exactly to their liking. They thought that the only thing which stood in their way was the popular leaders, the generals and admirals. If they could somehow or other get rid of them, they would be able to do as they wanted much more easily. Their first attack was made on Cleophon in the following way.

In the first session of the assembly to debate the question of peace, the Spartan delegation outlined the terms on which Sparta was ready to agree; simply that each of the Long Walls must be pulled down for a length of a mile and a quarter. You, fellow Athenians, were very upset to hear mention made of the destruction of your walls, and Cleophon in his speech voiced all your opinions when he said that this was quite unacceptable. He was followed by Theramenes, now as always plotting against the common people. He claimed that if you chose him as ambassador with full powers to discuss peace, he would manage to obtain terms which would mean that none of the walls would be destroyed, and that the city would not be weakened in any other respect. He thought that he could get still further benefits for the city from the Spartans. You were taken in by his promises, and elected as ambassador extraordinary a man whom you had rejected the year before in the election of generals, as you had felt that he was not well disposed towards the common citizens of Athens.

So Theramenes went off to Sparta and stayed there for some time, leaving you under siege, and in the full knowledge that the bulk of the population was in terrible straits, most of them in lack of even the necessities of life because of the war and disasters. He felt that, if he made you even more destitute than when he had left you, any terms which he wished to bring would be favourably received.

Meanwhile his confederates left behind at Athens were plotting to overthrow the Democracy, and brought Cleophon to trial on the pretext that he had not taken up his post for the night, but in fact because he had sided with you in resisting the destruction of the walls. So they established a court to try him, and witnesses came forward from among those in favour of changing the constitution to an oligarchy, and for this reason he was put to death.

A little later Theramenes returned from Sparta. He was met by some of the generals and brigadiers, including Strombichides and Dionysodorus and some others who were well disposed towards you, as they later showed. All were very upset. The peace terms which he had brought were those of which you have learnt from bitter experience. We have lost many good citizens and some of us have been exiled by the Thirty. For the terms were that all the Long Walls should be destroyed instead of the original mile and a quarter, and in place of some other benefits gained for the city, that the fleet should be handed over to the Spartans and the Peiraeus wall dismantled.

THE RULE OF THE THIRTY
404–403 B.C.

After the surrender of Athens, there was a Spartan garrison there for a time, until a group of oligarchs, called the Thirty, came to an agreement with the Spartans and took charge. Ostensibly it was a wider oligarchy than the name suggests, as there were meant to be three thousand hoplites enrolled to form the citizen body. But the names were never revealed. In 403 a democratic revolution, headed by Thrasybulus, overthrew the Thirty. Lysias' father, Cephalus, figures in the first book of Plato's Republic, together with his brother Polemarchus. The family were aliens resident in Athens and ran an arms factory. Plato makes Cephalus say that happiness depends on character rather than on wealth, while Polemarchus puts forward a doctrine that might have appealed to the Thirty, that Justice consists in doing good to one's friends and harm to one's enemies.

Source: Lysias, For Eratosthenes, 1.

Further Reading: Loeb translation by W. R. M. Lamb. Apart from Xenophon and Ferguson, as in last extract, see also C. Hignett in A History of the Athenian Constitution for a detailed analysis of the events. Plato's Republic is translated in the Loeb series by Paul Shorey, by H. D. P. Lee in Penguins, and also by B. Jowett.

My father Cephalus was persuaded to come to Athens by Pericles, and lived here for thirty years. Neither he, nor we, his sons, were ever involved in any suit, as plaintiffs or defendants. We lived so much at one with our fellows that we did them no injury and received no hurt from them. But when the evil tyrants, the Thirty, came to power with their perversion of the truth, they proclaimed that the city must be cleansed of wicked men and all the citizens be turned to paths of virtue and justice. But, for all their claims, they had the effrontery to act as they did, as I will try to show you by reminding you of your general sufferings and of my own case in particular.

Two of the Thirty, Theognis and Peison, stated that some of the resident aliens were a burden on the city. This seemed to give an admirable pretext for punishing them and thereby making money, for Athens was completely impoverished and the government needed revenue. Their audience was readily convinced; they thought nothing of murder, but highly of making money. So they resolved to arrest ten men, including two of small property to have a ready defence to the others that their actions had not been dictated by financial considerations, but had been done to benefit the state, a common justification for all their conduct. They divided out the houses and began their visits.

They found me dining at home with a few guests, whom they turned out, and handed me over to Peison, while the others went to our arms factory and freed the slaves. I asked Peison if he was prepared to release me on receipt of money. He replied that he was, if the sum was big enough. I said that I was ready to give him a talent of silver, which satisfied him. Although I realized that he respected neither god nor man, I felt that in the present circumstances it was inevitable to trust his word. When he had sworn a solemn oath on the lives of himself and his children that he would save me if he got the money, I went into another room and opened my chest. Peison followed me and, seeing what was in the chest, called two of his attendants and ordered them to take the entire contents. When he had seized not the one talent agreed upon, but three talents of silver, 400 Cyzican staters, 100 darics and four silver vases, I asked him to leave me some journey-money; whereupon he said that I would be lucky to get away with my life.

As Peison and I were leaving, Melobius and Mnesitheides met us on their return from the factory; they stopped at the door and asked us where we were going. Peison replied that we were on our way to my brother's, to find out what he had at home. When they told him to be off, bidding me follow them to the house of Damnippus, Peison came up close and whispered to me not to say a word, but to take courage as he would soon be there. We found Theognis in charge of other prisoners at the house, and, handing me over to him, my escort left. In these circumstances I seemed to be in great danger, as if my death was already fixed. Calling for Damnippus, I said, 'You're a friend of mine, I'm in your house, I've done no wrong. I'm being jailed for my money. Please give me all the help in your power to save me in my present plight.' He promised that he would, but he thought it better to have words with Theognis, whom he felt would do anything for money.

While he was talking to Theognis, I thought that the best plan would be to try to escape, for I was very familiar with the house and knew that there was a back door. My reasoning was that if I got out unseen, then I would be safe, while, if I were caught, I would be released just the same if Damnippus had succeeded in persuading Theognis to take the money; if he had failed, I would be killed in any case. With this in mind, as they guarded the main entrance, I made my getaway. I had to pass through several doors, which by good luck were all open. I arrived at the house of the shipmaster Archias and sent him to the city to get news of my brother. On his return he told me that he had been arrested by Eratosthenes in the street and had been taken to prison.

The night after hearing this, I sailed off to Megara. The Thirty gave their usual instructions to Polemarchus to drink the hemlock, before even telling him the charge on which he was to be put to death, thus depriving him of a chance of a court hearing or of making his defence. Even when his body was removed from prison, they did not allow him to be buried from any of our three houses, but hired a shack and put him there. And though there were many garments which his friends asked for, they gave nothing for his burial. So his friends each provided something, one a cloak, one a scarf and so on, just what they happened to possess.

THE GREEKS RETREAT
401 B.C.

Ten thousand Greek mercenaries had joined the abortive attempt of Cyrus to wrest the throne of Persia from his brother, Artaxerxes. After the battle of Cunaxa, the Greeks were left without leaders when their generals were treacherously murdered by a satrap. Xenophon, an Athenian, took over the command, and began the retreat through the rugged routes of Armenia. Harassed all the way, they also had other enemies to surmount. Xenophon writes in the third person.

Source: Xenophon, *Anabasis*, IV, 5.

Further Reading: Translation in Penguin Classics by Rex Warner, in Loeb series by L. Brownson and O. J. Todd. Apart from general histories, W. W. Tarn writes in *C.A.H.* vol. VI, ch. i.

After crossing the Euphrates, they marched about forty miles in three stages over a plain covered in snow. A northerly wind blowing right in their faces made the third stage particularly difficult, seering everything and freezing the soldiers. One of the priests suggested a sacrifice to the wind. His advice was followed, and everyone agreed that the violence of the wind did indeed drop. The snow was about six feet deep, and this caused the deaths of many of the animals and slaves, and of about thirty soldiers. They survived the night by lighting fires, for there was an abundance of wood at the halt. But the late arrivals did not get any wood, and those already there did not allow the stragglers to come near the fires they had lit, unless they shared with them their wheat or any other food they had. Private supplies were shared out amongst themselves. Where the fires blazed, deep holes melted in the snow right down to the soil, and the depth of the snow could there be measured.

The whole of the next day was spent on the passage of the snow-field, and many of the men suffered from hunger-exhaustion. Xenophon was bringing up the rear, and did not know what their complaint was as he came upon those falling out of line. One of the experts told him that they were clearly suffering from this exhaustion and would be able to get up if they had something to eat. So he went around the baggage animals, distributing any-thing edible he found there, and sent others to run along the lines if they still had strength and give food to the exhausted. When the latter had eaten something, they did indeed get up and con-tinue the march.

On the advance, Cheirisophus came to a village about dusk, and found some women and girls at a spring outside the walls who had come from the village to collect water. When asked who they were, the Greek interpreter replied in Persian that they were on their way from King Artaxerxes to the provincial governor. The women's reply was that he was not in their village, but about three miles away. Since it was late, the Greeks entered the walls with the water carriers, and approached the mayor. Cheirisophus encamped inside with as many of his troops as possible, but the remainder who had not been able to finish the stage spent the night outside without food or warmth, and this caused the deaths of some soldiers.

Picked enemy forces were following them, seizing the slow baggage animals and squabbling among themselves for them. Some of the Greek troops were falling back, suffering from snow-blindness or with their toes dropping off from frostbite. Some protection against the snow was afforded if a man marched with something black held in front of his eyes, and against frost-bite by continual movement and if shoes were taken off at night. Men who slept with their shoes on found the straps biting into their feet and their shoes frozen solid. Their old boots had fallen apart and their new footwear was a sort of mocassin made of new flayed skin.

THE TEN THOUSAND REACH THE SEA
400 B.C.

After their hazardous journey, the Greek mercenaries finally reached the Black Sea near Trebizond. Their joy was partly due to their arrival at a place originally colonized by Greeks, and partly because they knew that once they got to the sea they could get back home. The sea was to the Greeks as familiar and welcome as it is to the British.

Source: Xenophon, *Anabasis*, IV, 7.

Further Reading: Translation in Penguin Classics by Rex Warner, in Loeb series by L. Brownson and O. J. Todd. See previous extract.

After four days they arrived at the mountain which was called Theches. A great shout arose as the vanguard reached the top. Hearing it, Xenophon and the rearguard thought that further enemies were attacking them from in front. For others were following them behind from the blazing country, and his rearguard had set an ambush, killing some and taking some prisoners. . . . The shout now grew louder and closer as the new arrivals kept on running to join up with the men on top who continued their shouts. The noise naturally increased as the numbers grew. Xenophon thought that it must be something serious, and, mounting his horse, he went to investigate with Lycius and the rest of the cavalry. Soon they heard the soldiers shouting, 'The sea, the sea', and passing the news along. The whole army including the rearguard rushed up, driving with them the baggage animals and horses. When all had arrived at the summit, they hugged each other, generals, captains and all, with tears in their eyes. Suddenly, at someone's suggestion, the soldiers fetched stones and built a large cairn.

THE DEATH OF SOCRATES
399 B.C.

Socrates was accused of corrupting the youth in persuading them that the old gods were of no importance. He was, in fact, a scapegoat for the disillusioned element in Athens which tried to find some reason for the defeat by Sparta. Even so, he might easily have been acquitted or received some lighter sentence had it not been for his arrogance. Plato was a disciple of Socrates and, though he actually states that he was not present at the scene he describes, he certainly knew all those who were. The speaker is Phaedo.

Source: Plato: *Phaedo*, 117a.

Further Reading: Loeb translation by H. N. Fowler, Penguin translation by Hugh Tredennick. Among many works on Plato and Socrates are the two histories of Greek Philosophy from Thales, by J. Burnet and W. K. C. Guthrie. See also the *Legacy of the Ancient World* by

W. G. de Burgh, and the *Memorabilia* of Xenophon for various contemporary anecdotes about Socrates (Loeb translation by E. C. Marchant). Socrates' own defence is recorded by Plato in *The Apology,* translated in Penguin Classics by Hugh Tredennick. *C.A.H.* vol. V, ch. xiii, by J. R. Bury.

When Crito heard, he signalled to the slave who was standing by. The boy went out, and returned after a few moments with the man who was to administer the poison which he brought ready mixed in a cup. When Socrates saw him, he said, 'Now, good sir, you understand these things. What must I do?'

'Just drink it and walk around until your legs begin to feel heavy, then lie down. It will soon act.' With that he offered Socrates the cup.

The latter took it quite cheerfully without a tremor, with no change of colour or expression. He just gave the man his stolid look, and asked, 'How say you, is it permissible to pledge this drink to anyone? May I?'

The answer came, 'We allow reasonable time in which to drink it.'

'I understand', he said, 'we can and must pray to the gods that our sojourn on earth will continue happy beyond the grave. This is my prayer, and may it come to pass.' With these words, he stoically drank the potion, quite readily and cheerfully. Up till this moment most of us were able with some decency to hold back our tears, but when we saw him drinking the poison to the last drop, we could restrain ourselves no longer. In spite of myself, the tears came in floods, so that I covered my face and wept—not for him, but at my own misfortune at losing such a man as my friend. Crito, even before me, rose and went out when he could check his tears no longer. Apollodorus was already steadily weeping, and by drying his eyes, crying again and sobbing, he affected everyone present except for Socrates himself.

He said, 'You are strange fellows; what is wrong with you? I sent the women away for this very purpose, to stop their creating such a scene. I have heard that one should die in silence. So please be quiet and keep control of yourselves.' These words made us ashamed, and we stopped crying.

Socrates walked around until he said that his legs were becoming heavy, when he lay on his back, as the attendant instructed. This fellow felt him, and then a moment later examined his feet and legs again. Squeezing a foot hard, he asked him if he felt anything. Socrates said that he did not. He did the same to his calves and, going higher, showed us that he was becoming cold and stiff. Then he felt him a last time and said that when the poison reached the heart he would be gone.

As the chill sensation got to his waist, Socrates uncovered his head (he had put something over it) and said his last words: 'Crito, we owe a cock to Asclepius. Do pay it. Don't forget.'

'Of course', said Crito. 'Do you want to say anything else?'

There was no reply to this question, but after a while he gave a slight stir, and the attendant uncovered him and examined his eyes. When Crito saw that he was dead, he closed his mouth and eyelids.

This was the end of our friend, the best, wisest and most upright man of any that I have ever known.

THE BATTLE OF CORONEA
394 B.C.

Some years after Xenophon had brought the Ten Thousand to the sea, he linked up with the Spartan king, Agesilaus, who was making war in Asia Minor against the Persian satraps. In 395 B.C. the news came of the death of Lysander in the Corinthian War, which several states had started against Sparta. Duty called Agesilaus home, and Xenophon went with him. The battle he describes was an attempt to stop the Spartans from reaching the Peloponnese. This it failed to do, but the Spartan victory was not decisive and the war dragged on into a stalemate.

Source: Xenophon, *Agesilaus*, ii, 9.

Further Reading: Loeb translation by E. C. Marchant. The events are described in the general histories and by M. Cary in *C.A.H.* vol. VI, ch. ii. F. E. Adcock's *The Greek and Macedonian Art of War* is a short, overall account of all aspects of Greek warfare.

I will describe the engagement, for none of the battles in our time has been quite like it. The two forces converged on the plain near Coronea, Agesilaus's army from the River Cephisus, the Thebans and their supporters from Mt. Helicon. As the two sides faced each other, they saw that their infantry forces were nearly equal in number, and the cavalry was also evenly matched. Agesilaus was on the right flank with the Orchomenians on the extreme left. Opposite Agesilaus were the Argives, while the Thebans were stationed on their right.

On the advance to contact, both sides maintained absolute silence. But at about two-hundred yards range, the Thebans raised a shout, and came forward together at the double. While the two armies were still about a hundred yards apart, the detachment of Agesilaus' infantry commanded by Herissidas (made up of men who had been with him from the start together with some Cyreians) rushed out in front with the Ionians, Aeolians and Hellespontines. All these joined in the charge, and, coming to grips with the enemy, routed their opposite numbers. The Argives could not stand up to the attack of Agesilaus's own force, and fled to Mt. Helicon. Thereupon, some of the mercenaries were about to give Agesilaus a victory wreath, when news was brought that the Thebans had cut through the Orchomenians and were among the baggage. Agesilaus immediately wheeled his infantry against them. And the Thebans, when they realized that their allies had fled to Mt. Helicon, came rushing forward eager to join their own troops.

It may be said without question that at this juncture Agesilaus showed great courage, but the course he adopted was not the safest. He could have allowed the men who were trying to break back to pass through, and then have followed up behind and defeated the stragglers. But he did not choose to do this, preferring to attack and shatter the Thebans in frontal assault. Their shields locked, they pushed, fought, killed and died. There was no shouting, and yet not silence either, but rather such a noise as might be made by the angry clash of armed men. Finally some of the Thebans managed to break through to Mt. Helicon, losing many in the retreat.

Victory lay with Agesilaus. He had been frequently wounded, and, as he was being carried back to his lines, some horsemen galloped up with the news that eighty armed enemy soldiers were in the temple, and asked him what to do about them. Though he had received wounds all over his body from every sort of weapon Agesilaus did not forget his duty to the gods, but ordered his men to let the enemy go wherever they wanted and not to harm them, arranging for his personal cavalry guard to escort them to safety.

The battle over, one could see on the site of the struggle the ground covered with blood, friend and foe lying dead on one another, shields broken, spears shattered and unsheathed swords, some on the ground, some fixed in corpses, some still held in the hands of the dead. It was now getting late, and so they dragged the enemy corpses inside their lines, had a meal and went to rest. Early the next morning Agesilaus gave orders to his chief-of-staff, Gylis, to reform the army, set up a victory trophy, with every man wearing a wreath in thanksgiving to the god, and to get all the flute-players to play.

SPARTAN DOMINATION
404-371 B.C.

After the defeat of Athens, Sparta was undisputed mistress of Greece. But she was totally unsuited for the job, and in 387 B.C. had to ask Persia to impose peace on all. At the Olympic festival in 380 B.C. the Athenian statesman, Isocrates, pleaded for a crusade against Persia which would unite Greece once more. In the course of it he has much to say about Spartan policy. After the battle of Leuctra, 371, Thebes took over from Sparta.

Source: Isocrates, *Panegyricus*, 110.

Further Reading: Translated in the Loeb series by George Norlin. M. Cary has chapters on the Spartan supremacy in Greece in *C.A.H.* vol. VI.

This, then, is our character and this is the evidence that we have always given that we have no designs on other's property. Who are our denigrators? They are the pro-Spartans, men who formed the Commissions of Ten, who defiled their own country, who made the sins of the past seem small, who left no excess open for any future would-be criminal. They claim to serve Sparta, but practise the very opposite; while they decry the disaster suffered by the Melians, they have grievously wronged and brazenly afflicted their own citizens. What crime has escaped them? What wickedness and deceitfulness have they not indulged in? They have held the lawless as their trustiest friends, they have traitors as their benefactors, they have chosen to play the slave to one of the Helots (Lysander), and have brought dishonour on their own countries. They have respected murderers and assassins among their countrymen, not their past.

In time gone by, each one of us had many sympathizers in the event of minor misfortunes owing to the state of general prosperity. But such a degree of outrageous behaviour is now established among us that under their rule we have stopped lavishing pity on each other, overwhelmed as we all are by trouble. No one has had the leisure to take upon him another's burdens. Who has managed to escape their grasp? Who has been so remote from public life that he has not been forced to be friend to disasters into which men of such natures have brought us? But they feel no shame at thus managing their own cities so lawlessly or at accusing ours so wrongly. They even dare to bring up against us our state trials and impeachments, though they killed more people without trial in three months than this city judged and condemned in the whole duration of her Empire. Who could recount the whole list of their crimes, those they have exiled, the revolutions and illegalities they have countenanced, the changes of constitution, their violence to children, rape of women, theft of property?

I can say just this in summary, that anyone by just one decree could have easily put an end to all our mistakes. But no one can possibly find remedy for all the murders and crimes for which they are responsible. Surely our rule was preferable to this present 'peace' and independence? They are indeed guaranteed in treaty, but they find no place in our cities. Who could desire such a disastrous state of affairs, in which pirates hold the sea and mercenaries capture cities; when citizens no longer fight for their land against foreign foes, but within their own walls against their fellow countrymen; when more cities have fallen than in the years before we made peace and when men in power have less spirit than those whom they have exiled in the rapidity of the change that has taken place?

A MARINE INSURANCE FRAUD
c. 360 B.C.

Many of the private speeches of Demosthenes concern claims for fraud against shipowners. The system at Athens was as follows. A 'bank' would lend money to a trader with which the latter bought goods for export. The sale of these enabled him to buy other goods for reimportation. On his safe return the trader repaid the capital sum plus interest (minimum 12 per cent). In case of shipwreck, the whole debt was declared void. There were many ways of committing fraud, one of which was to raise loans from different 'banks' on the same surety. Most of them then involved the intentional scuttling of the ship. In private suits at Athens, it was the custom for a trained advocate, like Demosthenes, to compose a speech to be delivered by the litigant himself. So the use of the first person pronoun does not refer to Demosthenes, but to the plaintiff Damon.

Source: Demosthenes, *Against Zenothemis*, 4.

Further Reading: Loeb translation by A. T. Murray. Trade and Banking are discussed in Zimmern's *Greek Commonwealth*, H. Michell's *The Economics of Ancient Greece*, and in *Trade and Politics in Ancient Greece* by J. Hasebroek.

This Zenothemis was an agent of the shipowner Hegestratos. Although he gave evidence in his petition that Hegestratos died at sea, he omitted the manner of his death, and so I will recount it. He contrived the following crime with him. The two of them borrowed money at Syracuse. Hegestratos agreed to state, if any of Zenothemis's creditors asked, that there was corn in the ship to this amount, and Zenothemis undertook to assure the creditors of Hegestratos that the cargo of the ship belonged to Hegestratos. One was master, the other supercargo, and so their words about each other were believed. On receipt of the money they sent it home to Marseilles, but put nothing on board. The contract, as usual, stated that if the ship arrived safely, the money must be returned. But, in order to defraud their creditors, they planned to scuttle the ship.

So Hegestratos, when they were about two or three days' sail from land, went down in the night into the hold of the ship and cut through the keel. Zenothemis, feigning ignorance, was passing the time on deck with the other passengers. Those on board, hearing a noise, realized that something dreadful was happening in the hold, and rushed down to see. Hegestratos was caught and expected to pay for what he had done, but he fled and in his escape threw himself into the sea, missed the skiff in the darkness and was drowned. So he, a thoroughly evil man, suffered the evil fate that he so richly deserved, and met with the same end which he had planned for the others.

Zenothemis, his partner and accomplice, at first appeared thunder-struck in the ship at the crime as if he knew nothing. He tried to persuade the man at the bow and the sailors to get into the skiff and leave the ship at once, for there was no chance of saving her and she was sinking fast. But they realized that his plan was for just this to happen, for the ship to be lost and the contract thus made void. Zenothemis failed in his aim, for our representative opposed him and offered the sailors considerable rewards if they saved the ship.

So it docked safely at Cephallenia, thanks mainly to the gods, but also through the courage of the sailors. There, with the same Massaliots, fellow citizens of Hegestratos, Zenothemis tried once more to prevent the ship from sailing to Athens, maintaining that he and the property had come from there, and that the master and creditors were resident at Marseilles. This too was unsuccessful, for the Cephallenian magistrates realized that the ship was bound for Athens, its home port.

It is unthinkable that anyone should dare to come here with such crimes on his conscience, but Zenothemis was so shameless and brazen that he not only did so, but, on his arrival, challenged our right to the corn and took us to court.

PASSWORDS AT TROY
360 B.C.

With the rise of professional soldiers in the fourth century, several men wrote handbooks of military skills, like the *Cavalry Commander* of Xenophon. Aeneas Tacticus, so called, probably lived about the first half of the century, and seems to have served in mercenary armies in the south of Greece and in Asia Minor. Certainly all his examples which are in any way full are taken from events in those areas. So it is safe to assume that he was there in person. The attack on Troy was part of the never-ending feud between the provincial governors, satraps, of the Persian Empire. Greek mercenary armies were frequently used to settle these disputes (see page 47).

Source: Aeneas Tacticus, xxiv.

Further Reading: Loeb translation by the Illinois Greek Club. On sieges see F. E. Adcock's *The Greek and Macedonian Art of War.*

If an army happens to be one of mixed cities or races, care must be taken when issuing passwords to avoid giving ambiguous words, if one idea has two names. For example, Castor and Pollux can be called the Tyndaridae or the Dioscouri, two different names for one concept; likewise Ares can be Enyalios, Athene can be Pallas, you can talk of a sword or a dagger, a torch or a lamp and so on, all words which are hard to remember if contrary to the established vocabulary of different races, and harmful if a password is given in a special dialect instead of in a language common to all. Such passwords must be avoided in mixed mercenary forces, or where there are allies of different races.

As an example we can see what happened to Charidemus of Oreum in Aeolis when he took Troy. The way he actually captured the town was as follows. The ruler of Troy had a servant who was ever going out after plunder, especially at night, leaving and returning to the city each time with whatever he had taken. Charidemus found out that he was doing this and came to terms with him, persuading him in a secret interview to agree to venture forth on a stated night as if on his usual marauding raid. He arranged for him to come out that night on horseback, so that the main gates would be opened, which would mean that he would re-enter the town through them and not, as usual, through the passage or side-door. The servant duly got out, and after conferring with Charidemus, received from him about thirty mercenaries, wearing breastplates and carrying swords, arms and hidden helmets. Then in the darkness he led them off, dressed in shoddy clothes which concealed their arms and made them look like prisoners, together with some women and children, and entered the city through the main gates which were opened because of his horse. Immediately they had got in, they set to work, killed the gate-keeper, did other wild deeds and gained control of the gates. Other detachments under Charidemus were not far off and quickly came up and captured the city. Finally Charidemus entered in person with all his forces.

He also set part of his army in ambush, expecting that help would come to the place. This, indeed, happened. Athenodorus of Imbros, immediately he heard of what was going on, tried to bring assistance to Troy, for he was stationed quite near at hand with a force. He was, too, pretty shrewd, and did not approach the city by the ambushed roads, but marching another way in the dark, came up to the gates unnoticed. Some of his troops got into the city as members of Charidemus's army, quite unsuspected. Then, before more entered, they were recognized by the password, some of them forced out, and others killed around the gates. For the password they used was *Tyndaridae*, while Charidemus had issued *Dioscouri*. This was all that stopped the city from immediate recapture the very same night by Athenodorus.

[Aeneas goes on to give more complicated passwords, including the modern type of sign and countersign.]

THE BIRTH OF ALEXANDER
356 B.C.

Tradition tells us that Philip received three pieces of news on the same day—his general Parmenion had defeated the Paeonians, his horse had won at Olympia, and his son Alexander was born. This letter is probably not genuine, but it purports to be, and is included to show the very real connection between Alexander and Aristotle. Many of Alexander's young contemporaries attended Aristotle's 'school', and there gained ideas of the nature and duties of the true monarch.

Source: Quoted in Aulus Gellius, IX, iii, 21, who lived in the second century A.D. and collected interesting remarks and information. This letter might have been written long after Alexander's time, when his connection with Aristotle became well known. There is enough wild fantasy in the traditions of Alexander to leave considerable doubt.

Further Reading: The best ancient biography of Alexander is by Arrian (Loeb translation by E. J. Robson, Penguin translation by A. de Selincourt). The two major books on Alexander the Great are by W. W. Tarn and U. Wilcken. On Philip, see *C.A.H.* vol. VI, chs. viii and ix, by A. W. Pickard-Cambridge.

Philip sends greetings to Aristotle. I write to tell you that a son has been born to me. I thank the gods greatly for this, not so much for the birth of the boy, as for the fact that he has been born during your lifetime. For my hope is that, if he is brought up and educated by you, he will prove himself worthy of me and of succeeding to my kingdom.

PHILIP MARCHES SOUTH
339 B.C.

After a short lull, war broke out again between Philip of Macedon and Athens in 341 B.C. For a time Philip did nothing in Greece proper, but in 339 B.C. he marched south, ostensibly to visit Delphi. The road from Macedon divides just south of Thermopylae, the two forks leading to Delphi and to Thebes and Athens. Elatea is on the road to Thebes. It thus became clear that Philip intended to attack.

Source: Demosthenes, *De Corona* (a speech delivered in 330 B.C., which contains a complete account of his whole political life), 169.

Further Reading: Translated in the Loeb series by J. H. Vince. For Philip, see previous extract.

You will remember that it was evening when the Cabinet received news that Elatea had fallen. They immediately rose in the middle of their dinner, ordered everyone out of the booths around the market-place and hung up the warning signs. The generals were sent for, the town crier summoned, the whole city was in a state of uproar.

At dawn on the next day the Cabinet called a meeting of the Council, while all you citizens made your way to the assembly. In fact the whole population was up there in its seats before the Council had done anything or drafted any recommendations. Later, on the arrival of the Council, the Cabinet reported their news. The messenger was brought forward, and when he had given his account, the herald asked, 'Who wants to speak?' Not a soul moved. Although the herald kept on repeating his question, no one was stirred to speak though all the generals were present and all the public orators, and though the country herself was crying out for someone to speak on her behalf. . . .

I suggest that the crisis on that day called for more than patriotism and wealth. It needed a man who had followed events from the beginning and had a reasonable understanding of Philip's intentions and designs in this action of his. Ignorance of this and failure to grasp the course of events was likely to lead a man, however rich and patriotic he was, to a failure to know our future policy and an inability to give you proper advice. But such a man was found that day in me, and I came forward to address you.

Please pay close attention to what I then said, for two reasons; first that you may know that I was the only one of the normal speakers and politicians who retained his proper sense of patriotism in the crisis, putting forward, in the middle of the panic, concrete suggestions of what you must do. Secondly, if you spend just a short time now, you will gain for the future far greater knowledge and experience of the whole course of public business.

THE DEATH OF ALEXANDER
323 B.C.

The exploits of Alexander are known almost entirely from much later biographers. But these had recourse to the official Diaries which were kept on his march. Not many of the biographies contain obvious verbatim reports of what the Diaries said. But the death of Alexander is clearly such a report. The method of description is very similar to many of the case-histories recorded by the great physician, Hippocrates. Arrian, the best of the biographers, lived from *c.* A.D. 95 to A.D. 170, and wrote in Greek.

Source: Arrian, *Anabasis of Alexander*, VII, 24, 4.

Further Reading: Loeb translation by E. J. Robson, Penguin translation by A. de Selincourt. Apart from the books by W. W. Tarn and U. Wilcken, A. R. Burn has a concise account in *Alexander the*

Great and the Hellenistic Empire. For a very short account of Alexander's successors, there is a chapter by E. Badian in *The Greeks* (edited by Hugh Lloyd-Jones). The major work on the Hellenistic Age is the *Social and Economic History of the Hellenistic World* by M. Rostovtzeff. For Greek Medicine, see the next extract.

(The figures in brackets by the side of the narrative are not in the original, but they are included to make the style resemble that of a diary.)

A few days later he (Alexander) had performed the divine sacrifices, those prescribed for good fortune and others suggested by the priests, and was drinking far into the night with some friends. He is said to have distributed sacrificial victims and wine to the army by detachments and companies. Some state that he wanted to leave the drinking-party and go to bed, but then Medius met him, the most trusty of his Companions, and asked him to a party, for he promised that it would be a good one.

(*Day* 1)

The Royal Diaries tell us that he drank and caroused with Medius. Later he rose, had a bath and slept. He then returned to have dinner with Medius and again drank far into the night. Leaving the drinking, he bathed, after which he had a little to eat and went to sleep there. The fever was already on him.

(*Day* 2)

Each day he was carried on his couch to perform the customary sacrifices, and after their completion he lay down in the men's apartments until dusk. During this time he gave instructions to his officers about the coming expedition and sea-voyage, for the land forces to be ready to move on the fourth day, and for those sailing with him to be prepared to cast off a day later. He was carried thence on his couch to the river, where he boarded a boat and sailed across to the garden where he rested again after bathing.

(*Day* 3)

The next day, he again bathed and performed the prescribed sacrifices. He then entered his room, lay down and talked to Medius. After ordering the officers to meet him in the morning,

he had a little food. Carried back to his room, he lay now in
continual fever the whole night.

(*Day* 4)

In the morning he bathed and sacrificed. Nearchus and the
other officers were instructed to get things ready for sailing two
days later.

(*Day* 5)

The following day, he again bathed and sacrificed, and after
performing them, he remained in constant fever. But in spite of
that he summoned the officers and ordered them to have everything quite ready for the journey. After a bath in the evening,
he was now very ill.

(*Day* 6)

The next day, he was carried to the house by the diving place,
where he sacrificed, and in spite of being very poorly, summoned
the senior officers to give them renewed instructions about the
voyage.

(*Day* 7)

The next day he was carried with difficulty to perform the
sacrifices, and continued to give orders just the same to his
officers about the voyage.

(*Day* 8)

The next day, though very weak, he managed to sacrifice.
He asked the generals to stay in the hall, with the brigadiers and
colonels in front of the doors. Now extremely sick, he was
carried back from the garden to the Royal Apartments. As the
officers entered, he clearly recognized them, but he said not a
word to them.

(*Days* 9 *and* 10)

He had a high fever that night, all the next day and for
another day as well.

This information comes from the Royal Diaries, where we
also learn that the soldiers wanted to see him, some hoping to see

him before he died and others because there was a rumour that he was already dead, and they guessed that his death was being kept back by his personal guard, or so I think. Many pressed into the room in their grief and longing to see Alexander. They say that he remained speechless as the army filed past him. Yet he welcomed each one of them by a nod with his head or a movement of his eyes. The Royal Diaries say that Peithon, Attalus, Demophon, Peucestas, Cleomenes, Menidas and Seleucus spent the night in the temple of Serapis and asked the god whether it would be better and more profitable for Alexander to be carried into the temple to pray the god for his recovery. A reply came from the god that he should not be brought into the temple, but that it would be better for him to remain where he was. The Companions brought this news, and, shortly after, Alexander died; for this was what was better. That is the end of the account given by Aristoboulos and Ptolemy.

A VISIT TO ATHENS
c. 320 B.C.

Dicaearchus was a philosopher who lived about 320 B.C. Very little is known about his life and his works only survive in fragments. The most important of them seems to have been *Life in Greece*. His description of Athens is tantalizingly vague, but it has the advantage that it is nearly 500 years earlier than the work of the much more famous Pausanias. The Olympieion mentioned here was eventually finished by the Emperor Hadrian in A.D. 129.

Source: Dicaearchus, fragment.

Further Reading: The lavishly illustrated *Greek Temples, Theatres and Shrines* by H. Berve, G. Gruben and M. Hirmer, and *Greek Architecture* by A. W. Lawrence are the best guides to the public buildings.

His next visit is to the city of Athens. The road is pleasant, through cultivated land which is friendly to look at. But the city is a dry place, with no great supply of water, and the street plan is very bad because of the city's age. Many of the houses are of poor quality and only a few of a good size. A stranger who suddenly saw the place for the first time would be unready to believe that this was the famed city of Athens. But it would not take long to convince him.

The Odeion is the most beautiful in the world. The Theatre is justly famous, of great size and beauty. The Temple of Athene, called the Parthenon, stands above the Theatre. Lavishly built and clearly visible from a long way off, it is a worthy shrine to the goddess it honours. Anyone who sees it cannot fail to be quite amazed by it. The Olympieion is half-finished, but the mere outline of the building is astonishingly good. If it had been completed it would be excellent. There are three Gymnasia, the Academy, the Lyceum and the Cynosarges, all in precincts covered in grass and trees. There are flourishing gardens for every type of Philosopher, with things to beguile and give rest to the soul. There are so many ways of spending one's time, a continuous stream of things to see.

Of the inhabitants some are Attic, some Athenian. The Attics are exceedingly talkative and empty-headed. They love malicious gossip and prying into visitors' lives. The true Athenian is great of soul, simple and direct in his manners, and a man who preserves the proper value of friendship.

THE PHYSICIAN
c. 320 B.C.

Included among the works of Hippocrates are a considerable number that were clearly not written by him. They lack the accurate scientific description of case-histories that are obviously genuine. But the following short passage by an unknown author of the late fourth century B.C. gives an interesting account of what was then considered the proper bedside manner.

Source: 'Hippocrates', *The Physician*, 1.

Further Reading: Loeb translation by W. H. S. Jones and E. T. Withington. B. Farrington's *Greek Science* has much to say in praise of Greek medicine. The *Legacy of Greece* contains a chapter on Greek Medicine by Charles Singer. The works of Hippocrates (see especially the *Epidemics*) are translated in other volumes in the Loeb series. *C.A.H.* vol. VII, ch. ix, by W. H. S. Jones on Hippocrates.

The position of a doctor must make him careful to keep his complexion and weight at their correct natural standard. For most people think that those who fail to take care of their own physical condition are not really fit to take care of that of others. Secondly, he must have a clean appearance, and wear good clothes, using a sweet-smelling scent, which should be a totally unsuspicious perfume. This is pleasant when visiting the sick. Also he must observe rules about his non-physical effect, not only in being quiet but also in being self-controlled in all aspects of life, for this has the best result on his reputation. His character must be that of a gentleman, and, as such, honourable and kindly towards all. For people dislike forwardness and interference, even if these qualities sometimes prove useful. He must also pay attention to his technical ability, for people like the same medicine in small doses. In facial expression he should be controlled but not grim. For grimness seems to indicate harshness and a hatred of mankind, while a man who bursts into guffaws and is too cheerful is considered vulgar. This must especially be avoided. He must be just in every social intercourse, and a sense of fairness ought to help him in every dealing. The relationship between doctor and patient is a close one. Patients submit themselves to doctors, who are always likely to be meeting women and girls, and entering houses with valuable possessions. Towards all these, therefore, he must keep himself under strict self-control. The above, then, are the physical and psychological requirements for a doctor.

FESTIVAL AT ALEXANDRIA
c. 275 B.C.

The festival to which the two women in this famous scene are going is that of Adonis. The myth of Adonis is one of the many nature myths to explain summer and winter. He was a mortal loved by Aphrodite, who grieved so much at his death from a boar's wound that he was allowed to spend six months on earth every year. The origin of the myth is said to be Phoenician. Apart from Shelley's use of the name to commemorate the death of Keats, Virgil also called the subject of his fifth Eclogue Adonis (possibly Julius Caesar). The

Ptolemy mentioned is Ptolemy II, the son of Alexander's general, who seems to have made a treaty with Rome. Theocritus was a native of Syracuse, and may have been about forty when this Idyll was written in Alexandria.

Source: Theocritus, Idyll 15.

Further Readings: Loeb translation by J. M. Edmonds. Apart from the fundamental *Social and Economic History of the Hellenistic World* by M. Rostovtzeff, T. R. Glover has some pages on Alexandria in *The Ancient World*. Theocritus is considered by Auguste Couat (trans. J. Loeb) in *Alexandrian Poetry*, 324–222 B.C. The *C.A.H.* chapter (vol. VII, iv) is also by Rostovtzeff.

(Gorgo, with her maid Eutychis, calls on Praxinoa whose maid Eunoa answers the door.)

GORGO: Is Praxinoa at home?

PRAXINOA: Ah, Gorgo dear, here you are at last; I thought you were never coming. Yes, I'm here. Eunoa, see to a chair for her, and put a cushion on it.

GORGO: Thank you, it's very nice as it is.

PRAXINOA: Well, do sit down.

GORGO: My word, what an ass I've been. You should have seen the men and chariots; boots and long tunics all over the place. I only just got here alive. The road seemed endless, and your house would be the farthest of all.

PRAXINOA: That's my fool of a husband; came and took a place at the world's end, fit only for animals not human beings, just to stop us being neighbours and to stir up trouble, the old spoil-sport. He's always the same!

GORGO: Careful! Don't call your Dinon such things while Baby's around. Just look, dear, how he's watching you. Cheer up, little Zopyrus, my darling. She's not speaking of da-da.

PRAXINOA: Good Lord, the baby understands.

GORGO: Nice da-da.

PRAXINOA: That nice da-da of his!—the other day I said to him, 'Daddy, please buy some soap and rouge from the shop.' Do you know what he did? He came back with some salt, and him a grown man.

GORGO: Mine's just the same; he's terribly close with money, is Diocleidas. Yesterday he went and bought five old purses, shoddy old bits of dog's hair, all got to be repaired. And he paid 7/6d. apiece for them. But come on, get your dress and coat on We're off to see the Adonis of the mighty king Ptolemy. I hear the Queen's outfit's pretty staggering.

PRAXINOA: Oh, I don't know. I expect it's just the same as usual.

GORGO: But if you've been and someone else hasn't, you can have a fine old gossip about it all. We must get a move on.

PRAXINOA: I suppose that those with nothing to do are always on holiday. Oh, all right then. Eunoa, you go and put that spinning back with the rest and stop picking your spots. Cats love to have a nice soft sleep. Here, get busy, and hurry up with some water. Heavens, we first want the water, and she brings the soap. Give it me, then. Not too much, wastrel. Now pour out the water. You slut, you've wet my dress, stop. Now I'm clean and sweet, thank God. Where's the key of the large chest? Bring it here.

GORGO: I like that folding dress, Praxinoa. It suits you. Tell me, how much did you pay for the material?

PRAXINOA: Don't remind me, Gorgo. Well over a fiver, and I put my heart and soul into making it up.

GORGO: Well, it's come out excellently.

PRAXINOA: Very kind of you to say so. Fetch me my cloak and arrange my hat properly. I'm leaving you here, baba. Horses bite little boys. You can squawl as much as you like, but I won't have you lamed. We're off! Phrygia, take the baby and play with him; call in the dog and lock the outside door.

Heavens, what a crowd! How on earth are we to get through this mass? They're like ants. You've done us some wonderful good, Ptolemy, since your father was exalted to heaven. There aren't any crooks nowadays creeping around Egyptian-style, fleecing the pedestrians, and playing the sort of horrible games the dreadful, deceitful rascals played before.

Dear Gorgo, what's to become of us? Here are the king's war horses. Good sir, don't trample me down. Look how fierce the chestnut is and how he's rearing up. Eunoa, don't be so reckless; get out of the way. He'll finish off his leader. I thank my lucky stars that I left baby at home.

GORGO: Cheer up, Praxinoa; we've got left behind now and they're reached their places.

PRAXINOA: And I'm nearly myself again too. Ever since a child I've had a special dread of horses and clammy snakes. Hurry up! A big crowd's pushing down on us.

GORGO: Have you come from the Court, dear?

OLD WOMAN: Yes, ducks.

GORGO: Easy to get there?

OLD WOMAN: The Greeks got into Troy by trying, didn't they? Where there's a will there's a way.

GORGO: The old woman's gone off with her proverbs.

PRAXINOA: Women know everything, even about Adam and Eve.

GORGO: Oh, look, Praxinoa; what a crowd around the doors!

PRAXINOA: Staggering! Give me your hand, Gorgo. And you, Eunoa, take hold of Eutychis's. Hold on, lest you get separated. Let's all go in together. Hold on to me tight, Eunoa. Damn, my summer coat's already split, Gorgo. Heavens, man, take care of my coat, if you want to live.

IST STRANGER: It's really out of my power, but I'll try.

PRAXINOA: What a mass! They're shoving like pigs.

STRANGER: Chin up, ladies; we're O.K.

PRAXINOA: God bless you, Sir, for ever for looking after us. What a good, kind man! Eunoa's getting squashed. Come on, you coward, give a push.

Hurrah! 'Everyone in', as the bridegroom said as he shut the door on the bride.

GORGO: Praxinoa, do come here. Just have a look at the decorations, so light and graceful. You'd say that they were some god's work.

PRAXINOA: The goddess of handicraft! The weavers and embroiderers that worked on those detailed pictures must have been marvels. How real everything seems, standing still or moving about. And how alive they look, quite unlike things spun. What a wonderful piece of work is man! And just look at the Adonis on his silver bed, with the first down just coming on his cheeks. Oh, thrice-loved Adonis, loved even in Hell!

2ND STRANGER: Do stop chattering like a lot of birds. They'll bore the pants off me with their platitudes.

PRAXINOA: Ha, where's he from? What's it to him if we do chatter. Go and lord it over your own slaves. You're talking to ladies from Syracuse. Actually we are Corinthian by birth like Bellerophon. We are talking Peloponnesian. I suppose Dorians are allowed to talk Doric? Let's pray only to have one boss. Don't you waste your time on me, sir.

GORGO: Hush, Praxinoa. The Argive lady's daughter is about to sing the *Adonis*. She's a pretty skilled singer and won the competition for the dirge last year. She will do it beautifully, I'm sure. She's clearing her throat.

(The dirge is sung)

GORGO: Praxinoa, how wonderful we women are. She's lucky to know all that, and luckier still to be able to sing it so well. But it's time to go home. Diocleidas will be wanting his lunch. The man's as sharp as vinegar; you can't come near him when he's hungry. Good-bye, lovely Adonis, and I hope you find us well when you come again.

DUILLIUS AND THE BATTLE OF MYLAE
260 B.C.

In the first Punic war (264–241 B.C.), the Romans had to struggle against the much superior naval skill of the Carthaginians. The story is told that they captured an enemy ship and slavishly copied it with remarkable speed. A fleet of such ships, manned by sailors who had much of their training on dry land, engaged the Cathaginian fleet at Mylae, off the north-east coast of Sicily, and using the special boarding-plank, the *corvus*, managed to defeat them. The Roman admiral was Duillius, who, much to the annoyance of some of the reactionary Romans, paraded his victory, putting up reminders of exactly what he had done.

Source: Inscription, C.I.L. I, 2, 25, available in the Loeb Edition, *Remains of Old Latin*, iv, p. 129. For the argument about whether the Inscription is genuine, see the above.

Further Reading: For Carthage, see *C.A.H.* vol. VII, ch. xxi, by Tenney Frank and *Carthage* by B. H. Warmington. For the Roman navy, see J. H. Thiel's *A History of Roman Sea Power before the 2nd Punic War*. Anderson's *Oared Fighting Ships* has a discussion on the vexed problem of the trireme.

He (Duillius) lifted the siege of the Segestans. All the Carthaginian legions and their greatest commander fled openly from the camp by daylight after nine days. He took the town of Macela by storm. And in the same year of office, he, as consul, was the first to be successful in ships on the sea, and to equip and prepare naval forces and fleets. With those ships he conquered in battle in the deep sea all the Punic fleets and the greatest Carthaginian forces in the presence of their commander, Hannibal,[1] and forcibly captured ships with their crews—one septireme, thirty quinqueremes and triremes—and sank thirteen. 3,600 gold coins were taken. 100,000 [at least] silver coins were taken as booty. Total sum taken worth . . . [figure incomplete]. He was the first to donate naval booty to the people and the first to lead in triumph freeborn Carthaginians.

ZENON, MINOR OFFICIAL
259 B.C.

One of the attractions of the discovery of papyrus rolls in Egypt is the light which they throw on ordinary events (see page 77). Sometimes we get a lot of information about one man, like Zenon. He seems to have been an agent for Apollonius who was the Dioecetes or Financial Minister to Ptolemy Philadelphus (285–246 B.C.). In these extracts Zenon is seen to have been a busy man, required to use his influence and talents on a wide variety of subjects. Instructions from Apollonius, petitions for help, notes from contractors, a desk diary with matters needing attention, even a clothes list, all these tell a detailed story of a minor official.

Source: Various extracts from *Select Papyri*, vol. I, translated in the Loeb series by A. S. Hunt and C. C. Edgar.

Further Reading: The most detailed information about conditions in Egypt is given by M. Rostovtzeff in *Social and Economic History of the Hellenistic World*.

---

[1] Not the later, more famous one.

1. To Zenon—Urgent

Apollonius greets Zenon. Load on board the maximum number of the thickest logs from the seasoned timber and send it soonest to Alexandria in time to use it for the Festival of Isis. Farewell.

(From the dates mentioned in the letter, it appears that the order must have come too late.)

2. . . . Nicanor, son of Xenocles, of Cnidus, agent to Toubias, has sold to Zenon, son of Agreophon, of Caunus, agent to Apollonius the Dioecetes, a Babylonian slave-girl called Sphragis, aged seven, for fifty drachmas. . . .

3. To Zenon—Greetings from Hierocles

I hope that you are well; I am in good health. You wrote to me about Pyrrhus. You asked me to train him if I am fully confident of his ability, and if not, to avoid unnecessary expense and diverting him from his letters. The gods know best about any certainty I may have, but Ptolemaeus is as sure as a man can be that Pyrrhus is much better than those now in training who had a good start on him, and that he will be well ahead of them in a very short time. He is making excellent progress in this and his other studies and, with god's luck, I hope to see you receive the crown for his success. Please send him a bathing apron quickly, if possible of goatskin or, failing that, of thin hide. Also a tunic and a cloak, a mattress, blanket and pillows—oh, and the honey too. You write that you are surprised that I did not grasp that there is a toll on all these. I do realize it. But you are in a position to be able to arrange for their safe despatch.

(The last sentence would suggest that Zenon was being asked to use his official position as agent to the Finance Minister to help a friend.)

4. To Zenon—Greetings from Platon

The father of Demetrius who will hand you this letter happens, it appears, to be spending some time in the Arsinoe district. The boy therefore wants some job there too. Knowing of your kindness, certain of his friends have asked me to write to you about him. Can you possibly find him employment in your service? Please do us this favour and think of something for him to do, whatever you think suitable. If you can make use of him, please look after him in other ways too. As a mark of appreciation I have sent to you from Sosus two artabae of chick-peas, worth five drachmas each, and I will try to buy twenty more artabae if there are any at Naucratis and bring them to you. Farewell.

5. Memo to Zenon from Kydippus

The doctors have ordered me to get hold of the following items. I would not have bothered you if I could have bought them in the market. Apollonius suggested that I write to you of what I need. If you have any supplies, please send me a jar of Chian or Lesbian wine, the sweetest possible, and as much honey as you can, preferably a chous. And organize the vessel to be filled with salt-fish. The doctors think I have most need of these things. If I get better and go on holiday to Byzantium, I'll bring you back some good salt-fish.

6. Memo to Zenon from Theophilus the painter

Tender for the work on the house of Diotimus.

(i) The Portico: the cornice painted with a purple border, the upper wall decorated in different colours, the lower course in a vetch-seed pattern and the pediment with circular veining; supply of materials and labour—30 drachmas.

(ii) The dining-room with seven couches: to do the ceiling in the pattern you saw, to paint the lower course in a pleasing shade and to paint the Lesbian cornice; supply of materials and labour—20 drachmas.

(iii) The dining-room with five couches: to paint the cornices; supply of materials and labour—3 drachmas.

The total sum—53 drachmas. If you provide the materials the cost will be 30 drachmas.

7. [Two lists of matters requiring attention]

(a) See Herodotus about the goat-hair, and ask Ameinios how much he sold per mna.

Write to Dioscourides about the boat.

Settle with Timaeus about the pigs.

Draft the agreement with Apollodorus and write to him to supply.

Load the boat with timber.

Write to Jason to have Dionysius put the wool on board, and to transport it down river when washed (a quarter of the Arabian wool); also to transport the sour wine.

Write to Meliton to plant some Bumastus vines from Neoptolemus, and to Alkimus if he approves.

Write to Theogenes about twelve yokes of oxen.

Write to Iatrokles and Theodorus about corn before the water in the irrigation canal drops.

(*b*) Get the olive kernels.

Get the olive-oil from Heragorus.

Buy for the horses 4 strigils, 4 rubbing-cloths, 4 scrapers, and a strigil for Phatres.

Get the cuttings of the walnuts.

Find out the assignment of wine sent down river, and to what district it has been assigned.

To fetch Hermon's slave-boy.

8. Zenon's wardrobe containing:

linen wrap, washed	1
clay-coloured winter cloak, washed	1
,, ,, ,, ,, , worn	1
,, ,, summer ,, , half-worn	1
natural winter cloak, washed	1
,, ,, ,, , worn	1
vetch-coloured summer cloak, new	1
white sleeved-tunic for winter, washed	1
natural ,, ,, ,, ,, , worn	1
natural tunic for winter, worn	2
white tunic ,, ,, , washed	2
,, ,, ,, ,, , half-worn	1
,, ,, for summer, new	3
unbleached tunic for summer	1
,, ,, ,, ,, , half-worn	1

white outer-garments, washed	1
„ „ „ , half-worn	1
pillowcases	1 pr.
socks, clay-coloured, new	2 prs.
„ , white, new	2 prs.
girdles, white, new	2 prs.

COMPENSATIONS AT ALEXANDRIA
c. 250 B.C.

Alexandria, as already seen in the extract from Theocritus (page 65), was a cosmopolitan city. It adopted a mixture of Hellenistic and Egyptian ways of life, with Greek public institutions and codes, but retaining much of the private and religious customs of the old inhabitants. It is hard to disentangle in the following code the points of Greek Law from the aspects common to many oriental codes, like the laws of Moses and Hammurabi.

Source: Greek Papyrus, in *Select Papyri* (Loeb), vol. II.

Further Reading: Loeb translation by C. C. Edgar and A. S. Hunt. M. Rostovtzeff in *C.A.H.* vol. VII, ch. iv, and his *Social and Economic History of the Hellenistic World* gives the best background. Hammurabi's Law Code is found in *Ancient Near Eastern Texts* (ed. by J. B. Pritchard). A simple, general account is also given in W. M. Flinders Petrie's *Social Life in Ancient Egypt.*

Threatening with iron

If a free man threatens another free man with iron, bronze, stone or wood, let him be fined a hundred drachmas if he loses the case. If a slave man or woman threatens a free man or woman, he or she must receive at least a hundred lashes, or the slave's master must pay to the victim double the penalty than that prescribed for a free man, if he loses the case.

Drunken assault

Whenever anyone commits any personal injury when drunk, or after dark, or in a sacred place, or in the Agora, he must pay double the prescribed penalty.

Slaves striking free men

If a slave man or woman strikes a free man or woman, he or she must receive at least a hundred lashes, or his master must pay double the penalty granted if a free man had been the culprit, providing that he agrees on the facts. If the case is disputed, then the master must be sued for a hundred drachmas a blow. If he loses then he must pay treble the amount without appeal, and if a large number of blows is involved, then the plaintiff must assess the damages, and the defendant must pay treble whatever assessment is made by the court.

Blows between free men

If a free man or woman strikes another free man or woman, starting a wrongful assault, he or she must pay a hundred drachmas without appeal if defeated in the case. If the blows are more than one, the plaintiff must assess the blows and sue for them, and the defendant must pay double the assesssment made by the court. If anyone strikes a magistrate in the exercise of his official duties, he must pay treble the penalties if defeated.

Outrage

If anyone commits an outrage against another in a way not covered above, the victim shall assess the injury and bring the person to court, stating accurately the manner in which he claims to have been outraged and the date of the offence. The loser must pay double the assessment fixed by the court.

ROMAN CAMP DEFENCES
198 B.C.

Though written of a time of which Polybius had no first-hand experience, the following description must certainly have been based on personal observation gained at a later date, presumably about 150 B.C. Flamininus, the first Roman general in Greece, was a Philhellene and ended his short stay with the proclamation of the independence of all Greek states. Rome had been invited to Greece, and imperialist designs were not yet in their thoughts. For the life of Polybius, see page 81.

Source: Polybius, *Histories*, xviii, 18.

Further Reading: Loeb translation by W. R. Paton. On Roman warfare, read F. E. Adcock's *The Roman Art of War under the Republic.* F. R. Cowell has a brief passage in *Cicero and the Roman Republic* (ch. ii) and H. Stuart-Jones' *Companion to Roman History* (ch. iii) also deals with the subject. The relevant chapters in *C.A.H.* vol. VIII, vi and vii, are by Maurice Holleaux.

Flamininus could not find out the position of the enemy camp, but knowing definitely that they were in Thessaly, he ordered all his troops to cut stakes to carry with them against any possible need for them. This seems to be quite impossible by the Greek method, but easy if the Roman system is followed. For the Greeks have some difficulty in holding their own pikes on the march, finding them very heavy to carry, but the Romans hang their shields from their shoulders by leather straps, carry their javelins in one hand, and so can manage stakes as well.

There is also a considerable difference between the two sorts of stake. The Greeks think that the best stake is one which has many large branches off the stem, but the Roman stake has two, three, or at the most four side shoots, and these all on the same side. The result is that it is very easy to carry them—a man ties three or four together and lifts them up—and they certainly give greater protection when in use. When you put Greek stakes in front of the rampart, they are easy to pull up, for there is only one part that grips and is gripped by the earth, and its offshoots are large and numerous, which means that two or three men can stand around pulling on the offshoots of the same stake, and easily draw it up. When this happens, an immediate entrance is effected because of the width of the stake, and its neighbours are loosened because such a palisade has its stakes infrequently inter-twined and crossed over.

The opposite is the case with Roman stakes. They interweave them when putting them in, so that it is hard to see to which stake embedded in the earth the offshoots belong, or to which offshoots the stakes belong. Furthermore, it is impossible to pass the hand through and take hold of the stake, because they are planted thickly and intertwined, with the offshoots carefully sharpened. And if you can get hold of it, it is not easy to pull it out, for several reasons. Firstly, all attempts meet with almost absolute resistance from the earth. Secondly, anyone that pulls at one stake is forced to try to lift out many others that come with it because they are interwoven. It is not at all likely that two or three men will get hold of the same stake. And even if a man does succeed by brute force in pulling out one or two, the gap created is negligible. So this kind of palisade has great advantages: stakes of the sort are easy to carry, easy to find and give greater and more lasting protection. It is obvious, in my opinion at least, that this is one of the Roman military inventions above all others that is well worth imitation and adoption.

SUDDEN DEATH IN EGYPT
178 B.C.

These reports to officials date from possibly 178 B.C., A.D. 182 and A.D. 216, and all come from Egypt. It is interesting to note the existence of some sort of police in Egypt as early as the first extract, and also that accidents had to be reported.

Source: Select Papyri (Loeb), vol. II, pp. 384–8; translated by A. S. Hunt and C. C. Edgar.

(*a*) To Osoroeres, Royal Scribe:

On the 5th inst., as I was patrolling the fields around the village, I found a considerable quantity of blood. I learnt on inquiry from members of the village that Theodotus, son of Dositheus, had gone out and had not returned at the time I made this my report.

(*b*) To Aurelius Julius Marcellinus, Centurion; from Aurelia Tisais, daughter of Tais, formerly enrolled a member of the village of Teptunis in the district of Polemon.

Sir, My father, Kalabaleus, with my brother Nilus, left on a hunting expedition to hunt hares on the 3rd of this month, and up to the present time they have not returned. I suspect that they may have suffered some fatality. I make this report, hoping that it will be clear to you that, if they have met with a fatality, those found guilty may be answerable to me.

26th Choiak in the 25th year of Marcus Aurelius Severus Antoninus Caesar.

(*c*) To Hierax, Strategos, from Leonidas, also called Serenus, son of Tauris from Senepta.

Late last evening, the 6th, during the festival in Senepta, while castanet dancers were performing as usual at the house of my brother-in-law Ploution, his slave Epaphroditus, aged 8, leaning out of the window of the same house wishing to see the castanet dancers, fell and was killed.

BUYING A FARM
c. 170 B.C.

Farming was the only legitimate business enterprise in which a Roman Senator could engage. It is not surprising, therefore, that the die-hard old reactionary, Cato the Censor, should have left a book on agriculture. These extracts show quite clearly the coming crisis in Italian farming, for it can be seen that arable land was considered uneconomic compared with other uses to which farms could be put.

Source: Cato, *De Agri Cultura*, I, i.

Further Reading: Loeb translation by W. D. Hooper and H. B. Ash. Roman Agriculture is discussed in *Cicero and the Roman Republic*, ch. iii (F. R. Cowell), and there is a more detailed account by W. E. Heitland in the *Legacy of Rome*. Tenney Frank wrote the articles in *C.A.H.* vol. VIII, ch. xi, but also see a masterly summary by Hugh Last in *C.A.H.* vol. IX, ch. i.

When you are thinking of buying a farm, be sure not to complete the purchase over-hastily, take every trouble to visit it, and do not be satisfied with a single tour of inspection. If it is a good property, the more often you go, the more satisfaction it will give you. Pay attention to how the neighbours' farms look. In a good district they ought to look very well. Be sure not to commit yourself, but go into the farm and inspect it, leaving yourself a way of getting out of the deal. It should have a good climate and be free from storms, and the soil should be naturally fertile. If possible, the foot of a hill is best, facing south in a healthy spot, with a good supply of labourers. The water supply must be plentiful, and it must be near a large town, or the sea or a navigable river, or a good well-used road. You want your farm to be in a district where land does not frequently change hands, and where people regret having sold their property. Be sure that the buildings are in good condition, and do not be over-hasty in rejecting a former owner's advice or methods. A better purchase can be made from a man who is a good farmer and a good builder. When you visit the property, look around to see how many oil-presses and wine-vats there are. If the number is small, then you will know that the harvest is proportionately meagre. The farm should not necessarily have masses of equipment, but it must be well-sited. Take care to see that equipment is kept to a minimum to avoid extravagance on the land. Remember that fields are like men; however much profit they make, if they are extravagant, not much is left.

If I were asked what is the best kind of farm, I would suggest a vineyard of about 65 acres in the best situation with various types of soil, if, that is, the wine is good and plentiful. Next to it comes a watered garden, third an osier-bed, fourth an olive grove, fifth pasturage, sixth arable land, seventh a wood for timber, eighth an orchard and ninth a wood for acorns for feed.

[There was no large manufacturing industry in Italy. Individual towns got the reputation for producing the best machinery. This remained true in Italy for centuries.]

Tunics, togas, cloaks, aprons and clogs can be bought at Rome; caps, iron tools, scythes, spades, hoes, axes, harness, ornaments and chains at Cales or Minturnae; spades at Venafrum; carts and drags at Suessa or in Lucania; jars and pots at Alba Longa or Rome; tiles at Venafrum. Ploughs bought at Rome are best for tough soil, Campanian ones for rich dark soil. Roman yokes are the best. Detachable plough-shares are preferable. It is better to buy oil-mills at Pompeii and at Rufus's yard at Nola; nails and bars at Rome; pails, olive vessels, water pitchers, wine urns and other bronze vessels at Capua or Nola. Campanian baskets from Capua are useful. Pulley ropes and all other ropes can be had from Capua, and Roman baskets at Suessa. Lucius Tunnius of Casinum and Gaius, son of Lucius Mennius, of Venafrum make the best ropes for the wine-press.

KEEPING SLAVES
c. 170 B.C.

The early second century B.C. saw a great increase in the slave population of Italy, as Roman power began to spread through the Mediterranean. In particular they were used on the land, frequently in chain-gangs. To Cato, they were a valuable piece of equipment, and although we can detect no humanitarian feelings in him, he was conscious that slaves must be treated reasonably well if they were to repay the money invested in them.

Source: Cato, *De Agri Cultura*, LVI.

Further Reading: Loeb translation by W. D. Hooper and H. B. Ash. For Roman Agriculture, see the previous extract. For Slavery, see *Slavery in Classical Antiquity* (ed. M. I. Finley) and chapter 4 of Michael Grant's *The World of Rome*.

Rations for the slaves

For the actual labourers four pecks of wheat in the winter months, and four and a half in summer. The overseer, housekeeper, foreman and head-shepherd should receive three pecks. The chain-gang should receive four pounds of bread a day in winter, five from the time when they begin to dig the vines until the figs start to ripen, and then back to four again.

Wine for the slaves

For three months after the harvest, they should drink rough wine. In the fourth month, half a pint a day, or about two gallons a month. For the fifth, sixth, seventh and eighth months, the ration should be a pint a day, or four gallons a month. For the remaining four months, give them one and a half pints a day, or six gallons a month. For the feasts of the Saturnalia and Compitalia (December) there should be an extra ration per man of two and a half gallons. The total wine issue per man for a year should be about forty-two gallons. An additional amount can be given as a bonus to the chain-gang, depending on how well they work. A reasonable quantity for them to have to drink per annum is about sixty gallons.

Relish for the slaves

Keep all the windfall olives you can. Then keep the ripe olives from which only a small yield could be gained. Issue them sparingly to make them last as long as possible. When the olives are finished, give them fish-pickle and vinegar. Give each man a pint of oil a month. A peck of salt should be enough for a man for a year.

Clothes for the slaves

A tunic three and a half feet long and a blanket-cloak every other year. When you issue a tunic or cloak, take in the old one to make rough clothes. You ought to give them a good pair of clogs every other year.

POLYBIUS AND SCIPIO
167 B.C.

The occupation of Greece brought many educated Greeks to Rome, theoretically as hostages of good behaviour or as slaves. Several were befriended by influential Romans, like the comic playwright Terence. Polybius, a man of considerable importance in Achaea, was adopted by the family of Aemilius Paullus. The latter's sons had been adopted by the families of the Scipios and the Fabii. The Scipio in this story became, under the more usual name of Aemilianus, the leading man of his age, the final destroyer of Carthage, and the conqueror of the troublesome Spanish town of Numantia. He married the sister of the revolutionary tribunes, Tiberius and Gaius Gracchus, and was a well-known Philhellene. Polybius alternates between the first and third persons.

Source: Polybius, *Histories*, xxxi, 23.

Further Reading: Loeb translation by W. R. Paton. T. R. Glover in *C.A.H.* vol. VIII, ch. i, deals with Polybius and his Roman connections. H. H. Scullard's *Roman Politics* 220–150 B.C. gives a detailed analysis of the political background. Scipio appears as one of the imaginary group in Cicero's *De Amicitia* and *De Senectute* (Loeb translation by W. A. Falconer, Penguin translation of *De Senectute* by Michael Grant).

I promised to explain why and how the fame of Scipio grew so greatly in Rome and reached a dazzling height more quickly than might have been expected, and in addition to explain how his friendship with Polybius became so close that report of it circulated not only in Italy and Greece but men even further afield got to know of their affection and inseparability. We have already recounted above that their friendship originated in the loan of some books and subsequent discussion of them. This acquaintance flourished, and when the Achaean hostages were sent off to various cities, Fabius and Scipio, the two young sons of Aemilius Paullus, eagerly asked the general to let Polybius remain behind in Rome. This was allowed, and they became closer friends when the following incident occurred.

All three were leaving Fabius's house when Fabius happened to go off to the Forum while Polybius went the other way with Scipio. As they walked along, Scipio, speaking in a low gentle voice and blushing slightly, asked, 'Polybius, we are brothers, Fabius and I. Tell me, why do you speak and address all your questions and answers to him, and ignore me? I feel that your opinion of me is that shared by the rest of Rome, who, as far as I hear, think of me as a quiet, idle type, very different from the normal Roman man of action, just because I do not choose to plead in court. They say that my family is not in need of such a man as me as its champion, but a person of the opposite qualities. This greatly upsets me.'

Polybius was perplexed by the opening words of the young man (he was only eighteen at the time) and replied, 'Please, Scipio, don't say or think such things. My behaviour towards you is not because I condemn or ignore you. But your brother is older than you, and so I begin and end my conversation with him, and turn to him in replies and advice, thinking that you share his opinions. My heart warmed just now when I heard you say that you were upset at being thought over-meek and mild for a person coming from your family. It showed your greatness of heart. It would give me great pleasure to give you all my attention, and to help you to speak and act in a way worthy of your illustrious lineage. As for the intellectual studies which, as I see, win your admiration and interest, you will find plenty of ready assistants from the crowds of intelligent men whom I see flocking from Greece to Rome at the present time. And as for what upset you just now, you may be sure that you will find no one who will be more ready to support or assist you than me.'

Almost before Polybius had finished, Scipio clasped his hand warmly in both of his, and said, 'I hope to see the day when you put everything else second to devoting yourself to me and living with me. I am sure that then I will quickly show myself worthy of my family and my ancestors.' Polybius was delighted to see the spirit and affection of the young man, but was slightly worried when he considered the pre-eminence of the family and the prosperity of its members. But after this conversation, the young man never left Polybius's side, preferring his society to everything else.

ABSCONDING SLAVES
156 B.C.

The problem of keeping slaves under control was always recurring in the Greek and Roman worlds. Slave revolts at Rome reached their peak with the insurrection of Spartacus in 73 B.C. Attitude to slaves varied considerably, as already seen on pages 32 and 80. The slaves mentioned here must have been valuable, as the rewards for their return are very high.

Source: Select Papyri (Loeb), vol. II, p. 136.

Further Reading: Loeb translation by C. C. Edgar and A. S. Hunt. For slavery, see under Keeping Slaves (page 80). Also refer to M. Rostovtzeff's *Social and Economic History*.

A slave named Hermon, also answering to Nilos, belonging to Aristognus, the son of Chrysippus, the Alabandan ambassador in Alexandria, has run away. A Syrian by birth from Bombyce, he is eighteen years old, of medium height, clean shaven, thin legged, with a dimple on his chin, a mole on the left side of his nose, and a scar on the left of his face above the lips, with two foreign signs tattoed on his right wrist. He took with him three boxes of coined gold, ten pearls, and an iron ring on which were a flask and strigils. He was wearing a chlamys and a loin-cloth. Anyone who apprehends him shall receive three talents, two talents for pointing him out in sanctuary, or five talents for showing him to be at the house of a man answerable at law. Information should be lodged with the general's secretary.

Another slave, Bion, the property of Callicrates, a chief equerry at court, ran away with him. He is short in stature, broad across the shoulders, with fat legs and bright eyes. When he left he was wearing an himation and a slave's cloak, and took a woman's dress worth nearly seven talents of copper. The same rewards as above are offered for his arrest. Information to be lodged with the general's secretary.

THE END OF CARTHAGE
146 B.C.

Carthage had been conquered by Scipio Africanus in 202 B.C. But Rome was becoming frightened of signs of revival and by infringements of the peace treaty. A strong movement, led by the now aged Cato with his often repeated 'Carthage must be destroyed', insisted on its annihilation. After some unsuccessful campaigns, Scipio Aemilianus was given the task. He took Polybius with him. Unfortunately, the passage in Polybius describing the actual destruction of the town is lost, but this extract may show that the Roman fears were unfounded. Golosses, the Numidian king, was a Roman ally.

Source: Polybius, *Histories,* xxxviii, 7.

Further Reading: Loeb translation by W. R. Paton. B. H. Warmington's *Carthage* is useful, and see also T. R. Glover in *C.A.H.* vol. VIII, ch. i, for Polybius. B. L. Hallward wrote the chapter on the fall of Carthage in *C.A.H.* vol. VIII, ch. xv.

Now Hasdrubal, the Carthaginian general, was empty-headed and vainglorious, with a total lack of practical military ability. His faulty judgment can be seen in several particulars. To meet Golosses, the Numidian king, he went forward clad in full armour with a purple cloak over the top of it, escorted by ten armed attendants. Advancing about twenty yards from the escort with a ditch and palisade in front of him, he signalled to the king to come forward to meet him, though proper protocol demanded the reverse. But Golosses in a typically simple Numidian way advanced by himself, asking, as he drew near, what made Hasdrubal afraid that he came armed from head to foot. 'The

Romans' was the reply. . . . He asked Golosses to beg Scipio in the name of heaven and his own good fortune to spare the town, and to be sure that if this prayer was of no avail, the inhabitants would rather be slaughtered than surrender. The two separated after this conversation, agreeing to meet three days later.

When Golosses reported the request, Scipio said, with a wry smile, 'You dare to ask this, in spite of having shown such dreadful cruelty to our prisoners, and now seem to take hope in calling on the gods, though you have transgressed laws both human and divine'. King Golosses still wished to draw Scipio's attention to certain matters, especially that he must bring the siege to a hasty end. For, apart from natural accidents, the consular elections were at hand, and Scipio must take thought of these in case winter overtook him and a successor came out to reap the fruits of his labour without any pains to himself. Scipio listened carefully to what he said, and then asked him to inform Hasdrubal that he would grant a safe conduct to him, his wife and children, and to ten relatives or friends of the family. In addition he might take ten talents of his private money, and any hundred of his slaves.

Three days later, Golosses met Hasdrubal once again with this generous offer. Again Hasdrubal came forward to meet him in great pomp, dressed in purple and fully armed, leaving any king in a play far behind. He was naturally fat, and he now had a pot belly. His skin was unusually red, so that he looked as if he had been living like some ox fattened up for slaughter at a festival rather than as commander of a situation of such intense horror that it would be difficult for anyone to do justice to it in words. Yet when he met the king and heard the Roman terms, he kept on slapping his thigh, calling on fortune and the gods to witness that he, Hasdrubal, would not live to see the day on which the sun rose over a blazing city. For such a fire would be a fitting funeral-pyre for all true patriots.

When you consider this answer, you may wonder at the man's high-sounding words, but his practical actions will merely astound you by their futility and cowardice. First of all, at a time when the other citizens were dying like flies of hunger, he had repeated drinking parties, calling for rich second helpings, thus underlining others' helplessness by his own well-being. The number of the dying was almost unbelievable, as was the number which deserted to our side because of the famine. Secondly, by mocking, ill-treating and murdering many of the citizens, he held on to his power in a city that was in extremities in a way that a king in a prosperous state would hardly have dared to do.

ROMAN ARROGANCE
c. 130 B.C.

Not until 84 B.C. were all those who lived south of the Po granted full Roman citizenship. It needed the dangerous revolt of the Italian allies in 91 B.C. to remind the Romans of how precarious was their hold over the peninsula. The revolt had many causes, but not least was the high-handed treatment of a number of Roman officials. Gaius Gracchus, tribune in 123–122 B.C., tried to do something for the Italians, but he was unsuccessful.

Source: Speech of Gaius Gracchus, preserved by Aulus Gellius, x, iii, 5.

Further Reading: Histories of Gaius Gracchus are in H. H. Scullard's *From the Gracchi to Nero* and by Hugh Last in *C.A.H.* vol. IX, ch. ii. Chapter 3 of Michael Grant's *The World of Rome* deals with the social distinctions at Rome.

When a consul arrived at Sidicinum Teanum a few years back, his wife said that she would like to bath in the men's bath. The mayor of Sidicinum, Marcus Marius, was given the job of clearing the bath of those who were using it. But when the consul's wife told her husband that the baths had been made ready for her very slowly, and that they were not all that clean, a stake was put up in the square, and Marius, the leading man of the community, was brought forward. The clothes were stripped off his back and he was beaten with rods. The inhabitants of Calenum, on receipt of this news, decreed that no one should aim at washing in the public baths if a Roman magistrate were in town.

At Ferentinum a Roman praetor ordered the two local magistrates to be seized for the same reason. One of them thereupon threw himself off a wall, while the other was seized and also flogged. I will demonstrate by one example the extent of the arrogance and lack of control of some of our young nobles. A few years ago a young man came home from Asia, who had not even held a magistracy as yet, but had just served in an acting position. He was being carried in a litter. He was met by a Venusine farmer, who did not know what was in the litter, and asked as a joke whether it was a corpse they were carrying. On hearing this, the young man ordered the litter to be set down, and the yokel to be flogged with the straps that bound the litter, until he in fact died.

A ROMAN VISITOR TO EGYPT
112 B.C.

Egypt did not finally come into the Roman Empire till 30 B.C. But Roman influence had been felt long before that, and indeed asked for. Roman power was called in to settle the dynastic problem in 58–56 B.C. and there was a strong pro-Roman party in Egypt when Julius Caesar arrived in 48 B.C. Certainly it seems to have been diplomatic to extend a special welcome to a Roman as early as 112 B.C.

Source: Select Papyri (Loeb), vol. I, p. 416.

Further Reading: Loeb translation by C. C. Edgar and A. S. Hunt. M. Cary writes of Rome and Egypt in *C.A.H.* vol. IX, ch. viii.

To Asclepiades,

Lucius Memmius, a Roman Senator of considerable importance and position is sailing up from Alexandria on a sight-seeing tour to the district of Arsinoe. Receive him with proper ceremony, and see that accommodation is prepared in the usual places, landing-stages provided, and the under-mentioned gifts presented to him at the piers. Make sure about the appointments in the accommodation, the titbits to be given to Petesouchos and the crocodiles. Arrange for him to see the Labyrinth, and check up that the offerings and sacrifices are properly made. In every respect you must make certain that the man is contented, by showing the utmost zeal in your preparations.

ELECTIONS AT POMPEII
c. 80 B.C.

With annual magistracies, electioneering at Rome played a very important part in the life of any would-be politician. Quintus Cicero sent his brother, Marcus, a little manual called *De petitione Consulatus*, which included everything that he thought that a candidate should do. There are also many references in Marcus's own letters. Each country town in Italy had its own magistrates. At the head of these were the Duoviri, roughly the equivalent of Mayors. The usual Roman policy of dividing the authority was followed. It is obvious from these notices and from elsewhere that Elections at Rome were not always cleanly fought.

Source: Graffiti painted on walls at Pompeii, collected in *Remains of Old Latin*, vol. iv (Loeb series, translated by E. H. Warmington).

Further Reading: The letter of Q. Cicero is translated in the Loeb series by W. Glynn Williams. F. R. Cowell has a chapter on electioneering in *Cicero and the Roman Republic*, ch. 12.

1. Numerius Barcha, a fine man; I appeal to you to elect him member of the Board of Duoviri. So may Venus of Pompeii, holy, hallowed goddess, be kind to you.

2. Numerius Veius Barcha, may you rot!

3. Numerius Veius, a fine man; settlers, I appeal to you to elect him member of the Board of Duoviri.

4. Your best friend—Marcus Marius. Elect him Aedile.

5. Marcus Marius, a fine man: I appeal to you, settlers.

6. Quintus Caecilius, a generous man. To be Quaestor, I appeal to you.

7. Quintus Caecilius, a fair and generous man. To be Quaestor.

   (Nos. 8–10 are in R. H. Barrow's *Latin Inscriptions*, nos. 94, 95, and 97. They are of uncertain date, probably much later.)

8. The muleteers ask for Gaius Julius Polybius as a member of the Board of Duoviri.

9. I appeal to you to elect Gaius Julius Polybius Aedile: he makes good bread.

10. I appeal to you to elect Marcus Cerrenius Vatia Aedile; all members of the 'late-drinkers' club ask for this.

CICERO SWALLOWS HIS PRIDE
75 B.C.

Cicero undertook his first official public post in 75 B.C. as Quaestor at Lilybaeum in Sicily. There he was responsible to the governor of the province for financial matters, especially for dealings in corn. As a man whose family had never held high posts, he was naturally touchy about his reputation. Later in his life he was very prepared to criticize dreary activity in the provinces and to claim that anyone living away from Rome was little more than half alive. Puteoli, like Baiae on the Bay of Naples, was one of the fashionable resorts that well-to-do Romans favoured in order to avoid the malarial autumns in the city.

Source: Cicero, *Pro Plancio,* 64.

Further Reading: Loeb translation by N. H. Watts. F. R. Cowell's *Cicero and the Roman Republic* contains much interesting matter.

So much goes on at Rome that events in the Provinces hardly get a hearing. I am not very worried about seeming to boast if I speak of my Quaestorship. For although it was very successful, I think that I have proved myself later in the higher offices the type of man who does not need to claim much glory from any praise bestowed on the humbler post of Quaestor. But I am confident that no one will deny that my Quaestorship in Sicily was excellently and popularly conducted. Indeed I will make a confession. I was of the impression at the time that everyone at Rome had just one topic of conversation—that Quaestorship. When corn was very dear I had sent a large amount, I was friendly with the businessmen, just to the merchants, liberal and easy with the Controller, and careful of my conduct with the allied states. Everyone approved of my diligence in every duty I had to perform. Unprecedented honours had been discovered for me by the Sicilians.

So I left the Province with the hope that the Roman people would readily offer me anything. But on my journey home I happened to put in at Puteoli which is normally thronging with eminent men. There I nearly collapsed when someone asked me when I had left Rome and whether there was any news. I replied that I was just returning from my Province. 'Oh, of course,' he said, 'it's from Africa, isn't it?' I gave an angry and cold answer, 'Certainly not—from Sicily.' Then another man, an apparent know-all, volunteered, 'Of course, don't you know that he has been Quaestor at Syracuse?' That finished it. I gave up my annoyance and just pretended to be one of those who had come to take the waters.

PIRACY IN SICILIAN WATERS
71 B.C.

Piracy was an ever-recurring problem to the Romans. The young Julius Caesar was kidnapped by some whom he later returned to kill; a pirate fleet actually lay off Ostia, the port of Rome, and in the end things got so bad that Pompey was given special powers to destroy them. This he did in 67 B.C. Cicero's speech mentioning these special powers is still extant (*De Imperio Cnaei Pompeii*). This extract comes from a case in 70 B.C. when he was prosecuting Verres, theoretically for extortion in his province of Sicily. In fact, he mentioned anything that was likely to get Verres condemned, and Verres was so alarmed at the wealth of evidence that he fled from Rome before the case was nearly over. So Cicero did not actually deliver the part of the speech given below, but he had spent time searching for the evidence and he decided to publish it just the same.

Source: Cicero, *Against Verres*, ii, V, 86.

Further Reading: Loeb translation by L. H. G. Greenwood. The fullest account of piracy is by H. A. Ormerod in *Piracy in the Ancient World*. The career of Verres is shortly described by Hugh Last in *C.A.H.* vol. IX, ch. vii.

Cleomenes left harbour on board the quadrireme from Centuripa, followed by ships from Segesta, Tyndaris, Herbita, Heraclea, Apollonia and Haluntium. It had all the appearance of a fine fleet, but was actually feeble and weak because of the leave of absence given to the marines and sailors. Our wonderful, industrious governor only had his eyes on this fleet of his command for as long as it sailed past his notorious debauch. He had not been seen for several days, but he allowed the sailors a brief look at him then, as he, a governor of the Roman people, stood in sandles, a purple cloak and a tunic that reached the ankles, leaning on a woman on the beach. This was the dress in which very many Sicilians and Roman citizens had seen him.

The fleet moved on and finally reached Pachynus after four days' sailing, where the sailors in their agony of hunger collected the roots of the wild palms, which are very plentiful there as in most of Sicily, and on these the poor desperate men fed. Cleomenes, on the other hand, who considered himself a second Verres in point of luxury, wickedness and leadership, drank himself silly all day long in his tent erected on the shore. While he was incapable and the rest starving, news suddenly came of a pirate vessel in the port of Odyssea (our fleet still being at Pachynus). Cleomenes was relying on the theoretical but far from actual existence of some land forces to bring his complement of sailors and oarsmen up to strength. But the same greedy method of Verres was found to have been applied to these as well as to the fleets and there were only a few left, for most had been dismissed. First Cleomenes gave orders for the mast to be raised in his own ship, sails to be set, anchors to be weighed, and instructed the signal to be given for the rest to follow him. This vessel from Centuripa had a remarkable turn of speed under canvas, though no one knew a ship's potential under oars during Verres's governorship, in spite of the fact that Cleomenes was short of fewer oarsmen and marines as a mark of special honour and favour.

The quadrireme quickly disappeared as if in flight, while the remaining ships were struggling in one spot. But they had more courage. Although they were few and their situation critical, they shouted out that they were prepared to fight, and were willing to offer in battle the part of their lives and strength still left to them by hunger. If Cleomenes had not fled so far in front, there could have been some plan for resistance, for his was the only decked ship; it was of such a size that it could have protected the rest, and in a pirate battle would have seemed like a city among those pirate sloops. But hungry, in want, and deserted by their leader and admiral, they could do nothing except begin to follow him on the same course. Like Cleomenes, they made for Helorus, not so much in flight from the pirates' attack as in pursuit of their commander. As each dropped back last of the column, so it came first into danger, as the pirates attacked the rear ship. . . . While all this was happening, Cleomenes had reached the shore at Helorus, where he jumped out, leaving the quadrireme wallowing in the sea. The remaining commanders, once their admiral had gone ashore, could not fight back or make their escape by sea, and so they followed Cleomenes to Helorus. Then Heracleo, the pirate chief, suddenly finding himself the victor quite beyond his expectation, not by any valour of his own but because of the greed and wickedness of Verres, gave orders for the glorious fleet of the Roman people to be set on fire and burnt as it lay drawn up on the beach. The time was early evening. . . .

News of this dreadful tragedy was brought to Syracuse late at night. Everyone converged on the governor's residence. . . . Cleomenes, in spite of the dark, did not dare to show his face in public, but shut himself up at home, without even the company of his wife, who could perhaps have consoled her husband in his misfortune [she was with Verres]. The domestic discipline of our singular governor was so strict that in such a crisis and at the receipt of such momentous news, no one was allowed in, and no one dared to wake Verres from his sleep or interrupt him if awake. When the news was known throughout the city, a great crowd gathered. . . . The governor was asked for, and when it was agreed that no one had told him the news, there was a sudden rush on the house. . . . While he was still half-asleep in a drunken stupor, the crowd gained control of themselves, took their arms and manned the Forum and the Island, which comprises a great part of the city.

The pirates waited for just one night at Helorus, then left our ships still smouldering and proceeded on their way to Syracuse. The first part they approached was the summer quarters of the governor, that part of the beach where throughout those days he had placed his tents and camp of luxury. They found the spot deserted, and realizing that the governor had moved, they at once began to penetrate quite fearlessly into the harbour itself. When I say the harbour, I mean that the pirates entered the city and the inmost part of the city. For at Syracuse the buildings do not come to an end at the harbour, but the harbour is surrounded by and contained in the town, which means that the edges of the walls are washed by the sea, and the water, as it were, ebbs into a bay formed by the town. Here, under your governorship, Verres, the pirate Heracleo sailed at his fancy with his four little pirate sloops. . . . And as he passed the Island, the roots of the wild palms found in our ships were thrown out to let everyone know of the crimes of Verres and the disaster that had come upon Sicily.

A ROMAN CITIZEN CRUCIFIED
71 B.C.

This second extract from Cicero's speech against Verres shows what absolute power the governor of a province had during his term of office, even over Roman citizens. There was, of course, redress to be had at the end of the year, and a permanent court to deal with cases of extortion had been in existence since 149 B.C. But many governors relied on being able to bribe the jury to acquit them. Crucifixion was the punishment reserved for runaway slaves, and would have been a familiar sight to most Romans in the year 70 B.C. after the collapse of Spartacus' slave revolt when over 5,000 slaves were crucified along the Appian Way.

Source: Cicero, *Against Verres* ii, V, 160.

Further Reading: Loeb translation by L. H. G. Greenwood. See the preceding extract, and also *C.A.H.* vol. IX, ch. viii, by H. A. Ormerod.

This man Gavius, a citizen of Consa, whom I am telling you of, was thrown into prison by Verres with a number of other Roman citizens, but somehow managed to escape from the stone quarries at Syracuse and reached Messina. He now could see Italy and the walls of the Roman town of Rhegium so close at hand that, refreshed from the fear of darkness and death by the light of liberty and, so to speak, the sweet smell of legality, he recovered strength and began to give voice to his complaints at Messina that he, a Roman citizen, had been thrown into chains, that he was making straight for Rome and would be ready for Verres when he got back. . . . The poor wretch was immediately led off by the mayor of Messina. Verres, who happened to reach the town that very day, was informed of the facts, that there was a Roman citizen who was complaining that he had been in the quarries at Syracuse; he had just been embarking uttering loud threats against Verres when he had been dragged off the ship and kept in custody for Verres to decide what he wanted done with him. Verres thanked the men for their thoughtfulness and attention to his interests. He then went to the Forum, enflamed with his wild criminal lust, his eyes ablaze and his whole face betraying his cruelty. Everyone was agog to know to what lengths he would go and what he would do, when he suddenly gave orders for the man to be brought out, to be stripped naked and to be tied up in the middle of the Forum, and for the rods to be got ready. The man in his misery shouted out that he was a Roman citizen, a burgher of Consa; he had served with a well-known Roman knight, Lucius Raecius, who did business at Palermo, and Verres could find out the truth of all this from him. Verres maintained that he had found out that Gavius had been sent as a spy by the pirate chiefs to Sicily, though no witness was produced, no evidence given, and no one had the least grounds for suspicion. He then ordered the man to be severely thrashed. And so, in the middle of the Forum at Messina, a Roman citizen was beaten with rods, and all the time, amidst the pain and noise of the blows, not a groan or sound escaped his lips except the cry, 'I am a citizen of Rome'. He thought that by this mention of his nationality he would be rid of all the blows and physical torture. But so far from this diminishing the force of the blows, as he repeatedly mentioned his state in entreaty, a cross, I repeat a cross, was got ready for the luckless man, who had never before even so much as seen such an instrument. . . .

Why was it, Verres, that you, though by their old custom the Messinians had fixed any cross in the Via Pompeia behind the city, ordered it to be set up in that part of the city facing the straits, adding the remark that you chose this spot so that he who claimed to be a Roman citizen, could from his cross look across at Italy and gaze at his native land? This was the only time in Messina's history that a cross was placed there.

CATILINE AND THE STATE OF ROME
63 B.C.

The conspiracy of Catiline occurred during Cicero's consulship. Thwarted in attempts at becoming consul himself, Catiline resorted to armed insurrection. But his plot to kill Cicero and take over the city was betrayed, at which point he fled from Rome to a private army near Florence. He was defeated the next year after savage resistance. Cicero wrote incessantly of his part in the story, in prose, verse and rhetoric. The four speeches delivered against Catiline still survive, but they were delivered in the heat of the moment and are clearly suspect. The following character sketch was given in a speech delivered some years later, when Cicero was intent on trying to show why his client should have been friendly with Catiline.

Source: Cicero, *Pro Caelio*, 12–14.

Further Reading: Loeb translation by J. H. Freese and R. Gardner. Latin passages are collected in *Roman Politics 80–44 B.C.* by J. R. Hawthorn and C. Macdonald. *The Roman Republic* by T. Rice Holmes gives a factual account. F. R. Cowell in *Cicero and the Roman Republic* and *The Revolutions of Ancient Rome* has a lively approach to the period. R. Syme's *The Roman Revolution* is the fundamental work on this period. *C.A.H.* vol. IX, ch. ix, by M. Cary.

Some years after his first public appearance, Caelius became friendly with Catiline, following the example of many men of every class and every age. I think that you will remember that Catiline had just the vague outlines, not the clear-cut signs, of great virtues. His real friends were a collection of evil men, while he feigned devotion to the best. Many were the lusts that lured him on, though there were also things that drove him to hard work and feats of endurance. The vices of evil desire smouldered in him, while his dedication to military skills flourished. I do not think that there was ever such a monster on earth so compounded of such natural affections and desires of such a different, diverse and contradictory nature. No man could be found more affable with the famous, or closer to the wicked. Was there ever another who proved himself so much a member of the better party, or showed himself so vile an enemy to the state? Has ever a man been known more foul in his pleasures or more enduring in his toils? Who greedier, who more avaricious, but who more generous in his largesse? Good qualities he had. He included many men in his friendship, he protected them with his loyalty, he shared his possessions with all and strove to serve the difficulties of all his friends with money, influence, physical effort and, if need arose, with audacious crimes. He could change and direct his nature to suit the occasion, he could bend and twist this way and that, living severely with the serious, affably with the relaxed, gravely with older men, pleasingly with the young, brazenly with the criminal, lustfully with the libidinous. With his varied and manifold nature, he had collected every bold criminal from every land, while he held to him many a brave good man by an outward appearance of a simulated virtue. Such a criminal attempt to destroy the state could never have been made had not his great weight of vices been supported on roots of affability and endurance. So we must reject the prosecution's insinuation, and friendship with Catiline must not be imputed as a charge. Many men, some of them good, shared this friendship. I admit that he nearly deceived me, even me, when he gave the appearance of being a good citizen, an eager, firm, and faithful friend of all the best people. I found out his faults by my eyes sooner than in my understanding, by events sooner than by my suspicions. If Caelius, too, was a member of the great swarm of his friends, it is more important that he should feel repentance for the mistake he made (as I sometimes also repent my mistake about the man) that than he should fear a charge arising from that friendship.

Sallust was about twenty at the times which he describes. His own career in politics seems to have ended disastrously, and his own failure no doubt increased his bitterness against the city of Rome. But there is every reason to accept that this account is an accurate portrayal of a very real situation.

Source: Sallust, *Bellum Catilinum*, 37.

In my opinion, the Roman world during these years was shown up in its most depressing light. Although every nation from the rising to the setting of the sun gave obedience to her arms, though peace and prosperity, man's chief desires, flourished in Rome, yet

there were citizens who set out brazenly to destroy both themselves and the State. After the two Senatorial decrees, not one
man among the whole mass of citizens was found who was persuaded by the promised rewards to uncover the conspiracy, and
there was not a single desertion from Catiline's camp. This gives
some idea of the strength of the disease, or rather decay, in most
men's minds.

Those involved in the conspiracy were not the only ones to
show this corruption of mind; the whole plebeian throng supported Catiline's aims in their eagerness for revolution. This
seems entirely typical. In any state, those without wealth envy
honest citizens, and praise the wicked, hate traditional values and
long for new ones, keen to upset everything in their detestation
of their own lot. They find trouble-free nourishment in turmoil
and rebellion, since poverty stands to lose nothing. The city mob
was particularly liable to rush headlong into crime, for many
reasons. First of all, those especially notorious for vice or evil
character, those who had lost their inheritance through their own
disgraceful conduct, and, indeed, all those who had been driven
from home by wickedness or crime, all these flowed into Rome
as water into the bilges. Secondly, many remembered the result
of Sulla's victory, when private soldiers had been promoted, some
to the Senate, some to a wealth which let them pass their time in
a positively regal state of life and entertainment, and each man
hoped to gain such advantages for himself if he took up arms in
a victorious cause. Furthermore, the young men, who had
suffered from the great lack of manual employment on the land,
were induced by private and public largesse to prefer a life of
leisure in the city to unwelcome work in the country.

The poor state of national politics gave encouragement to
them and to all like them. So we must not be surprised if needy
men, of bad character and inflated hopes, thought that their own
and the State's good coincided. Besides, there were men whose
parents had been proscribed after Sulla's victory, whose property
had been sequestered, and who had lost the rights of freedom;
these, too, looked forward to the outcome of war in a similar

way. In addition, every member of any party, other than the Senate, preferred the collapse of the State to any lessening of their own power. This was the evil plight which had once again come upon the country after a lapse of some years.

RIOTS IN ROME
57 B.C.

With power at Rome rapidly developing into a struggle between a few major figures, law and order quickly degenerated. Two gangs in particular were very prominent, those led by Clodius and Milo. A few years before, Cicero had incurred the undying hatred of Clodius by trying to get him convicted on a charge of profaning the rites of some religious ceremony. In revenge, Clodius had procured Cicero's exile on a technicality connected with the Catiline conspiracy. Cicero claims to have been welcomed enthusiastically on his return. His reception by Clodius was a different matter.

Source: Cicero, *Letters to Atticus*, IV, iii.

Further Reading: Loeb translation by W. Glynn Williams and E. O. Winstedt. Apart from the works listed under the previous extract, see also L. R. Taylor's *Party Politics in the Age of Caesar. C.A.H.* vol. IX, ch. xii, by M. Cary.

On November 3rd some workmen were driven from my property by an armed gang. On the same day Catulus's Portico, which was being rebuilt by governmental decree and under consular tender, and had almost reached the roof, was pulled down, while the house of my brother Quintus was first shattered by a volley of stones thrown from my property and then set on fire by order of Clodius. The brands were hurled at it while the whole city watched, and a great cry of grief and sympathy arose, I will not say from good men, for perhaps not one is left, but from everyone else. Clodius rushed madly around, and after this frenzied outburst his only thoughts were for murdering his opponents, as he went from district to district openly promising slaves their freedom.

On November 11th I was walking along the Sacred Way, followed by Clodius and his gang. Suddenly shouts arose, stones were thrown, clubs and swords threatened us. I fled to the entrance way to Tettius Danius's house, the approaches to which were easily blocked by my companions. Clodius might easily have been killed, but I was beginning to look for a regimen, not surgery, to cure our troubles. When he saw by everyone's voice raised against him that the days of trial were over and those of punishment upon him, he made every Catiline seem like a perfect angel. On the 12th he tried to attack Milo's house in the Carmatian district. Quite brazenly, at 11 o'clock in the morning, he led a gang there with shields and swords drawn, while others carried blazing fire-brands. Clodius had adopted L. Sulla's house as his base for the attack. Then Q. Flaccus led out some brave men from another of Milo's houses and killed several notorious members of Clodius's robber gang. He was after Clodius himself, but the latter had shut himself up inside Sulla's house.

FESTIVAL AT ROME
55 B.C.

Public shows at Rome were frequent, for some were put on each year as election bribes. These described by Cicero were arranged by one of the consuls for the year, Pompey, to celebrate the opening of a new theatre. Cicero is writing to a friend who had been unable to get to the games.

Source: Cicero, *Letter to M. Marius* (*ad Fam.* VII, i).

Further Reading: Loeb translation by W. Glynn Williams and E. O. Winstedt. For the Roman theatre, see *The Roman Stage* by W. Beare. There is a short discussion and illustrations of animal shows in *Hellas and Rome* by W. Zschietzschmann. See also, *Animals for Show and Pleasure in Ancient Rome*, by G. Jennison.

The games, to answer your question, were excellently put on, but not to your taste. I can guess that from my own feelings. The first actors who came on stage to honour the occasion were the very people whom I thought to have retired for their own honour's sake. Your favourite actor, Aesop, was so bad that everyone wanted to see the back of him. As he began to take the oath, his voice dried up just as he was saying, 'If I wittingly fail. . . .' What else to tell you? You know the usual games that are put on, but they did not have the charm of even simple festivals. Any pleasure was removed by a spectacle of magnificence which I'm sure you would have been very glad to miss. What conceivable pleasure can there be in having 600 mules on stage in *Clytemnestra*, or 3,000 wine-bowls in *The Trojan Horse*, or the various ornaments of infantry and cavalry in some stage battle? They excited popular admiration, but would not have brought you any pleasure. If while the shows went on you have been giving time to your reader, Photogenes, provided that he read you something other than just my speeches, you will have got more satisfaction than any of us. I do not think that you pine for Greek or Oscan plays. You can see what is as good as an Oscan play any day in your own local parliament, and your opinion of the Greeks is so low that you do not even go to your house by the Greek Road! I don't see why you should regret having missed the athletes, if you dislike the gladiators. And Pompey admits that he wasted effort and hard work on the latter.

To end the celebrations, there were some wild beast shows, two a day for five days. Magnificently staged, I grant. But what pleasure can there be for a cultured person in seeing a weedy human being torn to pieces by a strong animal, or a magnificent beast pierced through and through with hunting spears? You have seen them all before, if they are worth seeing at all. I did go along, but there was nothing novel about them. The final day was given up to elephants, which won the amazement of the common crowd of spectators, but hardly their approval. Their emotion was rather one of pity and a feeling that those beasts had a sort of kinship with the human race. . . .

You remember you asked me in a recent letter to write to you something of this sort to lessen your disappointment at missing the games. I hope that I've achieved this. If not, I've got this comfort. I am sure that you will come to the next games and visit me, and not let every hope of your entertainment rest on mere letters of mine.

INVASION OF BRITAIN
55 B.C.

Julius Caesar's invasion of Britain was aimed at dissuading the Britons from interfering in Gaul. It also, no doubt, satisfied his curiosity and spirit of adventure. There is no evidence that he intended to make his conquest permanent. Caesar writes in the third person.

Source: Caesar, *Gallic War*, IV, 23.

Further Reading: Loeb translation by H. J. Edwards, Penguin translation by S. A. Handford. T. Rice Holmes's *Conquest of Gaul* is still the major work on Caesar's campaigns. For a concise history of the Romans in Britain, see I. A. Richmond's *Roman Britain*. Also see R. G. Collingwood's *Roman Britain*.

These matters settled, he waited for a suitable wind and set sail about midnight. The cavalry were ordered to go to another harbour to embark and follow him. This they were rather slow to do, and so it was about 10 a.m. when he arrived off Britain with the leading ships. Armed men could be seen stationed on all the heights, and the nature of the place was such, with the shore edged by sheer cliffs, that missiles could be hurled onto the beach from the top. Caesar considered this a totally unsuitable place for disembarkation, and waited at anchor till 3 p.m. for the rest of his invasion fleet to assemble. He then summoned a meeting of his brigade and battalion commanders, revealed the news he had from Volusenus, and outlined his orders. He wanted them to be ready to act immediately, on the slightest sign from him. For military practice demanded this, especially in a naval attack, which was liable to rapid, unexpected changes of circumstance. Dismissing his officers, he waited for a favourable combination of wind and tide, and then gave the signal to weigh anchor. Sailing on for about seven miles, he halted his line opposite an open, level beach.

The barbarians had discovered Caesar's plan by sending forward cavalry units and charioteers (a very common method of fighting with them). Their main force which had followed later was now in a position to prevent our men from disembarking. This caused considerable difficulty. The ships could only be drawn up in deep water because of their draught. The soldiers were faced with unknown ground and had their hands impeded, while they were burdened with a very heavy load of arms. And yet they had to leap down from the ships, keep their footing in the waves and fight the enemy. The latter, on the other hand, could either resist from dry land or by moving just a little forward into the shallows. So, completely unencumbered and with full knowledge of the ground, they boldly hurled their missiles, badly disturbing the horses which were totally unused to the conditions. Our men were shaken by these circumstances through lack of experience of this style of warfare, and failed to show the same dash and enthusiasm as they did in land battles.

As Caesar noticed this, he gave orders to the warships to row off slightly to the enemy's open flank away from the cargo ships. These ships were less well known to the barbarians and much more manoeuvrable. They were to halt, attack and move the enemy back by the use of slings, arrows and other missiles. All this helped our men considerably. The barbarians were affected by the strange shape of the ships, by the motion of the oars and the unusual type of catapult. Halting their advance, they slowly began to retire.

Our troops, however, were still hesitating, largely because of the depth of the sea, when the standard-bearer of the Tenth legion, with a prayer to the gods for a happy outcome for his legion, shouted, 'Jump down, men, unless you want the enemy to get your standard. You will not find me failing in my duty to my country or my leader.' This he yelled at the top of his voice, and then springing off the boat began to bear the eagle forward against the enemy. Our troops, with mutual words of encouragement not to commit a terrible wrong, all jumped down into the sea. Their fellows in the next boats saw what they were doing, followed suit and came to grips with the enemy.

DRUIDS IN GAUL
c. 54 B.C.

The Druids remain rather a mystery. Though popular fancy links them with Stonehenge, there is no evidence that it was built by them, and there is no satisfactory account of their origin. They certainly give all the signs of a priesthood dominating a primitive society. It is interesting to note that Roman religious toleration under Augustus specifically excluded the Druids, ostensibly because of the aspect of human sacrifice, only legally abolished in Rome by Senatorial Decree as late as 97 B.C. But no doubt the Romans feared the political hold exercised by the Druids.

Source: Caesar, *Gallic War*, VI, 13.

Further Reading: Loeb translation by H. J. Edwards, Penguin translation by S. A. Handford. See the preceding extract, and T. D. Kendrick's *The Druids*.

The Druids are in charge of all religious matters, superintending public and private sacrifices, and explaining superstitions. A large crowd of young men, who flock to them for schooling, hold the Druids in great respect. For they have opinions to give on almost all disputes involving tribes or individuals, and if any crime is committed, any murder done, or if there is contention about a will or the boundaries of some property, they are the people who investigate the matter and establish rewards and punishments. Any individual or community that refuses to abide by their decision is excluded from the sacrifices, which is held to be the most serious punishment possible. Those thus excommunicated are viewed as impious criminals, they are deserted by their friends and no one will visit them or talk to them to avoid the risk of contagion from them. They are deprived of all rights in court, and they forfeit all claim to honours.

There is one archdruid of supreme power. On his death, he is succeeded either by someone outstanding among his fellows, or, if there are several of equal calibre, the decision is reached by a vote of all the Druids, and the election is sometimes managed by force. At a fixed time of year they assemble at a holy place in the territory of the Carnutes, which is thought to be the centre of Gaul. Anyone with a grievance attends and obeys the decisions and judgments which the Druids give. The general view is that this religion originated in Britain and was imported into Gaul, which means that any keen student of Druidism now goes to Britain for information. . . .

The whole Gallic nation is virtually a prey to superstition, and this makes the serious invalids or those engaged in battle or dangerous exploits sacrifice men instead of animals. They even vow to immolate themselves, using the Druids as their ministers for this purpose. They feel that the spirit of the gods cannot be appeased unless a man's life is given for a life. Public sacrifices of the same sort are common. Another practice is to make images of enormous size, with the limbs woven from osiers. Living human beings are fitted into these, and, when they are set on fire, the men are engulfed in the flames and perish. The general feeling is that the immortal gods are better pleased with the sacrifice of those caught in theft, robbery or some other crime. But if a supply of such criminals is lacking, then they resort to the sacrifice of completely innocent victims.

A FAMILY QUARREL
51 B.C.

Not all of Cicero's life was spent worrying about himself or Rome. We do get personal touches about his own family from many of his letters—his love for his daughter, his treatment of his secretaries. The friendship of the two brothers seems very real, but there were occasions when Marcus was severely critical of Quintus. In 51 B.C. Quintus must just have returned from serving with Julius Caesar in Gaul, where he had distinguished himself in 54–53 B.C. Statius, who is mentioned in this letter, was a freedman of Quintus, and seems to have had considerable influence over him.

Source: Cicero, *Letters to Atticus*, V, i. The family name of Atticus was Pomponius. Girls were normally called after this name; hence Atticus's sister was Pomponia.

Further Reading: Loeb translation by E. O. Winstedt. For the character of Atticus, see the extract on page 116.

I now come to almost the last part of your letter, in which you speak of your sister. The situation is as follows. When I reached my estate at Arpinum, I was joined there by my brother, and we started talking quite a bit about you. In the course of this I mentioned the conversation about your sister that you and I had had in my Tuscan house. I have never seen a man so gentle or more affably disposed to anyone than my brother then was to your sister. Even if there was some tension because of high expenses, it certainly did not appear. That's all that happened that day.

Next day we left Arpinum. The date meant that Quintus had to stay at Arcae and I at Aquinum, but we lunched at Arcae— I think you know our villa there. When we arrived, Quintus said very politely, 'Pomponia, please look after the ladies, and I'll bring in the men'. Nothing, in my opinion at least, could have been more gentlemanly, the words, the intention, the expression on his face. But she, although we were all in earshot, replied, 'I am not even mistress in my own house'. I think that the reason was that Statius had arrived ahead of us to see to our lunch. Quintus turned to me, 'You see what I have to put up with every day?'

You will wonder what I think of all this. I can assure you that I was very distressed by the harshness of her words and expression, although I did manage to hide my discomfort. We all sat down for lunch except for her. When Quintus sent her some food from the board, she wouldn't have any. To sum up. I have never seen anything more gentle than my brother, more rough than your sister. And I have not included many things which displeased me at the time more than they did Quintus.

I then left for Aquinum. Quintus stayed at Arcae and visited me early next morning to tell me that Pomponia had not been ready to talk with him. She had been in the same mood as when I saw her, even though she was about to leave. If you ask me, you can tell her that in my opinion she showed a complete lack of manners that day.

CAESAR, POMPEY AND CICERO
50 B.C.

Intelligent people saw the inevitability of the Civil War between Caesar and Pompey. Cicero was in a particularly difficult position as he explains in this letter to his friend Atticus.

Source: Cicero, *Letter to Atticus* (ad. Att. VII, i).

Further Reading: Translations of all letters by R. O. Winstedt in the Loeb series. *The Fall of the Roman Republic* by T. Rice Holmes, and *The Roman Revolution* by Sir Ronald Syme are the best full accounts of the period. F. E. Adcock wrote the chapters in *C.A.H.* vol. IX, chs. xv and xvi. F. R. Cowell is also helpful.

I think I see ahead of us a struggle the like of which has never been before. The only hope is that the same god who exceeded our wildest hopes in freeing us from a Parthian war has regard for the state. I agree that I will be sharing this calamity with everyone else, but I ask you not to think of that. Please consider merely my own little problem. I suppose you realize that my friendship with both of them happened through your agency, and I wish that I had listened to your friendly advice from the start. But, as Homer said, 'You never persuaded the heart in my breast'. But you finally succeeded in urging me to embrace the friendship of one, because he had deserved so well of me, and of the other, because he was so powerful. Every move and step that I have taken has been to insure that I remained their dearest friend. I thought that, if I were united with Pompey, I would never be forced to any political indiscretion, and if I agreed with Caesar, I would never have to fight Pompey. They seemed so closely united.

Now, as you point out and as I realize so clearly myself, a terrific struggle is imminent between them. Both number me among their friends, unless one of them is just pretending. Pompey is quite certain and rightly judges that I strongly approve of his present political actions. I received letters from both of them along with yours, in which both claimed to value my friendship above that of anyone else. But what am I to do? I don't ask for the final solution; if it comes to battle, I see that it is preferable to be defeated with one (Pompey), than to conquer with the other (Caesar). But I want your advice about what the Senate will be discussing on my arrival. The motions are that Caesar should not be allowed to stand as candidate *in absentia*, and that he must dismiss his army. Someone will say, 'Your views, please, Marcus Tullius'. What am I to say? I can't very well answer, 'Just a moment, till I see Atticus'.

THE BATTLE OF PHARSALUS
48 B.C.

Eighteen months after crossing the Rubicon, which started the Civil War, Caesar brought Pompey to battle in central Greece at Pharsalus. He here describes the most important fight of his career.

Source: Caesar, *Civil Wars*, III, 88.

Further Reading: Translation in Loeb series by A. G. Peskett. There are very many books on Julius Caesar, the most accessible, apart from the general histories mentioned in the previous extract, including those by John Buchan and the imaginary *Ides of March* by Thornton Wilder. *C.A.H.* vol. IX, ch. xvi, by F. E. Adcock.

On approaching Pompey's camp, Caesar noticed that his line was drawn up as follows. On the left wing were the two legions which Caesar had given him under official pressure at the start of their quarrel. These were the First and Third, and Pompey took his stand there. The middle of the line consisted of the Syrian legions under Scipio's command. The Cilician legion and the cohorts from Spain were on the right flank, and formed Pompey's most trusted troops. The rest of the force was stationed between the centre and the wings, bringing the total number of cohorts to 110. This made the number of troops equal 45,000 plus about 2,000 reservists. . . . There were a further seven cohorts serving as garrison for the main camp and minor forts. Since his right flank was bordered by the steep banks of a river, Pompey had stationed all his cavalry, archers and slingers on the left.

Caesar retained his previous dispositions, with the Tenth legion on the right and the Ninth on the left, and since this had been badly mauled at Dyrrhachium, he brought it up to strength by adding to it the Eighth so that the two could protect each other. He had 80 cohorts of front-line troops, totalling 22,000 men. Two cohorts served as camp-guard. His commanders were Antony on the left, Sulla on the right, and Domitius in the centre. He placed himself opposite Pompey on his own right flank. In addition, noticing Pompey's arrangements and in fear that his right wing would be outflanked by the massed cavalry, he withdrew individual cohorts from the third rank. From these he formed a fourth rank, and stationed it to face the cavalry, showing it what he wanted done, and reminding them the day depended on their bravery. He further gave instructions to the third rank, and indeed the whole army, not to advance before ordered to do so. He himself would give the signal when ready.

Between the two armies there was sufficient ground for both sides to deploy. But Pompey had ordered his troops not to move and allow their ranks to be broken up, but to stand firm to receive Caesar's charge. Triarius is said to have advised this course, with the hope of weakening the first onset and disrupting their order. Pompey's troops, if they held their own ranks firm, could attack their enemies who would be in disorder Further, he hoped that the javelins would have a lighter impact if the troops were held in position than if they ran forward to meet the weapons. Perhaps, also, Caesar's troops would be exhausted and disheartened by running twice the distance. Our personal view is that Pompey was mistaken in giving this order. All men have an innate eagerness and natural enthusiasm which can be inflamed by keenness for battle. It is the general's job to foster this, not to repress it. The age-old custom of sounding off all the trumpets and of raising a general battle-cry also has its points. The feeling has always been that these alarmed the enemy and emboldened one's own men.

Our troops advanced when ordered with arms at the ready. But when they realized that Pompey's forces were not coming out to meet them, they used the skill and experience gained in previous engagements, and slowed down and halted about the half-way mark without further orders, to prevent engaging when they were tired. After a short rest, they started again, hurled their javelins, and, obeying Caesar's instructions, quickly drew their swords. Pompey's troops were a match for them. They managed to parry the javelins and hold the legions' charge, while preserving their own ranks. They too hurled their javelins and then turned to sword fighting. While this was happening, the cavalry on Pompey's left flank charged forward as ordered, followed by the whole mass of archers. Our cavalry could not check this attack, but was slowly forced to give ground. This encouraged Pompey's horse to press all the harder and, wheeling, they began to encircle our army on the open flank. Caesar noticed this, and gave his orders to the cohorts of the fourth rank, which amounted to six. They immediately charged at the double with such violence at Pompey's cavalry that not a single man stood his ground. They all turned tail and fled, not merely from where they were, but forced right back in flight onto the high ground. On their removal, all the archers and slingers were left unprotected and killed. In this same charge our cohorts surrounded Pompey's left flank where his troops were still resisting hard, and attacked them from the rear.

Simultaneously Caesar let fly his third line which had been in reserve and resting for this very moment. Whereupon Pompey's troops, finding themselves attacked by fresh and unwounded replacements instead of tired men and assaulted from the rear as well, could hold out no longer, and a general retreat began.

CICERO ENTERTAINS CAESAR
45 B.C.

Cicero's relations with Caesar were seldom cordial though usually polite. Caesar had pardoned his support of Pompey in the Pharsalus campaign, but Cicero lived in fear and hatred of the man whom he so assiduously flattered in public.

Source: Cicero, *Letter to Atticus* (ad Att. XIII, 52).

Further Reading: Translation of all the letters in Loeb series by E. O. Winstedt. See under the previous extracts. *C.A.H.* vol. IX, ch. xvii, by F. E. Adcock.

My word, I must say that my guest was pretty formidable but the whole thing turned out as you could wish it. It was all very pleasant. He arrived at Philip's on the evening of the 18th of December, and the whole house was packed so full of soldiers, about 2,000 of them, that there was hardly any space left even in the room where Caesar was going to have dinner. I was very alarmed at what would happen on the next day. But Cassius Barba came to my assistance and gave me some guards. They set up camp in the field and the house was defended. Caesar stayed at Philip's till 1 p.m. on the 19th and wouldn't see anyone. I

think he was going through his accounts with his secretary,
Balbus. Then he went for a walk along the shore. At 2 p.m. he
had a bath, when he got the news about Mamurra, but you could
not have told from his face. He got his rub down and then went
for a siesta.

Since he was on an emetic course, he ate and drank fearlessly
and with freedom. The dinner was rich and luxurious or even, I
might say, 'well cooked and seasoned, with talk exchanged
freely'. His retinue had a jolly good time in three other rooms,
and his less important freedmen and slaves were entertained as
well. The more important ones I welcomed with more ceremony.
In short, we seemed on equal gentlemanly footing. But he is not
the sort of guest to whom you want to say, 'Please come and
call on me on your return journey'. Once is enough. We did not
talk of matters of moment but rather about literature. He was
delighted and seemed pleased. He told me that he was going to
spend a day at Puteoli and another at Baiae. There, that's my
news about my hospitality, or rather billeting, which I did not
fancy, but was not very troublesome. I am waiting a little longer
here, and then going to my Tuscan estate. Nicias tells me that as
he passed Dolabella's house the whole armed troop formed up to
right and left of him. They only did it there!

CAESAR OFFERED A CROWN
44 B.C.

Lavish honours had been heaped upon Julius Caesar ever since his
victory over Pompey. These culminated in the event which Cicero
here describes. It is contained in a speech against Mark Antony which
Cicero had circulated towards the end of 44 B.C. The offer has been
made famous by Shakespeare in Antony's funeral speech in *Julius
Caesar*.

Source: Cicero, 2nd. Philippic against Antony, 84.

Further Reading: The speech is translated in Penguin Classics by
Michael Grant. It is one of the most vitriolic outbursts ever made,
and contains a complete record of Antony's life, including his actions
on the Ides of March. Loeb translation by W. C. A. Ker. For other
books, consult the previous extracts.

Let us turn to the Festival of the Lupercalia (February 17th). Your colleague (Caesar) was sitting on the platform on a golden chair, dressed in a purple toga and wearing his laurel wreath. You left your place, mounted to where he was sitting, and offered him a crown. A groan came from the whole forum. Whence came that crown? You hadn't picked up one that had been discarded, but had hatched and forged the plot in your own home. You placed the crown on his head, with uproar from the crowd. Caesar took it off to their cheers. . . . It is totally wrong that the man who offered the crown should still be alive when the man who refused it is rightly and generally agreed to have been justly killed. And yet you ordered an entry to be made in the public records of the Lupercalia: 'Mark Antony, consul, by popular request, offered the kingship to Gaius Caesar, dictator for life. Caesar refused to accept it.'

THE MURDER OF JULIUS CAESAR
March 15th, 44 B.C.

No eye-witness accounts have survived of the murder of Julius Caesar, although Cicero wrote on the evening of the 15th an ecstatic note to one of the conspirators. The sources that are best known are those of Plutarch and Suetonius, both of whom wrote after A.D. 100. Nicolaus of Damascus, a friend of Herod the Great (died in 4 B.C.), came to Rome some time during Augustus' reign, probably before the birth of Christ, and had the opportunity of speaking to people who may have had first-hand knowledge of the murder. But all three accounts have many similarities, and it would be safer to assume that all relied on the same, lost, original source. However, Nicolaus antedates the other two by 100 years, and was certainly alive in 44 B.C. Whatever the origin of his story, it contains so many small details that it must have been based on intimate knowledge of the events.

Source: Nicolaus Damascenus, in *Historici Graeci Minores* (ed. Dindorf), para. 24.

Further Reading: Life of Caesar by Suetonius is translated in Penguin Classics by Robert Graves and in the Loeb series by J. C. Rolfe. Plutarch's *Life of Caesar* is in Penguin Classics by Rex Warner. Thornton Wilder's *The Ides of March*, though stopping short of the murder, is an interesting fictional reconstruction of the private views of some of the protagonists. *C.A.H.* vol. IX, ch. xvii, by F. E. Adcock.

The conspirators never met openly, but they assembled a few at a time in each others' homes. There were many discussions and proposals, as might be expected, while they investigated how and where to execute their design. Some suggested that they should make the attempt as he was going along the Sacred Way, which was one of his favourite walks. Another idea was for it to be done at the elections during which he had to cross a bridge to appoint the magistrates in the Campus Martius; they should draw lots for some to push him from the bridge and for others to run up and kill him. A third plan was to wait for a coming gladiatorial show. The advantage of that would be that, because of the show, no suspicion would be aroused if arms were seen prepared for the attempt. But the majority opinion favoured killing him while he sat in the Senate, where he would be by himself since non-Senators would not be admitted, and where the many conspirators could hide their daggers beneath their togas. This plan won the day. Chance, too, played a part, for it made him settle on a definite day for the Senate to meet to discuss his intended measures.

When the day came, they assembled, with everything ready, in Pompey's Stoa, their normal meeting-place. The impression might be gained from his evil genius that all this was quite by accident and subject to chance, but in fact it led him into his enemy's place, in which he was to lie dead in front of Pompey's statue, and be murdered near the image of a man now dead whom, when alive, he had defeated. But if any attention is paid to such things, his destiny had the stronger force. For his friends were alarmed at certain rumours and tried to stop him going to the Senate-house, as did his doctors, for he was suffering from one of his occasional dizzy spells. His wife, Calpurnia, especially, who was frightened by some visions in her dreams, clung to him and said that she would not let him go out that day. But Brutus, one of the conspirators who was then thought of as a firm friend, came up and said, 'What is this, Caesar? Are you a man to pay attention to a woman's dreams and the idle gossip of stupid men, and to insult the Senate by not going out, although it has honoured you and has been specially summoned by you? But listen to me, cast aside the forebodings of all these people, and come.

The Senate has been in session waiting for you since early this morning.' This swayed Caesar and he left.

While this was happening, the conspirators were making their preparations and arranging their seats, some next to him, some facing him and some behind. Before he entered the chamber, the priests brought up the victims for him to make what was to be his last sacrifice. The omens were clearly unfavourable. After this unsuccessful sacrifice, the priests made repeated other ones, to see if anything more propitious might appear than what had already been revealed to them. In the end they said that they could not clearly see the divine intent, for there was some transparent, malignant spirit hidden in the victims. Caesar was annoyed and abandoned divination till sunset, though the priests continued all the more with their efforts. Those of the murderers present were delighted at all this, though Caesar's friends asked him to put off the meeting of the Senate for that day because of what the priests had said, and he agreed to do this. But some attendants came up, calling him and saying that the Senate was full. He glanced at his friends, but Brutus approached him again and said, 'Come, good sir, pay no attention to the babblings of these men, and do not postpone what Caesar and his mighty power has seen fit to arrange. Make your own courage your favourable omen.' He convinced Caesar with these words, took him by the right hand, and led him to the Senate which was quite near. Caesar followed in silence.

The Senate rose in respect for his position when they saw him entering. Those who were to have part in the plot stood near him. Right next to him went Tillius Cimber, whose brother had been exiled by Caesar. Under pretext of a humble request on behalf of this brother, Cimber approached and grasped the mantle of his toga, seeming to want to make a more positive move with his hands upon Caesar. Caesar wanted to get up and use his hands, but was prevented by Cimber and became exceedingly annoyed. That was the moment for the men to set to work. All quickly unsheathed their daggers and rushed at him. First Servilius Casca struck him with the point of the blade on the left shoulder a little above the collar-bone. He had been aiming for that, but in the excitement he missed. Caesar rose to defend himself, and in the uproar Casca shouted out in Greek to his brother. The latter heard him and drove his sword into the ribs. After a moment, Cassius made a slash at his face, and Decimus Brutus pierced him in the side. While Cassius Longinus was trying to give him another blow, he missed and struck Marcus Brutus on the hand. Minucius also hit out at Caesar and hit Rubrius in the thigh. They were just like men doing battle against him. Under the mass of wounds, he fell at the foot of Pompey's statue. Everyone wanted to seem to have had some part in the murder, and there was not one of them who failed to strike his body as it lay there, until, wounded thirty-five times, he breathed his last.

Cicero, who bitterly regretted that Antony had been allowed to live, wrote this interesting postscript to the murder about a year later:

'How I wish that you had invited me to that banquet on the Ides of March. There would have been no left-overs.'

TREATMENT OF SLAVES
c. 40 B.C.

Terentius Varro assisted Julius Caesar in many of his cultural and academic interests. Among other things he planned a huge library at Rome, to rival the one at Alexandria. His work *On Agriculture* often quotes Cato or other earlier writers, but his remarks on the treatment of slaves indicate a more humane approach, something that can clearly be seen in some of Cicero's letters, and later on in Seneca. The influence of Stoicism may have helped towards this.

Source: Varro, *de Agricultura*, I, xvii, 4.

Further Reading: Loeb translation by W. D. Hooper and H. B. Ash. For the Roman attitude to slaves, see the works cited under Keeping Slaves (page 80). E. E. Sikes writes on Varro in *C.A.H.* vol. IX, ch. xviii.

Slaves ought not to be kept in terror nor allowed to be over-spirited. Their overseers ought to be literate and have a little education, men of frugal habits, and slightly older than the labourers. The latter will obey them more readily than if they were younger than themselves. The vital necessity is that the overseers should be experts in agricultural matters. For their job is not simply to give orders, but to join in the work so that the labourers may have someone to emulate, and may realize that their overseer is rightly in charge of them because of his superior knowledge. The power which you delegate to the overseers must be to persuade men with words rather than by whips, if the same end can be achieved.

Not too many slaves of the same race should be bought, for petty squabbles are likely to result from this. The foremen should be encouraged by incentives, and you should be sure to give them some property of their own and some wives from among their fellow-slaves from whom they can have children. That will make their devotion to the farm closer and stronger. Slave families from Epirus are famous and fetch a high price because of this sort of relationship.

The goodwill of the foremen should be won over by giving them some respect, and you ought to consult the senior labourers about the work to be done. If you follow this practice, they feel less despised, and think that they are considered of some account by their master. Men go to work with a keener will if they get better treatment or larger rations, more clothes or holidays or remission of work or permission to graze some of their own cattle on the farm, or other things of this sort. In this way and by this sort of kindness, you can restore their feeling of loyalty to their master after heavy work or even after punishment.

Cato reckons the right number of slaves by two methods, the definite size of the property and the type of crop, giving two formulae for olive-yards and vine-yards. In the first he gives instructions of how an olive-yard of 160 acres should be appointed. He says that on this type of estate you should have thirteen slaves, comprising an overseer, housekeeper, five labourers, three cattle-men, one muleteer, a swineherd, and a shepherd. The other formula he gives is for 65 acres of vineyard, where he says that the following fifteen slaves are necessary: overseer, housekeeper, ten labourers, one cattleman, a muleteer, and a swineherd. Saserna writes that one man is capable of looking after six acres, which he ought to be able to dig in forty-five days. The rate for an individual acre should be one every six days; the extra nine days are necessary for effects of ill-health, weather, idleness and poor work.

ATTICUS THE BANKER
c. 40 B.C.

Atticus is best known as the addressee of the majority of Cicero's letters. A man of great wealth, he was a member of the Equestrian Order, the financial class at Rome. Apart from his business dealings, he spent much time studying Greek literature, and his refusal to engage in politics meant that he could remain on familiar terms with men of all persuasions. He was also one of the very few important men of his age not to die a violent death. His sister married Cicero's brother, and his daughter became the well-loved wife of Augustus's military expert, Agrippa. Cornelius Nepos was a contemporary, and gives us a picture of an entirely different type of Roman, the wealthy, cultured man of business and the intellect.

Source: Nepos, *Life of Atticus*, 13.

Further Reading: Loeb translation by E. S. Forster and J. C. Rolfe. For Economic matters, see Chapter 4 of F. R. Cowell's *Cicero and the Roman Republic*, and Tenney Frank's *Economic Survey of Ancient Rome*. *C.A.H.* vol. IX, ch. xix, by J. Wight Duff.

He was held to be as good a head of family as he was a citizen, for, although he was very rich, no one indulged less in overspending or extravagant building operations. But that did not mean that he did not live in as fine a house as any, and he had use of all the best things. His house on the Quirinal, which he had inherited from his uncle, was built by Tamphilus, and its chief attraction lay not in the actual building but in its trees. The house itself was an old one, more notable for good taste than extravagance, and he changed nothing in it unless forced to by its age. His household, if judged by standards of utility, was of the best, but in terms of appearance hardly even up to average. For his slaves were all highly literate, all excellent readers and most of them library slaves, which meant that there was not even a footman who could not do both of these jobs very well. In the same way, the rest of the craftsmen needed by his domestic wants were outstandingly good. Everyone of them had been born at his house and brought up there, a mark not only of his restraint but of his care and attention as well. For surely it is a sign of restraint not to desire inordinately what is normally desired by others, and a sign of no little care to get things by work rather than by money. He was elegant, not magnificent, lived well but not extravagantly, and his every aim was for simplicity not affluence. His furniture erred in neither direction, not too little and not too much.

Perhaps some will think it a small matter, but I cannot help mentioning that although he had the reputation of being in the first rank of Roman knights, and although he extended generous invitations to men of all classes to visit him, yet we know from his account books that he only spent about £75 a month. I can vouch that this is no hearsay but genuine fact, for I was often involved in his family affairs because of my friendship with him.

The only entertainment ever heard at his dinner parties was a reader, a most pleasant habit, I think. No meal passed at his house without some reading, which meant that guests found equal delight for their minds and their stomachs. The people he invited were those who shared his own interests. The acquisition of that great additional fortune made no difference to his daily habits or standard of living; he could not be accused of living rather frugally on the £200,000 inherited from his father or rather extravagantly on the £1,000,000 later gained. His expenses were just the same, whatever his fortune. He owned no gardens, no luxurious villas in the suburbs or on the coast, and he had no country property in Italy except his estates at Arretium and Nomentum. He relied for his income on his property in Epirus or Rome. This will show to you that he regulated his expenses not by how much he had but by how much he needed.

He never lied, and could not stand a lie. This meant that his affability was not without a measure of strictness, and his seriousness was coupled with an ease of manner which made it hard to understand whether his friends were more afraid of him or affectionate towards him. His response to any request made of him was cautious, for he thought it the mark of a fickle not a liberal man to promise what could not be fulfilled. In the same way, he used such care in any enterprise which he had undertaken, that it seemed as if his own personal interests were at stake, not merely someone else's business. Once embarked on a deal, he never gave it up; he thought that his own reputation depended on the affair, and that meant very much to him. As a result, he managed the financial affairs of the Ciceros, Marcus Cato, Quintus Hortensius, Aulus Torquatus, and many another Roman business-man. So it can be seen that it was not indolence that made him avoid politics but judgement.

JOURNEY TO BRUNDISIUM
38 B.C.

Horace's journey to Brundisium was made at the same time as an official mission of Maecenas to try and patch up an entente between Antony and Octavian. So the party had some of the advantages open to official travellers on the main roads of the Empire. Maecenas was the patron of Horace, Virgil and many other poets. He also did much to help Octavian (called Augustus after 27 B.C.) in his domestic plans. Horace was very lucky to have found such an influential friend so soon after fighting against Octavian at the battle of Philippi. Virgil was in Octavian's debt for saving his farm from confiscation in 42 B.C. (*Eclogue* 1 and 9).

Source: Horace, *Satires*, I, v.

Further Reading: Loeb translation by H. R. Fairclough. On Roman roads see F. R. Cowell, *Cicero and the Roman Republic*, pp. 122 ff. Gilbert Highet puts Horace into his setting in *Poets in a Landscape*. For the literary circle under Maecenas, see *Roman Literature* by Grant and other literary histories; also *C.A.H.* vol. X, ch. xvi.

When I left the great city of Rome, a small inn at Aricia was my first halt. I was accompanied by the teacher of rhetoric, Apollodorus, the most learned Greek I know. Our next stop was Forum Appii which was packed with boatmen and also some roguish inn-keepers. We were lazy and took two days over this stage, which more energetic travellers usually manage in one. But the Appian Way is less tiring if taken leisurely. Here I declared war on my stomach because of the appalling water, while I waited for my companions to finish their dinner with some impatience. Night was drawing its shadows over the earth and scattering the stars in the sky, when the slaves started hurling abuse at the boatmen and the boatmen returned it with interest.

'Pull in here.' 'You're packing thousands aboard.' 'Here, that's enough.' A whole hour passed while they haggled over the money and got the mule tied on. Sleep was quite impossible because of the dreadful mosquitoes and the marsh-frogs, while the boatman, who had drunk too much cheap wine, and one of the travellers sang about his absent girl-friend. In the end the traveller grew tired and went off to sleep. The lazy boatman put the mule to grass, tied its tether to a stone, lay on his back and began to snore.

Day had come and we could not sense any movement in the boat until some hair-brained chap leapt out and started belabouring the mule and boatman about the head and back with a willow switch. Finally we only landed at about 10 o'clock, when we washed in your waters, Feronia. After lunch, we dragged our way for three miles to Anxur, perched on its far-gleaming rock. My good friend Maecenas and Cocceius were to meet us here, both sent on official missions on important matters, and both well used to settling friends' differences. Here I smeared some black ointment on my aching eyes. While I was doing this, Maecenas and Cocceius turned up with Fonteius Capito, every inch a gentleman and one of Antony's best friends. We were glad to leave Fundi where Aufidius Luscus was Milord Mayor, though we had a good laugh over all the paraphernalia of the idiotic clerk, his embroidered toga, broad stripe and little pan of coals. What airs he gave himself! We spent the night in the city of the Mamurras, where Capito provided the board and Murena the lodging.

The next day was a very welcome one. We were met at Sinuessa by Plotius, Varius and Virgil, as shining lights as any on earth, and my very best friends. You can imagine how we hugged each other and how happy we were. When I'm thinking straight, I would say that there is nothing to compare with a pleasant friend. The stage-house by the Campanian bridge gave us a roof, and the officials offered their dutiful supply of wood and salt.

We got to Capua early, and took the saddle-bags off the mules. Maecenas went off to play, but Virgil and I to sleep. Ball games are not much good for those with bad eyes, and exercise is not any fun for the unfit. We were on our way again, and welcomed at the well-provided villa of Cocceius, which lies above the inns of Caudium. Now, muse of my verse, recall for me the squabble between the wag Sarmentus and Messius Cicirrus. [Horace recounts the row.]

We went straight from there to Beneventum, where our eager host almost got singed as he turned our lean thrushes before the fire. For the coals slipped and the flame spread through the old kitchen and soon began to lick the high ceiling. Then you could see the hungry guests and the panicky servants snatching up the food and trying to put out the flames.

From there on Apulia began to reveal to me its well-known mountains, burnt up by the Sirocco. We would never have got over them had not a villa near Trivicum taken us in, though it was smoky enough to bring tears to the eyes, for they were burning damp branches and leaves in the hearth. Here I was fool enough to lie awake till midnight for a jilt of a girl. But keen for love though I was, sleep finally got the better of me, though it was interrupted by dreams of her.

Next day we travelled twenty-four miles by coach to stay at a village that will not scan in verse, but can easily be indicated. You have to buy the water there, cheapest commodity as it is. But the bread is so marvellous that travellers who know about it often carry it with them on their shoulders; for the bread at Canusium is rather gritty, and a jug of water is no better. Canusium was founded long ago by brave Diomede, and here it was that Varius left us, his friends, with tears in all our eyes.

We reached Rubi tired out, for the stage was long and made worse by the rain. The weather was better next day, but the road was worse right up to the walls of the fishing port of Bari. Then the town of Gnatia, built with grudging waters, made us laugh as it tried to persuade us that incense burned on the sacred threshold without flame. The jew Apella might believe that, but not I. For I have been taught that the gods lead a carefree life, and if any natural miracle happens, it is not sent by the gods from the high vault of heaven. Brundisium was the end of our journey, and of my long story.

A BORE
c. 35 B.C.

Apart from being an entertaining and perceptive account of a bore, this extract has importance in showing the relationship that existed between Maecenas and his protégés. This has been noticed in the previous passage.

Source: Horace, *Satires*, I, ix.

Further Reading: See under the previous extract.

I happened to be taking one of my usual walks along the Sacred Way. I was totally immersed in some trifle or other I was thinking of, when someone I knew just by name came up. Clasping my hand, he asked 'How are you, my very dear friend?' 'Very well, thank you, and you?' When he began to follow me, I broke in with, 'Want anything?' 'You know me,' he replied, 'I'm a man of education.' I said that I valued him the more for that. I badly wanted to get rid of him, so I walked a bit faster or stopped or whispered something in my slave's ear. A cold sweat started to run down to my ankles. I envied old Bolanus his temper as the fellow kept up an incessant chatter, singing the praises of the city and its various districts. I didn't say a word. He said, 'You're aching to get away; I've seen that for some time. But it's no use; I'll cling on to you and accompany you wherever you're going.' 'No point in putting yourself out,' I said; 'I want to visit someone you don't know who lives way off across the Tiber, near Caesar's Gardens.' 'But I've nothing to do, and I like a bit of exercise. I'll come with you.' My ears collapsed like those of a stubborn donkey when a rather heavy weight gets put on its back.

He began again, 'If I'm not mistaken, you will come to value me as highly as Viscus or Varius. I can write more verses at greater speed than anyone, I can move my limbs about more nimbly, and—Hermogenes would be jealous—I can sing.' This was the moment to interrupt, 'Have you a mother or relatives who need to see you safe and sound?' 'Not one, I've buried them all.' 'Lucky them; that just leaves me. Do your worst.' . . .

We had now reached Vesta's Temple, about a quarter of the day gone, and he fortunately had to go to answer to a surety. If he did not do so, he would forfeit the suit. 'Please, stay here a moment,' he said. 'Damned if I have the strength to stand and wait. And anyway I don't know a word of civil law, and I'm off to you know where.' 'I'm not sure what to do—abandon you or the case.' 'Me please,' I answered. 'No, I won't,' he said, and began to walk on ahead. It's hard to fight when you're down, and so I had to follow.

Once more he started up, 'On what terms are you with Maecenas? He's a man of few friends and a very shrewd disposition. No one has used his fortune more cleverly. You would have a great supporter in me, one well prepared to play second fiddle, if you would be ready to introduce me. I'm sure that you will get the better of them all.' I said, 'Our relationship is not like that. There's not a house more pure or more averse to that sort of evil complex about prestige. It doesn't worry me if A or B is richer or cleverer than me; everyone has his proper place.' 'That's quite remarkable and truly magnificent.' I replied that it was so, nevertheless. 'You make me all the keener to get to know him.' 'Should you wish it,' I sneered, 'you will certainly succeed; your virtue is so great. He's a man who can be won, and that makes the first approach all the harder.' 'I won't fail myself. I'll bribe the slaves. If I'm shut out to-day, I won't give up. I'll find the right time, I'll meet him in the streets, I'll dog his footsteps. Man gets nothing in life without effort.'

While he was going on like this, Fuscus Aristius met us, a dear friend of mine and well acquainted too with my companion. We stopped and asked each other where we had come from and where we were going. I started to tug at his cloak and to grip his arms tightly, nodding, winking, begging him to rescue me. He with a smile on his face—the rogue—pretended not to understand. I was seething with rage and said, 'You told me that you had something private to say to me.' 'Oh, yes, I remember, but some other time. To-day's the Thirtieth Sabbath. Do you want to offend the circumcized Jews?' When I said that I was not superstitious, he continued, 'But I am. I'm one of the weaker brethren, one of many. Pardon me, but I'll tell you later.'

I could not imagine that the day had dawned so black for me. Fuscus villainously fled and left me to the executioner. Luckily the opponent in the case met us and shouted, 'Here, where are you off to, scoundrel? Can I call you as witness?' This to me, and I was very ready to listen. With that he rushed him off to court. There were shouts and crowds of each one's supporters. I was saved.

LETTER OF ANTONY TO OCTAVIAN
33 B.C.

One of the underlying reasons for the enmity of Antony and Octavian was that the former had deserted or divorced Octavian's sister, Octavia. He had then gone through a ceremony of marriage with Cleopatra, and had partitioned out the Roman Empire in the East between their children. This letter is contained in the *Life of Augustus* by Suetonius, but is claimed to be genuine. Of Antony's sex life we have abundant news in Cicero's Second Philippic. Suetonius is chiefly responsible for news about Octavian.

Source: Suetonius, *Life of Augustus*, ch. lix.

Further Reading: Loeb translation by J. C. Rolfe, Penguin translation by Robert Graves. *2nd Philippic* translated in Penguin Classics by Michael Grant. *The Architect of the Roman Empire* by T. Rice Holmes gives the historical background of the quarrel between Antony and Octavian.

What's upset you? Because I go to bed with Cleopatra? But she's my wife, and I've been doing so for nine years, not just recently. And, anyway, is Livia *your* only pleasure? I expect that you will have managed, by the time you read this, to have hopped into bed with Tertulla, Terentilla, Rufilla, Salvia Titisenia, or the whole lot of them. Does it really matter where, or with what women, you get your excitement?

VICTORY OVER CLEOPATRA
31 B.C.

There is no eye-witness account of the battle of Actium, which
finally gave to Octavian mastery over the Roman world. But it was
natural that poets should mention the event, and this we find. Virgil
found a way to introduce a picture of the battle, portrayed on Aeneas'
shield in the eighth book of the *Aeneid*. But this ode of Horace was
probably written in 30 B.C., and tells us something of the feeling at
Rome on the news of the victory. Cleopatra had lived in Rome just
before 44 B.C., and Horace clearly indicates the Roman horror at what
we might call the Eastern Menace.

Source: Horace, *Odes*, I, 37.

Further Reading: Loeb translation by C. E. Bennett. T. Rice Holmes
has a description and discussion of the battle of Actium in *The Architect
of the Roman Empire*, vol. i. There are also discussions of the battle in
the *Journal for Roman Studies*, vols. xxi, xxvii and xxviii. L. P. Wilkinson's *Horace and his Lyric Poetry* discusses Horace the Poet.

Now we can drink, now we can strike the dance-floor with
unrestrained feet, now, my friends, it is time to decorate the
couches of the gods with Salian feasts. Before this it was wrong
to bring out the best wine from the old bins, while that queen was
plotting her mad scheme of destruction for the Capitol and death
to our Empire, with her foul band of men, horrible with disease,
capable of hoping for the world and intoxicated with the sweet-
ness of her fortune. But her fury was brought low, for not one
ship returned safe from the blaze, and her mind, maddened by
the waters of the Nile, was, in her flight from Italy, restored to
a true sense of terror by Caesar. He pressed after her in his ships,
like a hawk pursuing gentle doves or a rapid hunter the hare in
the plains of snowy Haemon, to cast his chain upon the deadly
foe. But she sought a nobler death. She was no coward to fear
the sword or to make for secret shores in her swift ship. She
dared to return to her shattered kingdom with face serene, brave
enough to clasp fierce asps to her, and to drink the black poison
into her body. Wilder she was, now that she had resigned herself
to death, begrudging the cruel Liburnians their sight of her, a
queen no longer, being led in proud triumph, a woman of no
lowly spirit.

THE REIGN OF AUGUSTUS
44 B.C.-A.D. 14

We have very few first-hand accounts of any of the events during the reign of Augustus. But this unique document more than compensates for that. It is the record, written by Augustus himself, of all the major events and achievements of his life. It actually survives in a copy found at Ancyra, and other copies were probably put up in other places in the Empire. It certainly shows signs of revision, or at least of different dates of composition, and many of the things he describes are coloured by his own prejudices and the wisdom of hindsight. It remains the most important single document rescued from antiquity. Augustus was born in 63 B.C.

Source: Res Gestae Divi Augusti, sometimes known as the *Monumentum Ancyranum.*

Further Reading: Loeb translation by F. Shipley. There are very many books on Augustus. Perhaps the most readable is John Buchan's *Augustus.* For more detailed works, see *The Architect of the Roman Empire* by T. Rice Holmes and *The Roman Revolution* by R. Syme. Books on individual points may be found in the bibliographies to Syme and Michael Grant's *World of Rome. C.A.H.* vol. X.

(All dates in the inscription are of the normal Roman type, by the names of the consuls. I have taken the anachronistic step of changing them to years B.C. and A.D. The logical loss seems to be compensated for by the gain in clarity.)

At the age of nineteen I collected an army on my own initiative and at my own expense, by means of which I restored to freedom a state oppressed by the domination of a minority faction. For this the Senate, in an honorific decree, elected me to its number as a consular in 43 B.C., giving me magisterial powers and the right to voice my opinion in the House. At the same time it instructed me, as propraetor, to act with the consuls to see that no harm befell the state. In the same year, after the death in battle of the two consuls, I was elected consul by the people, and made a Triumvir to look after the state's interests.

I drove my father's murderers into exile, taking right and judicial vengeance on them for their crime. Later, when they made war on Rome, I twice defeated them in battle.

I often waged wars, foreign and domestic, by land and sea over the whole world, and in my victories I spared any citizen who asked for pardon. I preferred to preserve foreign powers which could safely be pardoned, rather than destroy them. Nearly half a million Roman citizens owed allegiance to my military command. Of these more than 300,000 were placed in colonies or demobilized at the end of their service. I allotted land to everyone of them or gave them a cash bounty. I captured 600 ships of trireme size or above.

Twice I celebrated a triumph with ovation, and three full triumphs, and I received the acclamation of Imperator twenty-one times. The Senate decreed me more triumphs, but these I refused. I consecrated the laurel from my fasces on the Capitol, when I had fulfilled the vows with which I had undertaken the war. The Senate decreed thanksgivings to the Immortal Gods fifty-five times for successes gained by me or by generals subordinate to my overall command. The total number of days on which these thanksgivings were rendered by decree was eight hundred and ninety. In my triumphs, nine kings or children of kings were led in front of my chariot. I had been consul thirteen times when I wrote this, and I had held the Tribunician Power for thirty-seven years.

I was offered the Dictatorship in my absence and again in 22 B.C. when I was in Rome, but I refused it. I did not, however, reject control of the corn supply at a time of great shortage, and my administration of it meant that within a few days I freed the whole state from its immediate fear and danger by my own efforts and expense. I also refused at the same time annual perpetual consulship which was offered. In 19 B.C. and again in 18 and 11 B.C. the Senate and People of Rome agreed to my election with supreme power as guardian of the laws and morals. I was unwilling to accept any office contrary to the customs of our ancestors. If the Senate wanted me to do anything, I did it through my Tribunician Power, in which I voluntarily asked and got a colleague five times from the Senate.

I was a Triumvir for administering the state for ten years on end. I was leader of the House right up to the day on which I write this, for forty years. In religious matters, I was Pontifex

Maximus, augur, a member of the board of Fifteen for the care of Sacred Rites, of the board of Seven for sacred feasts, an Arvil Brother, a Titian sodalis, a Fetial priest.

In my fifth consulship (29 B.C.), by the order of the Senate and people, I increased the number of the Patricians. I revised the Senate-list three times. In my sixth consulship (28 B.C.), I conducted a census, helped by my colleague, Marcus Agrippa. After a lapse of forty-one years I conducted a lustrum, in which the total Roman Citizenship amounted to 4,063,000. Again in 8 B.C., this time by myself with consular power, I made another one, and the figure then was 4,233,000. A third time with consular power in A.D. 14, with my son Tiberius as colleague, I did another in which the population was 4,937,000. By new laws carried on my instigation, I restored many traditions which were vanishing, and presented many examples for our descendants to imitate.

The Senate decreed that prayers for my health should be said by the consuls and priests every fifth year. In accordance with these vows, the four main priestly colleges and sometimes the consul held games in my honour. All the citizens, privately and in communities, unanimously and continuously said prayers for my health in front of all the couches of the gods.

My name was included by Senatorial decree in the Salian Hymn, and a law was passed giving me everlasting sacrosanctity and lifelong Tribunician Power. I refused to become Pontifex Maximus in the place of a colleague who was still alive, though the people offered me this priesthood which my father Julius had held. Some years later, when the man (Lepidus) died who had seized the office on the occasion of the civil war, I received it, in 12 B.C., when a great mass of people flocked to Rome from the whole of Italy in unprecedented numbers for the election.

In honour of my safe return, the Senate consecrated the altar of Fortuna Redux in front of the temple of Honour and Virtue by the Capena Gate, on which the priests and Vestal Virgins performed an annual sacrifice on the anniversary of the day in 19 B.C. when I returned to Rome from Syria. The day was called the Augustalia from my own name.

By Senatorial authority, some of the praetors and tribunes, together with the consul Quintus Lucretius and leading citizens, were sent to Campania to meet me, an honour previously accorded to no one. On my return from Spain and Gaul after a successful mission in 13 B.C., the Senate decreed that the altar of the Pax Augusta should be consecrated in my name in the Campus Martius, on which it ordered the magistrates, priests and Vestal Virgins to perform annual sacrifices. The temple of Janus Quirinus, which our ancestors wished to remain shut only when victories had won peace by land and sea over the whole Roman world, was shut three times during my principate by order of the Senate, although the tradition is that it had only twice been shut before my reign since the foundation of the city.

My sons Gaius and Lucius, stolen from me by fate while still young, were, to honour me, designated as future consuls by the Senate in their fifteenth year, to enter office five years later. The Senate also decreed that from their first public appearance they might be present at public discussions. The whole body of Roman Knights gave each of them shields and silver spears, and hailed them as Leaders of Youth.

In accordance with the will of Julius I paid £3 to each Roman plebeian, £4 in my own name from war spoil in 29 B.C., £4 again in 24 B.C. from my own pocket as bounty, twelve free corn distributions in 23 B.C. from privately bought corn, and in the twelfth year of my Tribunician Power (12 B.C.) I made a third individual donation of £4. All these bounties reached no fewer than 250,000 men. In my eighteenth year of Tribunician Power (5 B.C.) I gave £2½ per man to 320,000 urban plebeians. In 29 B.C. I gave £10 a head to the soldier colonists from war booty. About 120,000 settlers received this triumphal bounty. In 2 B.C. I gave £2½ to each plebeian who was then receiving public corn. The number involved was just over 200,000.

I paid the communities money for the land which I gave to the soldiers in 30 B.C. and again in 14 B.C. This amounted to about £6 million paid for estates in Italy, and about £2½ million for land in the provinces. I was the very first man to establish colonies in Italy or the provinces who did this. Later, in 7, 6, 4, 3 and 2 B.C., I gave cash bounties to time-expired veterans, whom

I returned to their own towns. On these I spent as an act of generosity about £4 million.

Four times I aided the treasury with a personal gift, to the sum of £1½ million. In A.D. 6 I paid just over that amount from my private purse to the military exchequer which I got established to arrange for military pensions for those who had served twenty years or more.

Beginning in 18 B.C., when taxes were short, I gave tickets for corn from my granary and money from my purse sometimes to 100,000, sometimes more.

My new buildings included the Senate-house, the Chalcidium next to it, Apollo's temple on the Palatine with its porticoes, the temple of Divus Julius, the Lupercal, the portico at the Circus Flaminius which I allowed to be called the Octavian Portico after the name of the founder of a previous one on the same site, temples on the Capitol to Jupiter Feretrius and Jupiter Tonans, a temple to Quirinus, temples to Minerva, Juno Regina, Jupiter Libertas on the Aventine, a temple of the Lares at the top of the Sacred Way, a temple of the Penates on the Velia, a temple of Youth, and a temple of the Great Mother on the Palatine.

I rebuilt the theatres on the Capitol and of Pompey at my own considerable expense, with an inscription mentioning my name. I remade aqueducts in several places where they were decaying from age, and I doubled the flow of the Aqua Marcia, by letting a new stream into its channel. I finished the Forum Julii and the lawcourts between the temples of Castor and Saturn, works begun and nearly finished by my father. When these lawcourts were destroyed by fire, I began to rebuild them on a larger site, under the names of my sons, giving instructions for my heirs to finish them if my death should intervene. In 28 B.C., by Senatorial decree, I rebuilt eighty-two temples in the city, neglecting none which needed repair. In 27 B.C. I relaid the Via Flaminia from Rome to Rimini, and all the bridges were repaired except the Milvian and Minucian.

I built from booty the temple of Mars Ultor and the Augustan Forum on private land. I built a theatre near Apollo's temple on land largely privately bought, to be called after my son-in-law Marcellus. I consecrated gifts of about £1 million on the Capitol, and in the temples of Divus Julius, Apollo, Vesta and Mars Ultor. I returned 35,000 pounds of coined gold in 29 B.C. which had been sent by the country towns of Italy to my triumphs. Later, whenever I was hailed Imperator, I would not accept this gold, though the country towns voted it with the same kindness as they had done before.

I gave three gladiatorial shows in my own name, and five in the names of my sons or grandsons, in which about 10,000 men fought. I gave the people two athletic shows gathered from all over the world in my own name and a third in my grandsons' names. I gave games four times in my own name and twenty-three times for other magistrates. With my colleague Agrippa I conducted the Centenary Games in 17 B.C. on behalf of the College of Fifteen. In 2 B.C. I instituted the Martian Games, thereafter by Senatorial decree and law conducted by the consuls. I gave twenty-three shows of African beasts in the circus, forum and amphitheatres on my own behalf or for my sons and grandsons, in which about 3,500 beasts were killed. I put on the spectacle of a naval battle across the Tiber, hollowing out an area 1,800 feet by 1,200 feet, in the place where Caesar's Grove now stands. In this show three hundred triremes and biremes fought and many more smaller vessels, and about 3,000 men took part in addition to the oarsmen.

After my victory I returned to the temples of all the states of the province of Asia what the man with whom I had fought had stolen from them and taken into private possession. Statues of me on foot or mounted, and silver ones driving a quadriga stood in the city to the number of about twenty-five. These I had removed, and from the money I put gifts of gold in Apollo's temple in my own name and the names of those who had honoured me with these statues.

I rid the sea of pirates. In that slave war, where men had fled from their masters and taken up arms against the state, I handed back about 30,000 slaves to their owners for punishment. Of its own accord the whole of Italy swore allegiance to obey me, and chose me as leader in the war which I won at Actium. The same oath was taken by the provinces of Gaul, Spain, Africa,

Sicily and Sardinia. Among those then fighting under my standard there were more than seven hundred senators, including eighty-three past or future consuls and about 170 priests.

I extended the frontiers of all the provinces of the Roman people bounded by tribes not obedient to our empire. I pacified the provinces of Gaul, Spain and Germany from the Atlantic near Cadiz to the mouth of the Elbe. I pacified the Alps from near the Adriatic to the Tuscan Sea, never wrongfully making war on any tribe. My fleet sailed the Ocean from the mouth of the Rhine to the East as far as the land of the Cimbri, which had never before been approached by land or sea. The Cimbri, Charydes, Sennones and other German tribes in that district sent envoys to seek friendship with me and the Roman people. By my command and under my auspices, two armies were led at about the same time to Ethiopia and Arabia (called 'Happy'), and large enemy forces from both these tribes were killed in battle and many towns were taken. In Ethiopia my armies reached Nabata next to Meroe; in Arabia they got as far as the town of Mariba in the land of the Sabaei.

I added Egypt to the empire of the Roman people. When I could have made Greater Armenia a province on the death of king Artaxes, I preferred to follow traditional policy in handing the kingdom over to Tigranes, son of Artavasdes and grandson of Tigranes, through the agency of Tiberius who was at that time my stepson. The same race later seceded and rebelled. When it had been subdued by my son Gaius, I gave control of it to king Ariobarzanes, the son of Artabazus, the king of Media, and after his death to his son Artavasdes. On his murder, I sent Tigranes, a member of the royal house of Armenia, to that kingdom. I recovered all the provinces east of the Adriatic and Cyrene as well, largely ruled by kings at the moment; before them I had recovered Sicily and Sardinia which had been seized in the Slave War.

I planted colonies of soldiers in Africa, Sicily, Macedonia, both Spains, Achaea, Asia, Syria, southern France and Pisidia. Italy too boasted of twenty-eight colonies founded by my authority which grew in prosperity and population during my lifetime.

I regained by conquest various military standards which other commanders had lost in Spain, Gaul and Dalmatia. I forced the Parthians to return to me the spoils and standards of three Roman armies, and to seek in supplication the friendship of the Roman people. These standards I placed in the sanctuary of the temple of Mars Ultor.

The Pannonian tribes which no Roman army had approached before my principate were conquered by my stepson Tiberius, and I subjected them to the Roman rule, extending the boundaries of Illyricum to the banks of the Danube. A Dacian army which crossed south of the Danube was defeated and crushed under my auspices. Later my army was led across the Danube and forced the Dacians to bear with the commands of the Roman people.

Delegations were frequently sent to me from India, the like of which no previous Roman leader had ever seen. Our friendship was asked for by envoys from the kings of the Bastarnae, Scythians, and the Sarmatae who live on either side of the Don; also by the kings of the Albani, Hiberi and Medes.

Various kings fled to me in supplication—Tiridates and later Phrates, son of king Phrates, kings of the Parthians; Artavasdes, king of the Medes; Artaxaies, king of the Adiabeni; Dumnobellaunus and Tincomnius of the Britons, Moelo of the Sugambri, and the kings of the Marcomanni and Suebi. Phrates, son of Orodes, king of the Parthians, sent his sons and grandsons to me in Italy, though he had not been overcome in war; he was seeking our friendship by pledging his children. Many other races experienced the good faith of the Roman people in my principate, with whom the Roman people had never previously exchanged envoys or had any dealings of friendship.

The Parthians and Medes through envoys received from me as chief men of those peoples the kings for whom they asked, the Parthians Vonones, son of Phrates and grandson of Orodes, the Medes Ariobarzanes, son of Artavasdes and grandson of Ariobarzanes.

In 28 and 27 B.C., after I had terminated the civil wars, when I had full power by universal consent, I transferred the body politic from my control back to the arbitrament of the Senate and people of Rome. For this reason and in my honour, I was called

Augustus by Senatorial decree. The doorposts of my house were publicly garlanded with laurels, a civic crown was fastened above my door, and a golden shield placed in the Senate-house of Julius, on which an inscription bore witness that it was given to me by the Senate and people of Rome because of my virtue, clemency, justice and filial devotion. Thereafter I exceeded all in authority, but I had no more theoretical power than any of my colleagues in each office.

In 2 B.C., the Senate, Equestrian Order and the whole Roman people gave me the title of Father of my Country, which they voted to be inscribed in the hall of my house, the Senate-house of Julius and in the Augustan Forum under the Quadriga which was put there by Senatorial decree.

I was seventy-six years old when I wrote this.

HOUSEKEEPING ACCOUNT
c. A.D. 1

No comment is needed on this extract except to point out the familiar attention paid to children and the apparent lack of proteins in the diet (see page 194 for another side to this). The correspondence with English dates is not quite certain.

Source: Select Papyri (Loeb), vol. I, p. 421; translated by A. S. Hunt and C. C. Edgar.

		drachmas	obols
Jan. 16th	Coraxian cloak	10	
	Turnips for preserving	1	2
	Hire of copper vessel for dyeing ..		2
	Salt ..		1
	Grinding 1 artaba of wheat on the 13th		3
	Rushes for the bread baking		2
	Wages for repair of Coraxian cloak		1½
	Entertaining the wife of Gemellus		4
	Myrrh for the burial of Phna's daughter ..		4

		drachmas	obols
Jan. 17th	Chous of olive-oil	1	4
	Wax and stilus for the children ..		1
	Pure bread for Prima		½
	Entertaining Tyche		3
Feb. 4th	Lunch for the weaver		1
	For the Serapeum		2
	Pure bread for the children ..		½
	Beer for the weaver		2
	Leeks for the weaver's lunch ..		1
	A pigeon		1
	To Antas	2	2
	Grinding 2 artabae of wheat for flour through Isas in town	1	2
5th	Grinding 1 artaba of wheat for flour in encampment		4
	Weaver's lunch		1
	Asparagus for Antas' dinner at the feast of the fuller..		½
	Cabbage for the boys' dinner ..		½
10th	Savoury		½
	Rushes for the loaves		2½
11th	Milk for the children		½
	Pure bread		½
12th	To Secuntas (? Secundus) for a cake for the children		½
13th	Barley gruel for the children ..		½
14th	Sauce		1
	Pure bread		½
	Entertaining Antonia		2
	Entertaining Taptollous		3
	Garlands for the birthday of Tryphas		2
	Birthday garlands		2
15th	Pomegranates for the children ..		1
	Toys etc. for the children		½
	Beer		3
	Sauce		1

		drachmas	obols
Feb. 16th	Sauce		1
	Thaesis—2 days (? stay or work) ..		5
	Taarpaesis—2 days		5
	Berous—10 days	4	1
18th	Grinding 1 artaba of wheat ..		4
	2 measures of salt for pickling ..		2
	Salt		1
	Needle and thread		1
	Grinding 1 artaba of wheat (through Theodorus)		4
	Weaving of a cloak	1	2
	White loaves	1	
	Pigeon for the children		1
	Pure bread for the children ..		½
	To Secundus for a cake for the children		½
	Dry finest flour		½
	Milk		½
	Myrrh for the burial of the daughter of Pasis		1

THE CHARACTER OF THE YOUNG CLAUDIUS
c. A.D. 10

Claudius, the future Emperor, was the son of Drusus. Drusus and his brother Tiberius were the sons of Livia, Augustus's second wife by a former marriage. He seems to have lacked the social graces, and was twice passed over as Emperor. How he gained power when dragged from a hiding-place behind a curtain on the murder of Caligula in A.D. 41 is well known. The reputation of Claudius has suffered much from the brilliant treatment by Tacitus, and also from the *Apocolocyntosis*, a satirical work by Seneca. This extract is a letter written by Augustus, who by this time had made up his mind about his successor, Tiberius.

Source: Letter found in Suetonius, *Life of Claudius*, 4.

Further Reading: Loeb translation by J. C. Rolfe, Penguin translation by Robert Graves. Translation of Tacitus' *Annals* in Loeb series by

J. Jackson, and in Penguin Classics by Michael Grant. Apart from *C.A.H.* vol. X, Momigliano's *Claudius* is very useful. The brilliant reconstruction by Robert Graves in *I, Claudius* is well worth reading, continued in *Claudius the God*.

To Livia,

I have done what you asked, and have spoken to Tiberius about what should be done with Claudius, your grandson, at the Martian festival. Both of us agreed that we must decide, once and for all, what policy to follow in his case. For if he is, forgive the expression, completely compos mentis, I see no reason why we should have any reservations about promoting him by the same stages and steps as his brother Germanicus. But if we feel him to be wanting and defective in soundness of body and mind, then the men who make it their business to mock and sneer at such things must not be given full scope for laughing at him and at us. If we have not made up our minds beforehand and base our considerations on particular moments of time, we will never know for certain if there is reason for believing that he could support such honours or not.

For the present, however, to reply to your letter, we are agreeable to his having charge of the arrangements for the sacred banquet at the Martian festival, provided that he is prepared to receive help from Silvanus's son, a relative of his, to avoid doing anything which might arouse attention or derision. We are not willing to have him watching the Circus Games from the royal box. For he will be too exposed and in the public eye in the front of the seats. We are also not prepared to let him go in procession to the Alban Mount, or indeed, to be in Rome during the Latin festival. If he can accompany his brother to the Mount, there seems no reason for refusing to give him similar charge over the city.

Those are my views; I always think that something definite should be decided about every matter to avoid perpetual vacillation between hope and fear. You may certainly, if you wish, let his mother Antonia read part of this letter.

Augustus.

TIBERIUS AS A GENERAL
A.D. 4-14

Tiberius had retired in disgrace or annoyance to Rhodes in 2 B.C. On the death of Augustus's grandsons, Gaius and Lucius, he became the heir apparent, was recalled and adopted as Augustus's son (he was, in fact, a stepson). From now until he became emperor in A.D. 14, he was almost continuously fighting to establish Rome's northern frontier. Ever since the death of Agrippa in 12 B.C. he had been the leading general and, whatever his faults as a civil administrator, he certainly gained the great respect of his troops, as Velleius shows.

Source: Velleius Paterculus, II, civ, 3.

Further Reading: Loeb translation by F. Shipley. For general history see *C.A.H.* vol X. For the historical background to this extract, read J. Buchan's *Augustus* or T. Rice Holmes' *Architect of the Roman Empire.* F. B. Marsh's *The Reign of Tiberius* is a standard work. A very interesting psychological history of Tiberius is by G. Marañon, *Tiberius: A Study in Resentment.*

It was at about this time that I became a soldier in the army of Tiberius, having previously served my tribunate. Immediately after his adoption by Augustus, I was sent to Germany as a cavalry commander under him, succeeding my father in that post. Either as a commander or as a general, I was a witness for nine solid years of his superlative achievements, and helped in them to the limit of my own poor ability.

I cannot think that mankind is likely to see a spectacle equal to the one which I enjoyed, when throughout the most populous parts of Italy and the whole expanse of the Gallic provinces, men saw once again their old general, a Caesar in actions of valour before he was in name. They were all fuller in congratulation of their own good luck than of him, as tears of joy welled from their eyes as they saw him. They eagerly and almost strangely rushed forward to salute him, wanting to touch his hand, and could not prevent themselves from crying, 'Do we really see you again, sir? Have we got you back safe?', and 'I served under you, sir, in Armenia—I was with you in Raetia—I was decorated by you against the Vindelici, I in Pannonia, I in Germany.' Words cannot describe the scenes which were almost unbelievable.

I will give you an example, which does not make very grand
telling, but which merits the highest praise for its solid and true
worth and for its service. Certainly it was most pleasant to
experience and showed wonderful humanity. For the whole
duration of the German and Pannonian wars, there was not one
member of the army, either above or below me in rank, who fell
sick, whose health and recovery did not mean so much to Tiberius
that his mind seemed to disengage itself from the mass of his
great exploits and have time for just that one invalid. A horse-
drawn vehicle was ready for those that needed it, his litter was
available to all, and I was one of those who benefited from its
use. Any invalid was helped by his doctors, his kitchen appointments and his bathing apparatus which had been brought for his
own personal use. Men only lacked their own homes and servants—nothing else which could be provided by those at home
or for which they could wish.

One further point I will add, which will be immediately
recognized as true—as indeed will everything else I have mentioned, by anyone present during those campaigns. He, alone of
generals, always rode on horseback, and for the greater part of
the summer season ate his meals sitting (rather than reclining)
with his guests. He ignored those who did not follow his own
high standards, provided that no damaging example was set. He
frequently employed admonishment, occasionally reproof but
rarely punishment, and followed a practice of turning a blind eye
to most things, while from time to time censuring a few.

TOMI AND THE BARBARIANS
c. A.D. 12

Ovid felt the same about being out of Italy and Rome as had Cicero
sixty years before. He was exiled to Tomi, on the Black Sea, for two
reasons, one of which we know to have been the publication of the
Art of Love which went against Augustus's avowed attempt to improve
the morals of Rome. The other is called by Ovid a 'mistake' but that
is all we can discover for certain. The land north of the Danube was
inhabited by the Dacians, who caused much trouble under Domitian

and were finally incorporated in the Empire by Trajan in A.D. 106. It is interesting to note that Ovid later learnt the language he so affects to despise.

Source: Ovid, *Tristia*, III, x and V, x.

Further Reading: Loeb translation by A. L. Wheeler. Apart from the books on Augustus mentioned under previous extracts, see L. P. Wilkinson, *Ovid Recalled*, and Gilbert Highet's chapter on Ovid in *Poets in a Landscape*.

The very Danube, which is as wide as the papyrus-bearing Nile and enters the vast sea through many channels, freezes as the winds harden its deep-blue waters and glides on beneath its covering of ice. You can now walk where once went ships, and the hooves of horses sound on the ice-packed waters. Over new bridges, with the stream flowing below, Sarmatian oxen drag the barbarians' carts. I know that I will scarcely be believed, but when the rewards for lying are nil, firm faith ought to be given a witness's tale. I have seen the mighty sea itself grow solid with ice, and a slippery coat press down on the unmoving waves. Seeing was not enough. I personally have trodden on the hard sea, and the tops of the waves lay under my feet without wetting them. . . . Ships will stand in the deep, shut in by the ice, and no oar can part the congealed waters. I have seen fish frozen into the ice, and part of them even then was alive.

So if the savage force of the north wind hardens the waves of the sea or the overflowing waters of the river, immediately the Danube is levelled by its dry blasts, the barbarian foes ride over on their swift horses. Strong in cavalry and the far-flying arrow, they ravage the neighbouring land far and wide. Some flee, and with no one to protect the fields, the unguarded wealth is snatched away, the wealth of a poor country, herds and creaking wagons, and the riches that the poor rustic has. Others are driven off into captivity, with their arms tied behind their backs, looking round in vain at their lands and small homesteads. Others fall miserably pierced by the barbed arrows, for there is poison smeared on the swift iron point. What they cannot take away or drive off with them they destroy, and enemy flames burn down the innocent houses. Even when there is peace, men are afraid in the fear of war, and no one ploughs the soil with weighted share. . . .

Nothing outside is safe; the hill itself is hard to defend by the scanty walls and natural strength. The enemy swarm in, like birds, when least expected, and drive off the booty almost before they are seen. We have often picked up harmful missiles in the middle of the streets which have come inside the walls even when the gates are shut. So there are few men who dare to cultivate the land, and the luckless farmer ploughs with one hand and holds his arms in the other. The shepherd wears a helmet as he plays on his pitch-joined pipes, and war, not wolves, is what alarms the frightened sheep. Our defences hardly help to protect us, and even inside the town the crowd of barbarians mixed with Greeks causes fear. For barbarians live with us with no distinction and live in more than half the houses. You may not actually be afraid of them, but you can still hate them as you see their chests covered in skins and shaggy hair. Even those believed to be of Greek descent are covered in Persian trousers instead of their native dress. They do their business in the common language; I have to gesture for what I want. Here *I* am the barbarian, understood by none, and the boorish Getae laugh at my words of Latin. They often quite safely and openly attack me, reproaching me with my exile. And as happens, they think that I have some sinister motive when I give a plain 'yes' or 'no' in answer to their questions. And, lastly, law is unjustly administered by the hard sword, and many a man lies wounded in the middle of the market square.

THE REIGN OF TIBERIUS
A.D. 14-37

The character and reign of Tiberius are known mainly from the accounts of the later writers, Tacitus and Suetonius. Both are biased, Tacitus because he saw in Tiberius the prototype of the infamous Domitian and because he used Senatorial sources for his history, Suetonius because he delighted in recounting the private vices and behaviour of the Emperors to the neglect of more public happenings. Velleius, as can be seen from a previous extract, was just as likely to be prejudiced in his favour. But a judicious comparison between this contemporary record and the later versions enables some degree of certainty to be reached. But the description of Sejanus, executed for treason in A.D. 31, seems wide of the mark.

Source: Velleius Paterculus, *History of Rome*, II, cxxvi, 1.

Further Reading: Loeb translation by F. Shipley. For other books, see the selection under Tiberius as a General (page 137).

It would be a bold man who would be prepared to recount in detail the events of the past sixteen years which are so well known to the eyes and minds of all. Tiberius demonstrated that his father was now a god, not by imperial command but by his own devotion, not by calling him a god but by assuming him to be one. Confidence and good faith were restored to the Forum, and strife was ended; election tempers were removed from the Campus, discord from the Senate; justice, fair play and hard work, which had lain buried and smothered in decay and disuse, were restored to the state. The political leaders recovered their authority, the Senate its prestige and the courts their dependability. Brawls no longer disturbed the theatres, and all were either encouraged to wish to act rightly or were forced to do so. Good actions were honoured, bad ones punished; the lowly respected but did not fear the powerful; the powerful led but did not despise the lowly. Corn was at its cheapest, peace at its most plentiful. The Pax Augusta spread into all lands East and West, from the Northern extremities to the Southern, and kept every corner of the world free from the fear of banditry. The Emperor's generosity took under its wing accidental losses not merely of private citizens but of whole cities too. Communities in Asia were restored and freed from the injustices of provincial governors; the deserving met with immediate honour, while the wicked faced penalties which, though sometimes slow in coming, came most inevitably. Influence gave place to equality, graft to merit. For this, the best of Emperors, taught his citizens how to act rightly by his own example, and though he had the pre-eminent power to do so, his example is all the greater for that reason.

Great enterprises need great assistants, and it is of advantage to a state if those whom she must use should be of outstanding dignity, and if their usefulness should be supported by official position. Tiberius followed precedent in choosing and retaining

Aelius Sejanus as his one great lieutenant in all imperial matters. Sejanus was the son of a leader of the Equestrian Order, and on his mother's side claimed relationship with illustrious, old and much-honoured families. He had brothers, cousins and an uncle who had served as consuls. He himself was a glutton for work and a model of loyalty, his strong body matching his mental vigour. A man of cheerful uprightness and old-fashioned gaiety, like the leisured in his actions, he claimed nothing for himself but achieved all, always valuing himself less than others' estimation of him, calm of face and calm in life, for ever mentally alert.

INTERVIEW WITH GAIUS
A.D. 40

Philo was a Jew from Alexandria, where the Jews had been savagely attacked in A.D. 38 on the pretext that they refused to worship the new Emperor, Gaius. An embassy, of which Philo was a member, brought two complaints to Rome, one against the desecration of the Temple and their synagogues, the other about some aspect of their right to citizenship in Alexandria. From the next extract it may appear that they claimed a dual citizenship, but the problem is undecided. Gaius, or Caligula, reigned from 37 until his murder in 41. His madness seems definitely authenticated.

Source: Philo, *Embassy to Gaius*, 349.

Further Reading: Loeb translation by F. H. Colson. Josephus's *Jewish Antiquities* is translated in the Loeb series by H. St. J. Thackeray and R. Marcus. For the state of Alexandria, see the index to M. Rostovtzeff's *A Social and Economic History of the Roman Empire*.

It is right to recount what we saw and heard when we were summoned to present our case on the question of citizenship. Immediately on entering, we realized from his face and gestures that we were in the presence not of a judge but of a prosecuting counsel, and that we would find him more firmly against us than our actual opponents. A proper judge would have sat with some colleagues chosen on merit, as this was a most important examination which affected many thousands of Jews in Alexandria for the first time in the city's history, after complete silence for nearly four hundred years. The litigants would have been standing on either side of him with their advocates, and, after listening in turn for a set time to the cases of the plaintiffs and defendants, he would have risen to discuss with his colleagues what was the fairest public judgement they should give. But the actual events were more like those of a cruel tyrant, with a scowl on his despotic brow.

He did not do one of the things I have just mentioned, but sent for the stewards of the two gardens belonging to Maecenas and Lamia. These gardens are situated together near the city, and he had been there for the past three or four days. That was the stage on which the drama against our whole race was to be enacted, and we were to be the audience. He gave instructions for all the rooms to be opened, as he wanted to carry out a detailed inspection of each of them.

When we were brought before him, we bowed ourselves to the ground in reverence and care, and saluted him, addressing him as Augustus Autocrator. His answer was couched in terms so kind and gentle that we surrendered any idea not merely of winning our case but even of saving our lives. In a sarcastic, sneering way, he said, 'You are the god-haters, who do not consider me to be a god but refuse to accept me as one, although all others have agreed that I am one'. Then, stretching his hands to heaven, he gave vent to an appeal which it was sin even to listen to, let alone repeat verbatim. You can imagine the delight which at once filled the delegates on the other side, who thought their case won from the opening remark by Gaius. They waved their arms about, danced around and called him by the name of every god they could think of. The bitter, sycophantic Isidorus saw that he was delighted with these more-than-human names, and said, 'Sire, you will find even more cause to hate these men and those of their race when you know of their ill-will and impiety towards you. When the whole world conducted sacrifices of thanksgiving for your recovery, these alone could not bear to join in. When I say "these", I include the other Jews.' We all cried in unison, 'Lord Gaius, this is slander. We did sacrifice, hecatombs too, not merely by sprinkling blood on the altar and carrying home the meat for a banquet and party, as is the way of some, but by giving all the offerings to the sacred flame. This we have done not once but three times to date; once when you became Emperor, again when you recovered from that dreadful disease which affected the whole world, and a third time in hope of a victory in Germany.' His reply was, 'All right, perhaps this is true, that you have sacrificed and on my behalf. But the sacrifices were offered to another god. What good is that if you did not sacrifice to me?' This, coming on top of his earlier remark, caused in us such a deep and immediate shudder that it was clearly visible on our faces.

During this conversation, Gaius was going round the villas, inspecting the men's and women's quarters, ground floor, second floor, everything, with criticism of some things as inadequately prepared and plans for others to be more lavishly equipped. We were tugged along behind as we followed him up and down, scoffed and jeered at by our opponents like knock-about comedians. In fact it was rather like a play. The judge had taken on the role of prosecuting counsel, the prosecuting counsel that of a poor judge who paid attention not to the nature of the truth but only to the dictates of his own personal enmity. When a judge of that sort accuses a man on trial, silence is imperative. For silence can be a defence, especially to those like us, who could make no reply to the questions which he wanted answered, since our customs and laws held our tongues and kept our mouths tightly stitched up.

When he had arranged some of the matters about the buildings, he asked us most importantly and solemnly, 'Why don't you eat pork?' A great peal of laughter broke out from our opponents at this question, partly from pleasure and partly from a definite policy to flatter him to make his remark seem witty and graceful. So loud was the laughter that one of his attendants who followed him was amazed at the insult to the Emperor in whose presence even a faint smile is unsafe unless you know him very well. We replied, 'Different people have different customs, and both we and our opponents are forbidden to use certain things'. Someone said, 'Many people don't eat lamb, which is so easy to get'. Gaius laughed and said, 'Quite right, for it's not nice'. We were in despair with these inanities and insults, when he at last said sarcastically, 'We wish to know what justice you have in your claim about the citizenship'. We started to outline our case, but when he had had a taste of the justice of our plea, and had recognized that it was a good one, he cut us short before we reached the main points and leapt off at the double into a large room, where he rushed about ordering windows to be fitted all round, with translucent stones like clear glass which do not stop the light but block out the wind and the heat of the sun. Then he slowly approached us and said equably enough, 'What is your case?' We were just beginning to go on with our points when he ran into another room in which he ordered original pictures to be painted. Thus our claims were scattered, disjointed, virtually amputated and obliterated. We gave up, for we had no strength left, and the only thing we expected was instant death. We had no spirit remaining, but in our agony we went out to pray to the true God that he might check the anger of this man, so falsely called a god. And he, taking pity on us, turned Gaius' wrath to mercy. Becoming gentler, he said, 'The men seem misguided rather than wicked, and stupid not to believe that my natural lot was that of a god'. Whereupon, he went away, bidding us go too.

CLAUDIUS AND ALEXANDRIA
A.D. 41

Clearly the row described in the previous extract had not been solved when Gaius was murdered. Claudius knew something of the Jews from his friendship with Herod Agrippa, and in spite of the suspicions of Augustus about his sanity, proved sensible in his dealings with the Empire.

Source: Letter of the Emperor Claudius; *Select Papyri* (Loeb), vol. I, p. 212.

Further Reading: The life of Claudius is reconstructed by Robert Graves in *I, Claudius* and *Claudius the God*. The history of his reign is partly preserved in Tacitus's *Annals* (Penguin translation by Michael Grant), and Suetonius's *Life of Claudius* is translated in Penguin Classics by Robert Graves. See also Momigliano's *Claudius*.

As for the discord and trouble, or, to give it its proper name, your war with the Jews, I have not wished to make an accurate enquiry as to where the guilt lies, although your deputation acquitted itself well before us in the confrontation, especially Dionysius, son of Theon. But I will harbour a merciless anger against whoever starts it off again. I warn you quite simply that unless you stop this deadly, hot-headed feud against each other, I shall be forced to show you what a difference there is in a kindly prince when moved to righteous indignation.

I hope, then, that you will give proof that the Alexandrians are gentle and kindly disposed towards the Jews who have lived in the same city for so long. You must pollute none of their religious observances, but allow them to follow the same customs as they did under the Blessed Augustus, which I personally guaranteed to them after an impartial enquiry.

To the Jews I give this definite order. Do not aim for more than you formerly owned, and, in future, do not send me a second delegation as if you lived in a second city. This has never happened before. Do not go to see the games presided over by the Gymnasiarch or the citizen-games, while you enjoy your own privileges and have advantage of countless other material blessings in a foreigners' city. Do not bring in, or allow in, Jews sailing from Syria or from Upper Egypt, which I would be forced to view with grave suspicion. If you disobey, I shall do all in my power to drive them out as the instigators of a nuisance that besets the world.

If both sides alter their present conduct and are prepared to live in amity and kindness with one another, I will show you my affection for the city, which dates back a long way, for my family has traditional friendship with you.

GLADIATORIAL SHOWS
c. A.D. 50

Many literary Romans disliked the shows in the arena, as has been seen in the case of Cicero. To Seneca the wholesale butchery of human life was a shocking negation of his Stoic principles of the Brotherhood of Man. Some of the early emperors, like Tiberius, were equally opposed, but the cruelties of Caligula and Nero (whom Seneca served for a few years, and by whom he was later ordered to commit suicide) are notorious. Many of them had private arenas built in their own palaces.

Source: Seneca, *Letters,* 7.

Further Reading: Loeb translation by R. H. Gummere. For gladiatorial shows, see J. Carcapino's *Daily Life in Ancient Rome,* ch. viii; R. W. Moore's *The Roman Commonwealth,* ch. viii, and pictures in Zschietzschmann's *Hellas and Rome.* There are many mosaics depicting gladiators, the most accessible being at the Roman villa at Bignor, Sussex (gladiators as Cupids). Stoicism is considered in R. W. Livingstone's *Mission of Greece* and T. R. Glover's *The Conflict of Religions in the Early Roman Empire.*

There is nothing so ruinous to good character as to idle away one's time at some spectacle. Vices have a way of creeping in because of the feeling of pleasure that it brings. Why do you think that I say that I personally return from shows greedier, more ambitious and more given to luxury, and, I might add, with thoughts of greater cruelty and less humanity, simply because I have been among humans?

The other day, I chanced to drop in at the midday games, expecting sport and wit and some relaxation to rest men's eyes from the sight of human blood. Just the opposite was the case. Any fighting before that was as nothing; all trifles were now put aside—it was plain butchery. The men had nothing with which to protect themselves, for their whole bodies were open to the thrust, and every thrust told. The common people prefer this to matches on level terms or request performances. Of course they do. The blade is not parried by helmet or shield, and what use is skill or defence? All these merely postpone death. In the morning men are thrown to bears or lions, at midday to those who were previously watching them. The crowd cries for the killers to be paired with those who will kill them, and reserves the victor for yet another death. This is the only release the gladiators have. The whole business needs fire and steel to urge men on to fight.

'But he was a robber.' What of it; did he kill anyone? 'Yes, he did.' Well, just because he committed murder, did he deserve to suffer this? And you, poor man, what have you done to deserve to have to watch it? 'Kill him, lash him, brand him! Why is he so frightened of running against cold steel? Why does

he die so feebly? Why is he so reluctant to die or to be driven
to his death by the lash? They must both inflict wounds on each
other's bare chests. Ah, now there's an interval. Let's have some
men strangled to fill in the time.'

THE SHIPWRECK OF ST. PAUL
c. A.D. 60

This extract from the Acts of the Apostles shows quite clearly the
hazards of winter sailing in the Mediterranean. The date of Paul's
'appeal unto Caesar' is not certain, but must be before 65. Malta was,
of course, part of the Roman Empire. The Acts of the Apostles was
written by St. Luke.

Source: Acts of the Apostles, ch. xxvii, v. 27.

Further Reading: Among a host of books, Werner Keller's *The Bible
as History* and L. Grollenberg's *Atlas of the Bible* are two readily
accessible modern works.

For thirteen days we were carried along in the Ionian Sea.
About midnight on the fourteenth the sailors felt that they were
approaching land, so they sounded and found the depth to be
twenty fathoms, and a little later they sounded again and found
fifteen fathoms. In their fear that we would be driven onto some
rocky coast, they threw four anchors over the bow and prayed
for daylight. The sailors aimed at getting off the boat, and
launched the skiff on the pretext of going to cut the anchor from
the bow. But Paul said to the Centurion and the soldiers, 'You
cannot be safe unless they stay on board'. So the soldiers cut the
skiff's ropes and let it fall overboard. Just before first light, Paul
encouraged everyone to have some food with these words: 'You
have now been on watch for thirteen days on end without proper
food, without a real meal. I do suggest that you take some
nourishment, for it would certainly help your chances of getting
off safely. Not one hair of your heads will be hurt.' Then he took
bread, said Grace before all, broke the bread and began to eat.
Everyone on board (the total number of us was 276) recovered
his morale and took some food. When they were satisfied, they
lightened the boat by throwing the grain into the sea.

At daybreak, they could not recognize the coast, but saw a bay with a sandy beach, where they hoped to steer the ship and so save it. They cut away the anchors and let them fall into the sea, and also undid the fastenings of the steering-oars. Then they raised the foresail to the breeze and made for the beach. They grounded on a small headland, where the prow stuck fast above the surf, but the stern was being broken up by the force of the swell. The soldiers wanted to kill the prisoners to prevent their escaping by diving off. But the Centurion, who wanted to save Paul, resisted their wishes and gave instructions to those who could swim to dive overboard first and get to land. The rest were to escape on rafts or pieces of the boat's timber. In this way everyone got safely ashore. When we were safe, we found out that the island was called Malta. The natives showed us uncommon kindness. . . .

After three months we set sail in an Alexandrian boat which had wintered in the island, and had Castor and Pollux as its figure-head. We reached Syracuse, where we spent three days, then sailing round we landed at Rhegium. After a day there we spent two days sailing under a southerly wind to Puteoli, where some brethren invited us to stay with them for a week. So we came to Rome.

THE GREAT FIRE AT ROME
A.D. 64

That 'Nero fiddled while Rome burned' is well known. Tacitus is the origin of the story. Little is known of the historian's early life, and it is not even certain when or where he was born. It is likely that he was about nine years' old in A.D. 64, and possible that he was actually in Rome during the fire. He could certainly have talked to many eye-witnesses who had been there. Some of his remarks about Christians are clearly a result of later events, but there is a strong tradition that Peter and Paul reached Rome by A.D. 62, and the Pauline *Epistle to the Romans* proves the existence of many converts. As in the Great Fire of London, there was a blessing behind the disaster. The new Rome was planned more carefully and more beautifully than before, as Tacitus mentions in a section omitted from this extract.

Source: Tacitus, *Annals*, XV, ch. 38.

Further Reading: Loeb translation by J. Jackson, Penguin translation by Michael Grant. The biography of Nero by Suetonius is translated in Penguin Classics by Robert Graves. Apart from general histories, such as H. H. Scullard's *From the Gracchi to Nero*, R. Syme's *Tacitus* deals with the author's origin and sources.

The disastrous fire which followed was more serious and severe than any which the city has suffered from the violence of flames. It is uncertain whether it started accidentally or by Nero's own instigation, for both theories have their supporters.

It began in the part of the Circus Maximus which joins the Palatine with the Caelian Mount. Once the fire had started there among the shops, which contained materials to feed the flames, it grew rapidly. Fanned by the wind it swept the whole length of the Circus. Neither houses, with all their protection, nor temples, in spite of surrounding walls, could check the spread at all; indeed nothing could. The blaze surged first over the level areas, rose to the higher ground and then returned to lay waste the lower districts. The speed of its advance and the awkward nature of the city forestalled any attempts to quench it. For this was Old Rome, and the streets twisted tightly in and out through large blocks of penthouses.

Everything combined to impede counter-measures—the shrieks of frightened women, the age of some and the youth of others, selfish or selfless interests, the delay or the haste in waiting for or pulling along the weak. Often, as they looked behind them, they found the flames surrounding them in flank or in front. If they reached the next district, they found, when that too caught fire, that places which they thought to be quite safe were actually in the same plight. Finally, completely at a loss as to what area to avoid or where to make for, they thronged the roads out of town and scattered in the fields. Some lost all their private possessions, even the means of daily sustenance. Others, from the love of their dear ones whom they could not get out, perished although an escape route was clear. No one dared to resist the flames because of the frequent threats of gangs of men who stopped them if they did so. And others openly threw on fire-brands, shouting that they had authority for this. They may well have received orders, or they may merely have wanted to loot with more freedom.

Meanwhile Nero was at Antium, and he did not return to the city until his house which joins the Palatine with the Gardens of Maecenas was threatened by the fire. But nothing could stop the fire from consuming the Palatine, his palace and all. However, as some comfort to the terrified fugitives, he did throw open the Campus Martius and the buildings put up there by Agrippa, and even his own gardens. He also built temporary accommodation to receive the destitute mob. Relief was brought from Ostia and neighbouring towns, and the price of corn was reduced to three sesterces a bushel. These apparently popular measures proved valueless, for the rumour spread that while the city was burning Nero had entered his private theatre, and had recited the story of the Fall of Troy, comparing the present misfortunes with that old disaster.

At last, after five days, the fire was stamped out at the foot of the Esquiline by widespread demolition of buildings so that the persistent violence of the flames met with nothing but empty ground and the open sky. But the fear of the city population continued, and no one could presume to have real hope, for fire started again in the more open regions of the city. This did mean that there were fewer casualties, but greater damage was caused to shrines of the gods and to porticoes designed for leisure. This second outbreak created more ill-feeling, because it originated in the property of Tigellinus in the Aemilian district, and people felt that Nero was eager to win the glory of founding a new city, and of calling it after his own name. Rome is divided into fourteen districts. Of these, four remained untouched and three were razed to the ground. In the remaining seven just a few traces of buildings remained, burnt and in ruins. . . .

No amount of human help, no largesse from the Emperor or appeasement of the gods could squash the rumour that the fire had been started on orders. So to try to put an end to the gossip, Nero punished with most refined tortures, on trumped-up charges, those who were hated because of their depravity and were commonly called Christians. Christ, the originator of the name of this sect, had been executed by the Procurator

Pontius Pilate during the reign of Tiberius. Though checked for a while, this deadly superstition was breaking out again, not only in Judaea, its birthplace, but in Rome too. For the city is like a sewer where it seems that everything horrible and noisome flows and thrives. The first seized were those who confessed to this faith. Large numbers were convicted on their evidence, not so much on a charge of complicity in the fire as because of their hatred of the human race. Macabre humour was extracted from their deaths. Some were covered in animal skins and were torn to pieces by dogs, others crucified or set fire to and burnt to provide illumination after dark. Nero offered his own gardens for this spectacle, and gave a show in the Circus, mixing with the crowd or riding in a chariot in an ordinary charioteer's dress. So although these actions were taken against guilty men who deserved exemplary punishment, the victims were actually pitied. It seemed that they were removed not for the public good, but to satisfy one man's cruelty.

THE STATE OF ROME
A.D. 69

Tacitus wrote his Histories before the Annals, and started them with A.D. 69, the year of the Four Emperors. He was born in about A.D. 54, and must have remembered the death of Nero. He later lived under the tyranny of Domitian, and many of his remarks here are no doubt drawn from incidents during the latter's reign. Unfortunately not much of the Histories is left, and a work that was possibly meant to go to the death of Trajan in A.D. 117 is broken off in 70.

Source: Tacitus, *Histories*, I, 2.

Further Reading: Loeb translation by C. H. More. For the lives of the Four Emperors, see Robert Graves's translation of Suetonius in Penguin Classics and Plutarch's *Lives of Otho and Galba*, translated in Loeb series by B. Perrin. R. Syme's *Tacitus* discusses the author and has much of a learned nature about the period.

I am undertaking the description of a time rich in disaster, grim with battle, rent by discord, and dreadful even when there was peace. Four emperors met a violent death, there were three

civil wars and many more against foreign enemies or a mixture
of the two. Things went well for Rome in the East, but badly in
the West. Illyria was in ferment, Gaul shaky in its loyalty,
Britain subdued but immediately lost to us again. The Sarmates
and Suebi rose against us, the name of Dacia became known from
disasters to both sides, even Parthia took up arms in contempt for
the false Nero. Italy, too, was afflicted by calamities of a novel
kind as well as those which followed age-old precedent. Cities
were sacked and laid waste, the fertile Campanian coastlands were
devastated, the city of Rome was destroyed by fire, the most
revered shrine was consumed in the flames, even the Capitol
itself was the victim of arson at the hands of Roman citizens.
Sacred ceremonies were corrupted, adultery was widespread.
The seas were full of exiles and the rocks were covered with their
blood. Savagery was even worse in Rome itself. Nobility,
wealth and position were won and lost by crime, and virtuous
conduct brought inevitable disaster. The rewards that informers
gained were no less appalling than their vices; some got priest-
hoods or consulships as their spoil, others jobs and power at
Rome, while all their mischief-making actions were prompted by
hatred and terror. Slaves turned against masters, freedmen
against patrons, and those without enemies were destroyed by
their friends.

Yet the age was not quite so barren of virtue that it failed to
produce some examples of noble conduct. Mothers followed
their banished children into exile, and wives their husbands.
Relatives showed courage, kinsfolk stood firm and slaves remained faithful and unshaken even under torture. The final grim
act of necessity for any man of fame was undertaken bravely, and
their ends equalled the honoured deaths of men of old.

Quite apart from the manifold disasters to men, in the sky and
on the earth there were prodigies and warnings from thunder-
bolts, portents of things to come, some propitious, some ominous,
some quite clear, some shrouded in mystery. No age has produced
more obvious signs, in the atrocity of the disasters to the Roman
people, that vengeance, not protection, was what the gods willed
for us.

THE DESTRUCTION OF THE TEMPLE AT JERUSALEM
September 8th, A.D. 70

The most serious revolt so far of the Jews was described by Josephus, a Jew himself who had been a general in the Jewish army. He had been captured by Vespasian, but his life was spared through the agency of Titus, and he stayed with Titus in a privileged position for the rest of the campaign. The revolt started in A.D. 66, and when Vespasian returned to Rome in 69 to become Emperor, Titus was left to complete the suppression of Jerusalem. The aftermath of this revolt can be seen in some of the Dead Sea Scrolls, as fugitives took refuge in the desert.

Source: Josephus, *The Jewish War*, VI, 6.

Further Reading: Loeb translation by H. St. J. Thackeray, Penguin translation by G. A. Williamson. Apart from the facts presented in *C.A.H.* vol X, ch. xxv, S. W. Baron's *A Social and Religious History of the Jews* is clearly relevant. Very many books have already been published on the Dead Sea Scrolls. Two readily available are John Allegro's *Dead Sea Scrolls* and G. Vermes's *Dead Sea Scrolls in English*.

At this moment one of the soldiers, not waiting for orders and without any dread of such an act but driven on by some frenzy, snatched a brand from the blazing fire and, lifted up by a comrade, hurled the torch through the golden door which gave access to the buildings of the Temple Precinct from the north side. As the flames surged up, a great cry to match their feelings arose from the Jews, and they rushed to the defence, reckless of their lives and prodigal of their strength once they saw that the purpose of their previous watch was gone.

A message was quickly brought to Titus, who was in his tent during a lull in the battle. He leapt up just as he was, and rushed to the Temple to control the blaze, followed by all the officers, with the common soldiers accompanying them in a flutter. The shouts and noise were on a scale to be expected from such a force in such a disorderly move. Titus by verbal orders and gestures signalled to those fighting to put out the fire, but they did not hear his voice as their ears were filled with the greater volume of noise, and they paid no attention to his hand-signals, distracted as they were by the passion of battle. As the legionaries rushed in, neither warning nor threat checked their frenzy, but fury was their general. Many, as they pushed about the entrances, were trampled on by each other or fell on the still hot, smouldering ruins of the porches, and suffered the same fate as the vanquished. As they approached the Temple, they pretended not to hear Titus's instructions, but encouraged those in front to throw in the brands. The rebels were by now incapable of resisting, and death and flight were everywhere. For the most part it was the weak, defenceless citizens who were butchered where caught, and the pile of corpses grew around the altar, as the blood ran deep down the Temple steps and bodies of the slain slipped down from above.

As the fire gained strength, Titus found that he could not restrain the surge of his enthusiastic soldiers. Going into the Temple with his officers, he gazed at the Holy of Holies and its contents, much finer than the normal report of them which is circulated, and not a whit below their reputation and glory among the Jews themselves. The flames had not yet got inside, but were consuming the surrounding buildings. Titus quite rightly thought that the Temple could still be saved, and, leaping forward, he tried to get the soldiers to douse the fire, ordering Liberalius, the centurion of his bodyguard of lancers, to strike with his club anyone who disobeyed, and force him to help. But their obedience to Titus and their fear of the officers who were trying to control them was mastered by their passion, their hatred of the Jews and the wilder lust for battle. Most were driven on by the hope of loot, for they thought that the inside of the building must be full of money if the outside, which they could see, was made of gold. One of those who had got in forestalled the attempts of Titus who had rushed in to check them, and hurled a brand against the hinges of the door. Suddenly flames appeared from within, which forced back Titus and his officers, leaving those outside to kindle the blaze unhindered. In this way, though much against Titus's will, the Temple was burnt. . . .

From its first foundation by King Solomon until its present destruction, which happened in the second year of Vespasian's rule, the interval was 1,130 years, 7 months and 15 days. From its second foundation by Haggai in the second year of the reign of Cyrus until its capture by Vespasian (*sic*) was 639 years, 45 days.

TRIUMPH IN ROME
A.D. 71

On the completion of the Jewish War, a triumph was held jointly by Vespasian and Titus. Josephus came back to Rome with Titus, and gives us this full account. We may suppose that the proceedings were much as usual.

Source: Josephus, *The Jewish War*, VII, 3.

Further Reading: Loeb translation by H. St. J. Thackeray; Penguin translation by G. A. Williamson. See also general works, such as Friedlander's *Roman Life and Manners under the Early Empire* and J. Carcopino's *Daily Life in Ancient Rome*.

The date on which the victory festival was to take place was announced well in advance, and there was not a single person in the whole countless mass of citizens who stayed at home that day. Everyone went out and seized whatever spot they could find where it was possible merely to stand, leaving just enough room for the passing of the procession which they were to see.

During the hours of darkness the whole military force had been led out in companies and battalions by its officers and had been drawn up—not, as usual, near the gates of the palaces on the Palatine, but near the temple of Isis. For Titus and Vespasian had spent the night there, and now, as dawn began to break, they emerged, crowned in laurel wreaths and wearing the time-honoured purple clothes, and walked to the Octavian colonnade. There the Senate, the magistrates and those of Equestrian status were waiting for their arrival. A tribunal had been erected in front of the colonnade, with ivory chairs placed on it for them. As they walked forward to take their seats, all the soldiers raised an immediate cheer, paying abundant testimony to their valour, while Titus and Vespasian sat unarmed, dressed in silk garments and wearing their laurel wreaths. Vespasian acknowledged their acclaim, and, although they were keen to continue cheering, made a sign for silence. As all fell completely quiet, he rose, and, covering most of his head with a veil, made the traditional prayers. Titus followed him in doing likewise. After the prayers, Vespasian said a few words to the whole throng, and then dismissed the soldiers to have the customary breakfast provided at the generals' expense. He then walked to the gate, which got its name from the fact that all triumphal processions passed through it, where he and the others had a light meal. Afterwards, donning the triumphal robes and sacrificing to the gods stationed at the gate, they sent the procession on its way through the theatres to give the crowds a better view.

It is impossible to do justice in the description of the number of things to be seen and to the magnificence of everything that met the eye, whether in skilled craftsmanship, staggering richness or natural rarity. For almost all the remarkable and valuable objects which have ever been collected, piece by piece, by prosperous people, were on that day massed together, affording a clear demonstration of the might of the Roman Empire. The quantities of silver, gold and ivory, worked into every conceivable form, were not like those usually carried in a triumph, but resembled, as it were, a running river of wealth. Purple cloth of extreme rarity was carried along, some of it fashioned by Babylonian skill into accurate pictorial representations. Translucent gems, embedded in diadems or other objects, were borne in such profusion as to dispel any idea that they were rare. Images of the Roman gods passed by, wonderfully big and very skilfully worked, all of them made of expensive materials. Many kinds of beast were led along, all with their individual trappings. In charge of each part of the procession was a number of men in purple and gold costumes, while those selected for the triumph itself wore choice clothes of astonishing richness. Even the prisoners were worth seeing—no disordered mob, but the variety and beauty of their clothes diverted the eye from the disfigurement of their injuries.

The greatest amazement was caused by the floats. Their size gave grounds for alarm about their stability, for many were three or four stories high, and in the richness of their manufacture they provided an astonishing and pleasurable sight. Many were covered in cloth of gold, and worked gold or ivory was fixed on all of them. The war was divided into various aspects and represented in many tableaux which gave a good indication of its character. Here was a fertile land being ravaged, here whole detachments of enemy being slaughtered, others in flight and others being led off into captivity. Here were walls of colossal size being pounded down by siege-engines, here strongpoints being captured, and here well-defended fortifications overwhelmed. On one float the army could be seen pouring inside the walls, on another was a place running with blood. Others showed defenceless men raising their hands in entreaty, firebrands being hurled at temples or buildings falling on their owners. On yet others were depicted rivers, which, after the destruction and desolation, flowed no longer through tilled fields providing water for men and cattle, but through a land on fire from end to end. It was to such miseries that the Jews doomed themselves by the war. The craftsmanship and magnificence of the tableaux gave to those who had not witnessed the events as clear an idea of them as if they had been present. Standing on his individual float was the commander of each of the captured cities showing the way he had been taken prisoner. Many ships followed the floats.

Spoil in abundance was carried past. None of it compared with that taken from the Temple in Jerusalem, a golden table many stones in weight and a golden lampstand, similarly made, which was quite unlike any object in daily use. A centre shaft rose from a base, and from the shaft thin branches or arms extended, in a pattern very like that of tridents, each wrought at its end into a lamp. There were seven of these lamps, thus emphasizing the honour paid by the Jews to the number seven. A tablet of the Jewish Law was carried last of all the spoil. After it came a large group carrying statues of victory, all of them made of ivory and gold. The procession was completed by Vespasian, and, behind him, Titus. Domitian rode on horseback wearing a beautiful uniform and on a mount that was wonderfully well worth seeing.

The procession ended up at the Temple of Juppiter on the Capitol, where the generals got down. They still had to wait for the traditional moment when the news was brought of the death of the enemy leader. In this case he was Simon, son of Giovas, who had passed in procession with the captives, and had been dragged under the lash, with his head in a noose, to a spot near the Forum. That is the traditional place at Rome for the execution of those condemned to death for war-crimes. When his end was announced and a general cheer had arisen, they started the sacrifices, and after completing them with the customary prayers, they retired to the palace. There they entertained some of the citizens to dinner, while for all the others preparations for banquets at their own homes had already been made.

For on that day the city of Rome made holiday for their victory in the war against the Jews, for the end of civil disorder, and for the rising expectations of peace and prosperity.

AGRICOLA, GOVERNOR OF BRITAIN
A.D. 78

We have already seen some of the results of bad governorship in the case of Verres in Sicily. Unfortunately it was all too common. So the picture given by Tacitus of his father-in-law, Agricola, is a welcome change. There is no evidence that Tacitus ever came to Britain, but he probably had access to official papers as well as the benefit of conversation with Agricola and his subordinates.

Source: Tacitus, *Agricola*, 19.

Further Reading: Loeb translation by M. Hutton, Penguin translation by Michael Grant. Apart from the general books already mentioned, Richmond's *Roman Britain* and Collingwood's *Roman Britain*, A. R. Burn's *Agricola and Roman Britain* and R. Syme's chapter in *C.A.H.* vol. XI, ch. iv, together with references in his *Tacitus*, are more specific.

He tried to understand the temper of the province, and was warned by others' experiences that force profits little if followed by injustice. So he decided to cut out the initial causes of rebellion. Beginning with himself and his staff, he first restrained his own household, which many find as hard to do as to govern a whole

province. No public business was transacted by freedmen or
slaves, no promotion or enrollment of centurion or soldier was
effected by private interests, recommendations or requests. Those
who proved themselves best were considered the most trust-
worthy. He knew everything, but not everything was followed
up. Small misdemeanours were pardoned, large crimes suitably
and severely punished. He did not always demand punishment,
but was often content with repentance. He tried not to put
likely wrong-doers in charge of official posts, rather than have
to punish them when once they had done wrong. He softened
the tribute of corn and money by levelling out the duties, putting
an end to any which had been invented for pure gain and proved
a harsher burden than the tribute itself. For the natives were
forced in mockery to sit in front of closed granaries, to buy and
then surrender corn at a fixed price as if of their own free will.
Cross-country routes were ordered and remote places named as
centres, so that districts, in spite of the closeness of their winter
quarters, had to carry off their tribute to faraway isolated places,
until what had been easy for all became profitable for just a few.

By checking these abuses in his first year, he won a much
better name for peace, which formerly had been feared no less
than war because of the lack of care or harshness of previous
governors. The next summer he collected his army and was
always on the march, praising good conduct and checking the
stragglers. He personally chose the camp sites and explored the
estuaries and forests. Meanwhile he allowed the enemy no respite
from devastation in sudden raids. After a suitable display of
terror, he then showed once more how attractive peace could be
by his leniency. Many states had up till then considered themselves to be on a par with Rome, but this made them surrender
hostages, and lay aside their antagonism. They were then
garrisoned and forts were built with such intelligence and care
that no part of Britain came over to Rome so readily.

The next winter was spent in very salutary measures. To get
men living rural lives in scattered communities and so prone to
war to grow accustomed to peace and leisure as welcome additions
to their lives, he gave private encouragement and public help for
them to build temples, fora, and homes, by praising the energetic

and reproving the indolent. In this way men vied for his approval, which destroyed the necessity for force. He instructed the chieftains' sons in the liberal arts, and showed a preference for the native wits of the Britons over the pursuits of the Gauls, so that those who quite recently had rejected out of hand the Latin language now began to wish for a knowledge of even oratory. Our dress became respected and many a toga was to be seen. Little by little they were brought to alluring vices, porticoes, baths and elegant banquets. This was called culture by those who did not realize that it was really part of their enslavement.

Agricola never greedily claimed for himself the credit for things done by others. Centurion and officer alike found in him a reliable witness of their conduct. Some held him over severe in his strictures; his affability to good men was coupled with harshness to the wicked. But in his outbursts of anger there was no residue of unspoken malice, so that no one construed his silence as meaning terror for themselves. He believed it more honest to offend people openly than to harbour a grudge of hatred against them.

ERUPTION OF VESUVIUS
August 24th, A.D. 79

The famous eruption of Vesuvius which overwhelmed the towns of Pompeii and Herculaneum was watched by Pliny the Younger when he was staying with his uncle on the bay of Naples. About twenty-five years later he wrote this account in two letters to the historian Tacitus, who wanted information to include in his Histories. We do not know what use Tacitus made of it, since the relevant parts of his work are lost.

Source: Pliny the Younger, *Letters*, Book VI, 16 and 20.

Further Reading: Translation in Penguin Classics by Betty Radice; Loeb translation by W. M. Melmoth. There are many books on Pompeii. Perhaps the most attractive is *Pompeii and Herculaneum: The Glory and the Grief*, by Marcel Brion. *A Picture History of Archaeology* by C. W. Ceram and other histories of archaeology also have sections on the excavations. *Pompeii* by R. C. Carrington contains a full description of the town and excavations.

My uncle was at Misenum in personal command of the fleet. At about 1 p.m. on August 24th my mother pointed out to him that a cloud had appeared of extraordinary size and type. He had been sunbathing, and after a cold bath and a lunch taken at his ease, he was now reading. Asking for his shoes, he climbed up to a place from which the marvel could best be seen. A cloud was rising from some mountain which was later found to be Vesuvius, though we could not be sure at that moment as we watched from a distance. The best description that I can give would be that in shape and appearance it seemed very like a pine tree. For the cloud surged up high into the sky, like a tall tree-trunk, and then split into branches, possibly because its uplift was caused by fresh currents of air and when these weakened the cloud dissolved, or it may be that it was overcome by its very weight and dispersed out sideways. It varied in colour according to whether it carried up with it earth and ash, being sometimes white and at others dark and mottled.

My uncle, in the way a scholar will, thought that it looked interesting and should be investigated at closer range. So he ordered his light skiff to be launched and offered me the chance to go with him if I so desired. But, as a matter of fact, he had given me the topic for an essay, and I replied that I preferred to work. Just as he was leaving he received a message from Rectina, the wife of Bassus whose house was situated below the mountain, and who was terrified by the danger which threatened her. There was no escape except by sea, and Rectina asked my uncle to rescue her from her awful predicament. So he changed his plan, and his trip which he had started in a spirit of inquiry was accomplished in the most noble way. Ordering the warships to be launched, he embarked, determined to bring help not merely to Rectina but also to all the many others who thronged that most lovely shore. He hurried to the place from which everyone else was fleeing, and ordered the tiller to be set straight and a direct course steered for the scene of danger, though he remained so free from fear himself that he dictated and made notes of all the eruptions and disturbances of the volcano as he noticed them.

By now ash, which became hotter and thicker the nearer they approached, was falling on the boats. This was followed by pieces of tufa and stones blackened, burnt and cracked by the fire. They suddenly found themselves in shallow water as the shore was blocked by landslides. He wondered whether he should turn back, and his helmsman certainly advised that course. But after a moment he ordered, 'Make for the villa of Pomponianus. Fortune favours the brave'. Pomponianus lived at Stabiae, half the width of the bay away (for the sea sweeps in on gently curving beaches, which fold around it). Although the danger there was not immediate, it was very obvious and would be on top of him if it increased. So Pomponianus had put all his baggage on board boat, and had decided to make his escape if the sea-breeze died down. My uncle, of course, was carried in by this breeze, and clasped the trembling Pomponianus to him in his fear, offering words of comfort and encouragement. He even tried to lighten his panic by showing how unconcerned he himself was and asking to be shown to the bathroom. After his bath, he had a rest and then ate a meal very cheerfully, or, equally remarkable, seemingly so.

Meanwhile sheets of flame and tall columns of fire were belching forth from several parts of Vesuvius, their flash and intensity heightened by the darkness of the night. My uncle tried to lessen the alarm by insisting that the glare was caused by fires left burning by the panic-stricken farmers, and by their abandoned houses blazing on their own. Then he took himself off to bed and had a very real sleep. This was verified by those who were watching on the threshold, for they heard his breathing which was deep and resonant as he was a big man. But soon the corridor which led to his room was filling with pumice-stone and mixed ash to such a depth that if he had stayed any longer in the room he would not have been able to get out. When he was woken up, he went outside and rejoined Pomponianus and the others who had stayed awake. A discussion followed about whether they should stay indoors or walk about in the open. There was danger in both courses; the buildings were being frequently and violently shaken, and seemed as they tottered backwards and forwards to be being moved from their foundations; on the other hand there was some fear in the open from the fall of pieces of pumice-stone, even though they were light and half burned away.

But compared with the danger of the other alternative, this seemed the better course. So this my uncle adopted, obeying the dictates of logic whereas others would have listened rather to their fear. They put pillows on their heads and tied them with pieces of string as some protection against the falling objects.

It was now light everywhere else, but there it was the darkest and blackest night you can imagine, though this was relieved by the many torches and other lights. My uncle decided to make for the beach to see from close at hand whether the sea was calm enough to use. But it was still wild and surging on shore. The others began to run from the flames and the smell of sulphur which preceded the flames, but he was merely aroused by them. Leaning on two servants he got up, but immediately collapsed again. I think his throat and stomach which were naturally weak and constricted and frequently inflamed were blocked up and choked by the dense fumes. Two days after he died light returned. His body was found unharmed and with no injuries, still dressed in the clothes he had been wearing. He seemed to be like someone asleep rather than to be lying there dead.

Meanwhile my mother and I were still at Misenum. On my uncle's departure I had spent some time at my work, for I had remained behind for that very purpose. I then had a bath, dinner and a short, restless sleep. Earth tremors had been occurring for the past few days, but they were usual in Campania and did not cause much alarm. But they grew so violent that night that they seemed more likely to destroy than merely shake everything. My mother burst into my room just as I was getting up to wake her if she were still asleep. We sat down in the courtyard, a little distance from the house and the sea. I do not know whether to call my action bravery or foolhardiness, for I was only eighteen at the time, but anyway I asked for my Livy, and read on calmly, even copying extracts as I had started to do before. One of my uncle's friends, who had lately arrived from Spain, caught sight of us both sitting there, and me with a book in my hands, and violently attacked her stoicism and my false sense of security. But it made no difference—I continued with my book just the same.

It was now six o'clock in the morning, but the light was still
faint and slow in coming. Situated as we were in a narrow space
in the middle of tottering buildings, even though we were in the
open there was great danger from the seemingly inevitable
collapse of the house. So finally we decided to leave the town,
followed by a panic-stricken mob who seemed to prefer others'
ideas to their own, which may be the wisest thing to do when
afraid. They surged around us in a dense mass, pressing us on.
Halting when we had got away from the houses, we found many
things to cause us astonishment and many to make us afraid.
The carts which we had had brought out were rolling away in
different directions although the ground was quite flat, and they
could not be kept in their place even when wedged with stones.
In addition we noticed the violent undertow of the sea, which
was being battered back from the beach by the tremors. The
shore, indeed, had gone out a long way, and there were many
sea-creatures stranded on the dry sand. Looking the other way,
we saw the black cloud belching out with horrible fiery gusts and
flickering twisting forks of flame of great length. They seemed
rather like flashes of lightning, but much longer.

That same Spanish friend ran up and urged us with words
now more pressing, 'If your brother and your uncle is still alive,
he would want you to be safe. If he has died, then he would wish
you to survive him. Why don't you hurry up and get away?'
We replied that we could not possibly think of our own fate while
still uncertain of his. Our friend stayed no longer, but made off
at the double out of the danger. Soon the cloud seemed to drift
downwards and to cover the sea, hiding Capri in its folds and
blotting out Cape Misenum from our view. My mother begged,
urged, even ordered me to make good my escape; I was a young
man and could do so, but she was stricken in years, weak in body
and would not mind death so long as she did not cause mine.
I replied that I would not survive without her, took her hand and
forced her to go along with me, while all the time she showed
reluctance and kept on blaming herself for slowing me down.

Ashes were now falling on us, but not very thickly as yet.
Turning my eyes, I saw the dense pall pressing after us and
rolling over the ground behind us like a torrent. I suggested that

we should leave the road while we could still see, to avoid being trampled under foot by the mass of our fellow fugitives in the darkness. Scarcely had we sat down when the gloom of night descended upon us, not just like one moonless and overcast, but like the darkness you find in enclosed spaces when all the lights are out. All around us we could hear women screaming, children crying and men shouting. People were crying out for their parents, children and wives, and recognizing each other from their voices. Some mourned their own disaster, others that of their dearest. Some, even, in their terror of death prayed for death. Many lifted up their hands to the gods. But more felt that gods did not exist and that this was the last night of the world.

Certain people increased the general alarm by spreading completely false rumours. They announced that some buildings at Misenum were in ruins, others on fire—all quite false but they were believed. Soon it got a little lighter, though we felt that this did not mean the return of day but rather the approach of the flames. But the fire stayed far off and darkness returned, with renewed heavy falls of ash. From time to time we got up and shook it off us, for we would have been smothered and crushed by its weight if we had not. I might have boasted that I did not utter one groan or raise my voice at all in this appalling calamity, were it not that I in fact took comfort in the depressing but valid consolation that I was perishing in the general destruction of humanity.

Gradually the blanket of smoke thinned out to form a cloud or mist. Soon the sun was shining and it was really day, even though the sun seemed dark as it does during an eclipse. Our frightened eyes found everything changed and covered in deep ash like snow. Returning to Misenum, we refreshed our bodies as best we could and spent an anxious night in a mixture of hope and fear. But fear prevailed. For the earth tremors continued, and many poor people turned mad by the disaster were making a grotesque mockery of their own and others' misfortunes. But we had no thought of leaving until we had news of my uncle, however great the danger we had suffered and indeed still expected.

That is my story. I do not suppose that you will think it worthy of writing in your History, and perhaps not even fit subject for a letter. But you must blame yourself, for you it was who asked me for it.

A SOCIAL MENACE
c. A.D. 80

In the touchy days of the late first century, writers turned from history to some safer subject. Martial was very much a product of his times, writing epigrams and short satirical poems. Many are vulgar and many amusing. Most are written with a keen eye for satire; the original of 'I do not like thee, Doctor Fell' belongs to Martial. The theft of table-napkins seems to have been a fairly common practice at Rome. Catullus wrote of another thief in about 55 B.C. The reason was the absence of forks, and the necessity of cleaning hands which were used for eating good.

Source: Martial, *Epigrams*, XII, xxix.

Further Reading: Loeb translation by W. C. A. Ker. *Daily Life in Ancient Rome* by J. Carcopino deals with all social matters (entertainments in ch. viii).

> Beware Hermogenes, a thief
> Of napkins, skilful past belief;
> The way that Massa got his wealth
> Could hardly equal H's stealth.
> Hold fast his left, his right hand catch,
> He'll yet find ways to napkin-snatch.
> Like jellied eels they seem to be,
> He sucks them down so easily.
> The Circus waves[1]—Myrinus lives!
> But this to H. four napkins gives:
> The praetor drops his starting-flag;
> Hermogenes this flag does bag.
> No diners-out, in fear of theft,
> Brought napkins lest no more be left;
> But Hermo's counter-move was able—
> He stole the cloth from off the table.

[1] The crowd waved kerchiefs if they wanted a gladiator spared.

If none is laid, he does not fear
To strip the covered couches bare.
The sun's too hot for watching, but
At his approach the awnings shut.[1]
And sailors reef their sails in fright
Whenever Hermo heaves in sight.
The linen-wearing balding priest
Of Isis flees, with those that feast:
He's filled with fearful perturbation,
For Hermo's in the congregation.
When going out to dine, I guess,
Hermogenes was napkinless;
But when he left them late at night,
His hosts were always napkins light.

DAY-SCHOOL OR BOARDING-SCHOOL?
c. A.D. 90

Education for the Roman aristocracy tended to be even more
stereotyped than it is for us. A boy usually went to one of a very few
provincial schools and then automatically to Rome. For a university,
Romans went to Athens or Rhodes. Teachers were not plentiful and
the good ones became household names, like the great Orbilius. The
syllabus was very narrow, consisting of a study of Literature and the
art of public speaking or rhetoric. Pliny was born at Como, about
thirty miles from Milan, certainly a shorter distance than Virgil had to
go to school in Milan from his Mantuan farm. Most of the Roman
well-to-do merely affected an interest in the provinces and were, like
Cicero, profoundly unhappy if they were too long away from Rome.
Pliny, in this letter to Tacitus, seems to have been genuinely different.

Source: Pliny the Younger, *Letters*, Book IV, 13.

Further Reading: Translation in Penguin Classics by Betty Radice.
Loeb translation by W. Melmoth. A. Gwynn's *Roman Education from
Cicero to Quintilian* is a full treatment. Chapters in more general works
include B. W. Henderson's *Five Roman Emperors*, Carcopino's *Daily
Life in Ancient Rome* (ch. v) and, for earlier education, W. Warde
Fowler's *Social Life at Rome in the Age of Cicero* (ch. vi). Also R. W.
Moore's *The Roman Commonwealth* (ch. iv).

---

[1] Awnings were pulled over the Amphitheatres to protect spectators against the
sun.

A short time ago, when I was last in my native town, I was visited by the young son of one of my fellow citizens. When I asked him if he was at school he replied that he was. 'Where?' 'At Milan.' 'But why not here?' His father had brought the boy along and was with him, and he it was who answered, 'Because we haven't got any schoolmasters here'. 'What? None? It must be of considerable importance for all you fathers (there were several fathers present) for your children to go to school in Como. You must agree that the most pleasant place for them to spend their time is in their native district. Their manners will be better controlled under the eyes of their parents and they will cost less at home. It would be fairly inexpensive to collect the money to engage teachers if you added to their salaries what you now spend on boarding, journey money and all the other extras which you have to buy when away from home—and that means everything.

I haven't any children yet, but I am prepared to contribute a third of whatever sum you provide on the state's behalf, as though it were my daughter or dependent. I would promise the lot, were it not for my fear that my benefaction would be converted to private use, as I have seen happen in many places where schoolmasters are appointed by the local authorities. The only remedy for this state of affairs is for the appointment to be in the hands of just the parents, and they will be bound to make a good choice, for they will be paying the salary. Those who may be careless about spending other people's money will be careful about spending their own, and will take precautions that only a good man gets my money for he will be getting theirs too. So come to some common agreement and be encouraged by my example. I hope that my share of the debt will be very large. You can do nothing more beneficial for your children or for your town. Let children who are born here be educated here, and from their earliest days grow up to love and live in their native soil. I hope that you engage such good teachers that neighbouring communities seek their education here, and that children from other towns may soon come flocking to Como just as ours now go there.'

I thought I ought to put the whole matter quite plainly to you to make sure that you know how pleased I will be if you

undertake what I ask. The matter is very important and so I
earnestly entreat you to search, among the crowd of scholars who
throng around you admiring your intelligence, for teachers to
whom we can offer the job, but on condition that I am not
connected with them in any way. I leave it to the parents to
decide on whom to choose. My share will merely be my interest
and my financial contribution. So, if you find anyone who has
some confidence in his own ability, let him take on the job, but
he must remember that as far as I am concerned this confidence
is all he has.

UPBRINGING OF CHILDREN
c. A.D. 90

Once a schoolmaster has been chosen, it still remains to think about
what he should reach. Pliny did not mention this point. But Tacitus
had some views. This extract comes from an imaginary dialogue in
which various public figures discuss the state of present-day oratory.
They are not all critical, but there is no doubt that Tacitus himself,
while being a considerable orator, viewed his contemporary world
with a severe eye. Rhetoric as a main subject in the schools had
gradually been creeping in since the first century B.C. The closing
down of the 'schools of impudence' to which he refers happened in
92 B.C. There seems nothing very unusual about criticism of the
modern teenager!

Source: Tacitus, *Dialogue about Orators,* 29.

Further Reading: Loeb translation by W. Peterson. See under the
previous extract for other reading.

Nowadays a young child is handed over from birth to some
feeble Greek serving-girl and one of the slaves, usually the
cheapest and the one least fitted for any serious service. Its
tender, unformed mind is steeped in the stories and lies of these
slaves, and no one in the whole house cares a jot what he says or
does in front of the young master. Furthermore, parents do not
bring up their children in ways of virtue and discipline but of
wilfulness and pertness, which means that they gradually learn
to be cheeky, without respect for themselves or others. Indeed,

the peculiar vices of this city seem to me to be conceived almost in the mother's womb, devotion to actors and obsession with gladiators and horses. When a child is totally concerned and preoccupied with such things, what room is left for the nobler arts? Their sole topic of conversation at home is about these subjects, and if you join the discussions of young men, you will find that they, too, are talking about the same things. Even teachers engage in such chatter as often as anything else. For they attract their pupils not by the rigour or imagination of intellectual discipline, but by currying favour in early calls and other ways of adulation.

I omit the pupil's early lessons, which usually involve too little hard work. Too little time is spent in getting to know authors or interpreting the past or understanding events, their fellow human beings and the times in which they live. Instead they seek the tuition of the so-called rhetoricians ... which started up just before Cicero's day. The disapproval which they met with from our ancestors is quite clear from the order for them to be shut down, these 'schools of impudence' as Cicero called them, which was given by the Censors Crassus and Domitius. But, as I was saying, boys are taken to these establishments, in which it is difficult to say what causes more harm to their minds—the place itself, their fellow pupils, or the nature of their study. For the place has no atmosphere as every entrant is equally unskilled, there is no advantage to be gained from their fellow pupils as boys among boys and youths among youths find an easy and safe audience for their remarks, and the pursuits themselves are mostly self-destructive. Two kinds of subject are dealt with by these teachers of rhetoric, the 'persuasive' and the 'controversial'. Of these the 'persuasive' topics are allocated to the boys as they are lighter and demand less intelligence, the 'controversial' to the older students. But what appalling quality and how stupidly selected! On top of a subject which is so untrue to life, a pompous declamatory style is affected. So it comes about that subjects like 'The Tyrannicides' Reward', 'Choices for the Raped', 'Remedies for Plague', 'The Incestuous Mothers' or something of this kind are dealt with daily in the schools, but never, or seldom, pursued in public in noble phraseology.

DECLINE IN AUDIENCES
c. A.D. 90

In the absence of literary magazines and periodicals, recitals of poetry played a large part in the intellectual life at Rome. All the great poets used this means to make their name and the literary community was very much united. Pliny, an intellectual snob, devoted every minute of his leisure hours to writing, and here bemoans the lack of real interest in poetry.

Source: Pliny the Younger, *Letters*, Book I, 13.

Further Reading: Translation in Penguin Classics by Betty Radice. Loeb translation by W. Melmoth. Histories of Roman literature, by H. J. Rose, Michael Grant, and J. Wight Duff (*Literary History of Rome in the Silver Age*) should be consulted, as well as the social histories mentioned in previous extracts.

This year has produced a great crop of poets; in April hardly a single day passed without a recital by someone or other. I am delighted that these pursuits thrive, and that men's abilities are brought to light and revealed, even though audiences are pitifully small. Most of the listeners sit in an ante-room whiling away the time of the recital in idle chatter, and ask for news to be brought them when the poet has arrived, when he has got through his introduction, and when he is most of the way through his work. Then and only then they enter slowly and reluctantly, staying for just a short time and leaving before the end, some sidling out furtively, others going quite openly. In years gone by there is a story that when the Emperor Claudius was walking on the Palatine he heard a noise, and on asking the cause, was told that Nomianus was giving a recital. Whereupon he dropped in suddenly and unexpectedly on the recitation. But nowadays, however much time a man has on his hands, even though he has had plenty of warning and been frequently reminded, he either fails to turn up, or, if he does, complains that he has wasted his time, simply because he has in fact not wasted it.

But this increases the approval and praise we should bestow on those poets who are not deterred from their enthusiasm for composition by the apathy and conceit of their audiences. I have attended virtually every recital, and most of the poets were indeed my friends, for there is scarcely anyone who has a regard for literary pursuits who has not also a regard for me. These reasons have made me spend rather longer in Rome than I had intended. Now I can go to my country retreat and compose something myself. But I do not want to hold a recital, for I do not want to seem to be claiming that the men whose recitals I attended are in my debt. After all I merely went along to listen. For in attendance at recitals, as in everything else, any favour bestowed loses its force if a counter favour is requested.

DINNER PARTIES
c. A.D. 95

Extravagance on meals at Rome was no new thing. The Dictator Sulla had passed laws in 82–80 B.C. limiting the amount that could be spent. Naturally this failed to have any effect, and many famous names come down to us as bon-viveurs, perhaps the chief being Lucullus. The heights to which culinary extravagance might go are found in the fictional satiric work of Petronius, *Trimalchio's Feast*. Most of Pliny's dinner seems to have been from the hors d'oeuvres, but the main courses are concealed in the expression 'hundreds of other good things'. Snow was used for cooling purposes.

Source: Pliny the Younger, *Letters*, Book I, 15, and Book II, 6.

Further Reading: Translation in Penguin Classics by Betty Radice; Loeb translation by W. Melmoth. Recent translations of *Trimalchio's Feast* are by Jack Lindsay and W. Arrowsmith (both in paperbacks). The Loeb translation is by M. Heseltine. Any of the social histories can be read, such as *Daily Life in Ancient Rome* by J. Carcopino, or *Everyday Life in Ancient Rome* by F. R. Cowell.

1. To Septicius Clarus,

Now look here, you promised to come to dinner, but didn't turn up. The judgment of this court is that you will defray my expenses, which were considerable, to the last penny. This was the menu I had ready—a lettuce and three snails each, two eggs, barley-water with honey-wine and snow (yes, you must include that too, perhaps more than anything else, because it melts away in the tray), olives, beetroots, gourds, onions and hundreds of other good things. Your entertainment would have been a comedian or a reader or a lyre-player, or, for such is my generosity, all three.

But you preferred to go to someone else with his oysters, vulvas, eels and dancers from Cadiz. You will pay for this, I won't tell you how. You have been cruel and have done me a disservice. You may not think so, but you have probably done yourself one too. What fun, laughter and edification we would have had. You can certainly get a more lavish dinner elsewhere, but nowhere one more jolly, simple and friendly. In short, try me and if after that you don't make your excuses to others rather than to me, then stay away from my table for good. Goodbye.

2. To Junius Avitus,

It would take too long to explain, and it doesn't really matter, how it happened that I was dining with a man I knew vaguely. In his own eyes he was a mixture of elegance and frugality, but in mine of extravagance and niggardliness. He served himself and a few others with the choicest dishes, but the rest just had poor, cheap fare. He had divided the wine into three sorts in small goblets, not to give people the chance to choose but no opportunity to refuse. One type was for himself and us, a second for his lesser friends (for he was the sort of man who graded his friends) and a third for his and our freedmen. The man next to me at table noticed this and asked me if I approved. I replied that I certainly did not. 'Then what practice do you follow?' 'I serve the same to all, for I invited them to give them dinner not distinction; and I feel that those who share the same couch and table should share everything else as well.' 'Even freedmen?' he asked. 'Yes, for when they are at table, they are in my eyes not freedmen but fellow-diners.'

My friend replied that it must be very expensive, and when I assured him that it was quite the contrary, he asked me how I did it. 'It's possible for the very good reason that my freedmen do not drink what I do, but I drink what they do.' I maintain that if you restrain your greed, then it isn't very expensive to share with many what you have yourself. If you want to spare expense, then greed is what must be checked and brought to heel. You will look after expense much better by your own restraint than by insulting others.

CUSTOMS OF THE GERMANS
c. A.D. 100

Tacitus, like his friend Pliny, combined a public with a literary career. He was thus in a good position to write about the Germans with whom Rome had been intermittently at war for 150 years. It is supposed that he must have been to Germany, even though he no doubt relied in the main on hearsay evidence. Germany to the Romans included modern Alsace and Lorraine as well as the land across the Rhine.

Source: Tacitus, *Germania*, 14.

Further Reading: Loeb translation by M. Hutton, Penguin Translation by Michael Grant. A good annotated edition of the *Germania* is by J. G. C. Anderson. Prof. R. Syme's *Tacitus* is the most recent large-scale book on the author. *C.A.H.* vol. XI, ch. xiii, is by R. G. Collingwood.

When battle is joined, it is thought disgraceful for a prince to be surpassed in courage, and for his followers not to rival their prince's valour. Above all, the disgrace and infamy if a man survives his prince and returns safe from battle lasts for the rest of his life. It is the chief clause in their military oath to defend and protect their prince and to assign all their deeds of valour to further his glory. So princes fight for victory and their retinues for them. If the tribe in which they have been brought up is resting in a state of long peace and quiet, most of the young warriors go off on their own to other tribes which are at war, for peace is not welcome to the Germans. Fame, too, is more easily obtained in dangerous situations, and a large retinue cannot be maintained except by deeds of war and violence. For warriors make demands on their prince's generosity for their war-horses and their blood-stained shields of conquest. Banquets and goods, rough but plentiful, serve as wages. Any luxury comes from war and plunder. Germans can be more easily persuaded to challenge

the foe and to win wounds than to plough the soil or wait for
the harvest. What is more, it is felt to be a mark of idleness and
supineness to gain by the sweat of one's brow what could be won
by blood.

When they are not at war, they pass some of the time in
hunting, but most in doing nothing, devoting themselves to sleep
and food. All the bravest and most warlike do nothing, while
the household duties and the care of the larder and fields is handed
over to the women, old men and the weaker members of the
family. The menfolk laze around showing a remarkably divergent
propensity, for the same men are so fond of laziness but absolutely
hate inactivity and peace.

No other nation is so totally devoted to feasts and hospitality.
It is considered a sin to shut anyone out of your house. Strangers
are welcomed as they come with elaborate meals. On their departure, the host takes it upon himself to point out the next stop and
to accompany the wayfarer. They enter the next lodging quite
without warning, but it makes no difference to the welcome they
receive. As far as the laws of hospitality go, stranger and friend
are treated alike. One custom is to give to the departing guest
whatever he asks for, and there is the same tradition in asking for
things in return. Presents delight them, but they do not reckon
up their gifts, and do not feel themselves under any obligation
when they receive them. . . .

They have a wash immediately they wake from their sleep,
which normally ends late. The water is usually warm, as is
natural among people with whom winter lasts long. After their
bath they eat. Each diner has a separate chair and an individual
table. Then they go out to business or to a drinking party, but
always armed. It is nothing disgraceful to continue drinking
right round the clock. As is only too likely among the drunk,
quarrels end in blood and wounds more often than in mere
argument. They choose their drinking sessions to settle enmities,
to arrange marriage alliances and to elect their chiefs, and especially to decide about peace and war. They feel that it is at that
time that their minds are most open for simple thoughts, and
most ardent for important ones. A race not naturally clever or
intelligent finds its innermost secrets of the heart revealed by the

freedom of the occasion. Everyone's mind is opened and laid bare. On the following day they go over their findings again, and anything agreed to on both occasions is adopted. They make their deliberations when they have not the sobriety to lie, and they decide on action when they are sober enough not to make mistakes.

The liquid for their drink comes from barley or grain, fermented rather like wine. Those living near the Rhine trade in wine. Their food is simple—apples, fresh meat or curded milk. They satisfy their hunger without extravagance or fancy additions. But there is not the same temperance against the calls of thirst. If their drunkenness were indulged to the limit of their desire, their defeat would be easier to accomplish by playing on these vices than it is by force.

CHARIOT-RACING
c. A.D. 100

Chariot-racing at Rome steadily increased in popularity under the early emperors. Nero is said to have enlarged the Circus Maximus to seat 200,000 spectators. The fans were divided in loyalty by the racing colours worn by the drivers. At the time Pliny writes the 'Greens' and the 'Blues' were ousting the older 'Reds' and 'Whites' in popular esteem. Partisanship became intense, and feeling ran as high as in any Celtic *v*. Rangers match in Glasgow.

Source: Pliny the Younger, *Letters*, Book IX, 6.

Further Reading: Translation in Penguin Classics by Betty Radice; Loeb translation by W. Melmoth. Public amusements are dealt with in R. W. Moore's *The Roman Commonwealth* (ch. viii), J. Carcopino's *Daily Life in Ancient Rome* (ch. viii) and in pictures in Zschietzschmann's *Hellas and Rome*. Edward Gibbon gives a graphic account of horse-racing at Constantinople in Justinian's day in *Decline and Fall*, ch. xl.

I have spent the past few days very pleasantly and restfully among my books and papers. You may wonder how that was possible in Rome. Well, the games in the Circus Maximus were on, and I'm not in the least bit interested in that kind of show. There's nothing new, no variety, nothing for which once is not enough. This makes me all the more surprised that so many thousands of grown men are prepared to see over and over again in such childish fashion galloping horses and men driving the chariots. If they were attracted by the horses' speed or the drivers' skill, there might be some sense in it. But as it is, they merely support a piece of cloth; that is what they follow, and if two colours were changed over in the middle of the actual race their support and allegiance would change too and they would immediately desert the drivers and horses they recognize from their seats and whose names they shout.

Fancy such influence and power wielded by one worthless shirt, not merely among the common crowd, which is more worthless even than that, but even among some men of taste. When I see this sort of person so insatiably fond of a sport which is so empty, meaningless and repetitive, I must admit to a feeling of pleasure that that pleasure is not for me. So for the past week I have readily spent my idle hours in writing while others have been wasting theirs in the most idle pursuits.

WATER SUPPLY AND WATER THIEVES
c. A.D. 100

In the second century A.D. the population of Rome grew to over a million, and the problem of a good water supply became acute. A commissioner of the water supply had long been appointed, and public figures had spent money on new aqueducts. Frontinus was appointed commissioner in A.D. 97, under Nerva, but spent most of his years of office under Trajan. He had between 74 and 78 been Governor of Britain, with successes against South Wales to his credit. Luckily he wrote down an account of his stewardship, with full details about all the aqueducts that fed the city. The complete details are too long to quote, but these extracts tell something of the problem that faced Rome and of the means used to by-pass the regulations. It seems unlikely that any century until our own has used more water per head of the population. In 100 the possible maximum was about ninety gallons per day, but it is improbable that this was ever available.

Source: Frontinus, *de Aquis*, I, 15.

Further Reading: Loeb translation by C. E. Bennett. There are sections about aqueducts in H. Stuart Jones's *Companion to Roman History* (ch. ii) and in *The Legacy of Rome*. A major work on the subject is T. Ashby's *The Aqueducts of Ancient Rome* (ed. I. A. Richmond).

The New Anio is drawn from the river in the district of Sinbrinum, at about the forty-second milestone along the Via Sublacensis. On either side of the river at this point are fields of rich soil which make the banks less firm, so that the water in the aqueduct is discoloured and muddy even without the damage done by storms. So a little way along from the inlet a cleansing basin was built where the water could settle and be purified between the river and the conduit. Even so, in the event of rain, the water reaches the city in a muddy state. The length of the New Anio is about 47 miles, of which over 39 are underground and more than 7 carried on structures above the ground. In the upper reaches a distance of about two miles in various sections is carried on low structures or arches. Nearer the city, from the seventh Roman mile-stone, is half a mile on substructures and five miles on arches. These arches are very high, rising in certain places to a height of 109 feet.

... All the aqueducts reach the city at different levels. So some serve the higher districts and some cannot reach loftier ground. For the hills of Rome have gradually increased in height because of the rubble from frequent fires. There are five aqueducts high enough at entrance to reach all the city, but they supply water at different pressures. ...

Anyone who wants to tap water for private consumption must send in an application and take it, duly signed by the Emperor, to the Commissioner. The latter must take immediate action on Caesar's grant, and enrol one of the Imperial freedmen to help him in the business. ... The right to water once granted cannot be inherited or bought, and does not go with the property, though long ago a privilege was extended to the public baths that their right should last in perpetuity. ... When grants lapse, notice is given and record made in the ledgers, which are consulted so that future applicants can be given vacant supplies. The previous custom was to cut off these lapsed supplies at once, to make some profit by a temporary sale to the landowners or even to outsiders. Our Emperor felt that property should not suddenly be left without water, and that it would be fairer to give thirty days' notice for other arrangements to be made by the interested party. ...

Now that I have explained the situation with regard to private supply, it will be pertinent to give some examples of the ways in which men have broken these very sound arrangements and have been caught red-handed. In some reservoirs I have found larger valves in position than had been granted, and some have not even had the official stamp on them. When a stamped valve exceeds the legal dimensions, then the private advantage of the controller who stamped it is uncovered. When a valve is not even stamped, then both parties are clearly liable, chiefly the purchaser, but also the controller. Sometimes stamped valves of the correct dimensions open into pipes of a larger cross-section. The result is that the water is not kept in for the legal distance, but forced through a short, narrow pipe and easily fills the larger one which is joined to it. So care must be taken that, when a valve is stamped, the pipes connected to it should be stamped as of the correct length ordered by Senatorial decree. For then and only then will the controller be fully liable when he knows that only stamped pipes must be positioned.

When valves are sited, good care must be taken to see that they are placed in a horizontal line, not one above the other. A lower inlet gets a greater pressure of water, the upper one less, because the supply of water is taken by the lower. In some pipes no valves are positioned at all. These are called 'free' pipes, and are opened and closed to suit the watermen.

Another of the watermen's intolerable practices is to make a new outlet from the cistern when a water-grant is transferred to a new owner, leaving the old one for themselves to get water from for sale. I would say that it was one of the Commissioner's chief duties to put a stop to this. For it affects not only the proper protection of the supply, but also the upkeep of the reservoir which would be ruined if needlessly filled with outlets.

Another financial scheme of the watermen, which they call 'puncturing', must also be abolished. There are long separate stretches all over the city through which the pipes pass hidden under the pavement. I found out that these pipes were being tapped everywhere by the 'puncturers', from which water was supplied by private pipe to all the business premises in the area, with the result that only a meagre amount reached the public utilities. I can estimate the volume of water stolen in this way from the amount of lead piping which was removed when these branch pipes were dug up.

ARE FIRE-BRIGADES REALLY NECESSARY?
c. A.D. 112

In about A.D. 111 Pliny was sent as governor of Bithynia. He took the opportunity to write to the Emperor, Trajan, about anything, big or small. This letter from Pliny is followed by Trajan's reply. Political clubs, referred to by Trajan, were a recurrent threat to Rome, and they had been banned from as far back as 55 B.C. In the absence of political parties, these clubs became the hotbed of revolutionary ideas. One of the main objections to early Christianity was the secret nature of the meetings as can be seen from the next extract. An official fire brigade at Rome had been started by Augustus, with a high official as Prefect of the Vigiles. This replaced a previous racket run by the wealthy Crassus for buying up burning property and putting out the fire with a private brigade.

Source: Pliny the Younger, *Letters,* Book X, 33 and 34.

Further Reading: Translation in Penguin Classics by Betty Radice, Loeb translation by W. Melmoth. Michael Grant considers political clubs and kindred points in *World of Rome,* ch. 2. Crassus's Fire Brigade is described by Plutarch in his *Life of Crassus* (Penguin translation by Rex Warner). Trajan's policies are described by R. P. Longden in *C.A.H.* vol. XI, ch. v. A full account of the duties and organization of the Vigiles is by Baillie Reynolds in *The Vigiles of Imperial Rome.*

While I was in another part of the province, a violent fire at Nicomedia destroyed many private houses and two public buildings, an old men's hostel and a temple to Isis, even though they were the other side of the street. It spread rather more widely than it need have done partly because of the strength of the wind, but partly because of the apathy of the public. I am reliably informed that men stood idly by doing nothing but watch the calamity. Furthermore, there were no hoses, buckets or any other public apparatus for controlling the blaze. I have given orders for these to be prepared. But, Your Majesty, I wonder if you think it would be right to form a fire-brigade of up to 150 men. I will make it my personal business to see that only genuine firemen are allowed to be members, and that this concession is not used for any other purpose. It will not be hard to keep a check on such a small number.

It has occurred to you, Pliny, to follow the example of other places and to consider the possibility of setting up a fire-brigade at Nicomedia. I remember that your whole province and especially that district has been troubled by societies of that sort. Whatever name we give them, and with however good a reason, men who are banded together will become in a very short time a political club. Your duty, then, is to be satisfied with getting ready things to assist in controlling fires, and to give advice to property owners to take fire precautions, and if the situation is serious enough to get the public to come to their aid.

PERSECUTION OF CHRISTIANS
A.D. 113

This famous letter from Pliny to the Emperor Trajan, and his reply, serve as an invaluable picture of the reaction of an intelligent and civilized nation to a force that they could not understand. We see the narrow-mindedness and hypocrisy of the Roman religion, its insistence on the outward show of piety and the inevitable fear of political implications. Pliny, the loyal Governor, is outraged by the lack of respect for Rome and the Emperor, but we seem to see also Pliny the man of culture and intelligence making the same reply as did Pilate—'I find no fault in Him.' Christianity had, of course, already reached Rome by A.D. 64, when Nero found the Christians convenient scapegoats to blame for the Great Fire.

Source: Pliny the Younger, *Letters*, Book X, 96 and 97.

Further Reading: Loeb translation by W. Melmoth; Penguin translation by Betty Radice. The Acts of the Apostles and other books of the *New Testament*. Tacitus briefly mentions Christ in his account of the fire in *Annals*, Book XV (translated by Grant in Penguin Classics). On the early church and persecution, also see Gibbon, ch. xv, Edwyn Bevan's *Christianity*, B. W. Henderson in *Five Roman Emperors*, and the *Atlas of the Early Christian World*.

It is my rule, Your Majesty, to report to you anything that worries me, for I know well that you are best able to speed my hesitation or instruct me in my ignorance. I have never in the past been present at the investigations into Christians, and so I am at a loss to know the nature and extent of the normal questions and punishments. I have also been seriously perplexed whether age should make some difference, or whether the very young should be treated in exactly the same way as the more mature. Should the penitent be pardoned, or should no mercy be shown a man who has recanted if he has really been a Christian? Should the mere name be reason enough for punishment however free from crime a man may be, or should only the sins and crimes that attend the name be punished?

Till I hear from you, I have adopted the following course towards those who have been brought before me as Christians. First I have asked them if they were Christians. If they confessed that they were, I repeated my question a second and a third time, accompanying it with threats of punishment. If they still persisted in their statements, I ordered them to be taken out. For I was in no doubt that, whatever it was to which they were confessing, they had merited some punishment by their stubbornness and unbending obstinacy. There were others possessed by similar madness, but these I detailed to be sent to Rome, for they were Roman citizens.

Soon, as I investigated the matter, types began to multiply as so often happens, and charges started to spread. An anonymous notebook was presented with many names in it. Those who denied that they were or ever had been Christians I thought should be released, provided that they called on the gods in my presence, and offered incense and wine to your statue (which I had expressly brought in with the images of the gods for that very purpose), and, above all, if they renounced Christ, which no true Christian, I am told, can be made to do. Others informed against admitted that they were Christians but later denied it; they had been, but had given up, some three years past, some further back, and one person as long as 25 years ago. All of them reverenced your statue and the images of the gods, and renounced Christ.

They stated that the sum total of their fault or error was as follows. On a fixed day they used to assemble before dawn to sing an antiphonal hymn to Christ as to a god, and to bind themselves by oath not for any criminal purpose, but to commit no fraud, no robbery or adultery, to bear no false witness, and not to deny any debt when asked to pay up. After this it was their custom to separate and to reassemble to eat a common meal, all together and quite harmless. They claimed that they had stopped even that after my edict in which I followed your commands in banning society meetings. So I felt it all the more necessary to find out the truth under torture from two slave girls whom they called Deaconesses. But I found nothing but a depraved and groundless superstition.

So I postponed my enquiry to consult you. The matter seemed worth your attention, especially since the number of those slipping is great. Many people of all ages and classes and of both sexes are now being enticed into mortal peril and will be in the future. The superstition has spread like the plague, not only in the cities but in the villages and the countryside as well. I feel it must be stopped and checked. It is true that everyone is agreed that temples once deserted are now being attended once again, and that sacred ceremonies once neglected are again being performed. Victims for sacrifice are everywhere on sale, for which only an odd buyer could be found a short while ago. All this goes to show how many men could be saved if there is room for repentance.

You have acted quite properly, Pliny, in examining the cases of those Christians brought before you. Nothing definite can be laid down as a general rule. They should not be hunted out. If accusations are made and they are found guilty, they must be punished. But remember that a man may expect pardon from repentance if he denies that he is a Christian, and proves this to your satisfaction, that is by worshipping our gods, however much you may have suspected him in the past. Anonymous lists should have no part in any charge made. That is a thoroughly bad practice, and not in accordance with the spirit of the age.

MARCUS AURELIUS
c. A.D. 162

Marcus Aurelius, the son-in-law and adopted heir of Antoninus Pius, became Emperor in 161, taking as his colleague Verus, the subject of the next extract. He is chiefly famous as a philosopher who propounded the noble doctrine of Stoicism in the work which we still have, the *Meditations*. Perhaps the most talked-of event in his reign was the battle in 174 which is said to have been won because of a violent storm prayed for by a legion largely composed of Christians. This has given rise to the story of the Miracle of the Thundering Legion. Without entering into this argument, it is necessary to say that one of the few blemishes on his reign was the persecution of the Christians. Fronto, a teacher of Rhetoric, was responsible for the education of Marcus and his colleague, and wrote a great number of letters to them both. Many are on private matters, often about Fronto's own health, but they do give an indication of the civilized nature of the times. The official name of Marcus was Antoninus.

Source: Fronto, *Letters to Antoninus Imperator*, i, 2.

Further Reading: Loeb translation by C. R. Haines. On Stoicism see Livingstone's *The Mission of Greece*, *The Roman Mind* by M. L. Clarke and T. R. Glover in *The Conflict of Religions in the Early Roman Empire*. *The Meditations of Marcus Aurelius* are translated by J. Jackson. See also *C.A.H.* vol. XI, ch. ix (Wilhelm Weber) and Gibbon, chs. i–iii.

I see you, Antoninus, as outstanding an Emperor as I ever wished, as just and pure in life as I ever guaranteed, as pleasant and agreeable to the Roman people as I ever hoped, as fond of me as I ever wanted, and eloquent to the heights of your own desire. For when you started once more to pay attention to oratory, it was no handicap to have had a lay-off. I see you daily increasing in eloquence, and that makes me as glad as if I were still your master. I love and adore all your good qualities, but I confess that I take the most immediate and highest pleasure from this eloquence. Parents recognize the features of their own faces in their children, and I notice in your speeches traces of my own skill, and, as Homer says of Leto, 'this gladdens the heart'. For I cannot express the force of my joy in my own words. Believe me when I tell you that no person whom I have ever met has had a richer vein of eloquence than you.

The historian Herodian (see pages 192 and 196) has this to say about the death of Marcus Aurelius.

He survived for one more day and night, and his death left a longing in the hearts of all men of his age, and an everlasting memorial of his goodness for all ages to come. When the news spread of his end, the whole army in Rome and all the ordinary people were alike filled with grief. There was not one person in all the Roman Empire who received the news without tears in his eyes. All with one voice shouted out that he was a fine father, a good Emperor, a valiant soldier, a prudent and efficient ruler. And not one of them lied.

LUCIUS AURELIUS VERUS AS A GENERAL
c. A.D. 163

L. Aurelius Verus, the colleague of Marcus Aurelius, was sent to fight the Parthians from 162–165, which he did with great success. Later he commanded Roman armies on the Northern frontiers. He died in 169. As already mentioned, Fronto was Verus's teacher of rhetoric, and no doubt got his news of action in the East direct from Verus. The trouble among the Syrian legions probably sprang from the general peace and tranquillity throughout the Empire which had been so much a part of the reign of Antoninus Pius.

Source: Fronto, Preface to *History of the Parthian War*, 12.

Further Reading: Loeb translation by C. R. Haines. Wilhelm Weber writes on Varus and the Parthian War in *C.A.H.* vol. XI, ch. ix. Gibbon, chs. i–iii.

But the most ill-disciplined of all were the Syrian soldiers. They were mutinous and disobedient, scarcely ever on parade, strayed from their appointed posts, wandered about like scouts, and were drunk from the middle of one day to the next. Unused even to carrying their arms, they left off one by one each piece of armour and in their hatred of hard work went about half naked like skirmishers or slingers. Apart from this sort of demoralization, they had been so dispirited by unsuccessful engagements that they turned to flee at the first sight of a Parthian, and interpreted the blare of trumpets as a signal not for advance but for retreat.

Lucius tried to check this bad collapse of military discipline as best he could, by making his own eagerness for battle an example to the troops. He marched at the head of his column, more frequently tiring himself out on foot than riding on his horse. He bore with the hottest sun as readily as a bright day, and dust storms meant no more to him than mere clouds. Sweating in his armour troubled him as little as sweating at sport. His head was bare in sunshine, rain, hail and snow, and unprotected even in battle. He took pains to review the soldiers in the field and to visit the sick. He inspected the troops' quarters with a keen eye which missed nothing; in an apparently casual way he noticed the cleanliness of the Syrians and the crudeness of the Pannonians, for he used a man's appearance to make some estimate of his character. He washed late after finishing his business, and kept a simple board, eating a soldier's fare in camp and drinking local wine and water at the natural temperature. He was always awake at the first watch of night, and the last in the morning found him still alert. Work pleased him more than leisure, which he passed in doing even more work. Any time free from military duties was spent busying himself in civil affairs. In sudden penury, he used branches and leaves for furniture, resting occasionally on turves as easily as on a bed. The sleep he asked for was earned by work, and silence was not demanded. He punished serious crimes severely, but turned a blind eye to more trivial ones, thus leaving room for repentance.

JULIANUS BECOMES EMPEROR
A.D. 193

One of the tragedies of the second century was that Marcus Aurelius left his son, Commodus, to succeed him. During his reign (180–192) the Principate deteriorated badly and, in spite of a short three months' respite under Pertinax, reached its worst state so far on his murder in March 193. Cassius Dio was a Syrian who had come to Rome on the death of Marcus Aurelius, and, as can be seen, achieved a position that well enabled him to write of Imperial matters. As so often, the Praetorian Guard dominated proceedings. The final outcome of this story was that Septimius Severus, who had been proclaimed Emperor by his troops, marched on Rome in that same year, killed Julianus and took over control of the state.

Source: Cassius Dio, Epitome of Book LXXIV, 11.

Further Reading: Loeb translation by E. Cary. On Commodus see Gibbon, ch. iv, and *C.A.H.* vol. XI, ch. ix, by Wilhelm Weber. For Julianus, *C.A.H.* vol. XII, ch. i, and Gibbon, ch. v.

When the news of the murder of Pertinax became known, the thoughts of all were centred on their own safety, as some ran home and some to the barracks. Sulpicianus had been sent by Pertinax to see to affairs in the camp, so he stayed there and tried to get himself appointed Emperor. Meanwhile Didianus, who had been sent back to his native town of Milan because of his marked revolutionary tendencies, a man who made his money by lending at extortionate rates and spent it in wasteful extravagance, had heard of Pertinax's death. He quickly made for the camp where he stood by the gates of the defences, asking the soldiers for the Imperial power. This resulted in an affair which brought shame and disgrace on the name of Rome. For the city herself and her Empire were put up for auction as in the market or sale-room. Those who offered it were those who had killed their Emperor, and the prospective buyers were Sulpicianus and Didianus, one inside and one outside the camp, trying to outbid each other. They were slowly increasing their 'bids', and had reached an offer of 5,000 drachmas to each soldier, for men would come and tell Julianus (Didianus) that Sulpicianus had offered such-and-such and ask if he added anything to that, and then go to Sulpicianus with the news that Julianus had reached a certain sum, asking what additional amount Sulpicianus would promise. Sulpicianus would have won the auction, for he had the advantage of being inside the camp, being city prefect and of having been the first to reach 5,000 drachmas. But now Julianus stopped rising slowly, and with loud shouts and wild gestures increased his offer by 1,250 drachmas. Captivated by his higher bribe and fearing, anyway, that Sulpicianus would take steps to avenge Pertinax, as Julianus himself had suggested to them, they welcomed him and appointed him as Emperor.

Towards evening he hurried to the Forum and the Senate-House, escorted by a packed throng of armed soldiers with massed standards, aiming, perhaps, to frighten us Senators and the people, and to win us over. All the time the soldiers cheered him and hailed him as Commodus. As this news reached each one of us, we were filled with terror of Julianus, especially those of us who had done anything helpful for Pertinax. I was one of these, for Pertinax, in addition to other honours, had appointed me praetor, and I had frequently proved in court that Julianus had often broken the law. In spite of, or possibly because of this (for not one of us thought it safe to stay at home lest this too be construed against us), we went to the Senate without a bath or even a meal, pushing our way through the soldiers. We heard Julianus making some typical remarks, such as, 'I see that you need an Emperor, and I, if anyone, am the best person to lead you. I would outline all my advantages did you not know them already from your previous experience of me. That was the reason why I did not ask for a large military escort, but came to see you by myself alone for you to ratify what the soldiers have given me.' This was his claim, but he had picketed the whole of the outside of the Senate-House, with many soldiers in the Chamber itself, and his mention that we knew him already only resulted in hatred and fear of him.

After he had managed to get a Senatorial decree passed which confirmed him in his position, he went up to the Palace where he found the dinner ready laid for Pertinax, which caused him much amusement. Sending for anything expensive that could anywhere be found, he ate a full meal, though Pertinax's body was still lying in the building. Indeed, he unconcernedly played at dice, joined, among others, by the dancer Pylades.

The next day we went to court, putting on a false front and pretending not to be grief-stricken. But the common people were openly scowling and said what they felt, ready to do what they could. Finally, when Julianus came to the chamber and was just about to sacrifice to Janus in front of the door, everyone shouted out as if by agreement, accusing him of having stolen power and calling him a patricide. He pretended not to be annoyed at this and promised them money, which infuriated them. They shouted in unison, 'We do not want it and will not take it'. The fearful echo of their words reverberated back from the surrounding buildings, and Julianus could no longer put a brave face on it, but ordered those standing in front to be killed. The people became even more excited, saying repeatedly how much they longed for Pertinax. They heaped abuse on Julianus and cursed the soldiers, calling on the gods to help them. Many were wounded and killed in various parts of the city, but still they persisted. Finally they seized arms and ran to the Circus Maximus where they spent the night. The following day, having had neither food nor drink, they renewed their uproar, yelling for Pescennius Niger and his followers in Syria to come to their assistance. After a time they became exhausted by their shouting, hunger and lack of sleep, and separated quietly, waiting for help from abroad.

ENTERTAINMENT IN EGYPT
A.D. 206–322

These three extracts explain themselves and underline the bureaucratic nature of Egyptian administration. The first dates from A.D. 206 and the third from A.D. 322. The second one was written some time in the third century A.D.

Source: Select Papyri (Loeb), vol. I, pp. 62–4; translated by A. S. Hunt and C. C. Edgar.

(a) To Isidora, a castanet dancer: from Artemisia of the village of Philadelphia:

I wish to engage you and two other castanet dancers to perform at my house for six days from the 24th of the month Pauni in the old calendar. Your wages will be 36 drachmas a day, and you will be provided with 4 artabae of barley and 20 double-loaves for the whole stay. I will ensure the safety of any clothes or gold ornaments you bring with you. I will provide you with two asses on arrival and two again on departure. Signed, the 16th of Pauni in this the 14th year of the reign of L. Septimius Severus. . . .

(*b*)   Onnophris and the four other Presidents of the village of Souis, and Copreus, son of Sarapammon, the leader of an orchestra of flute-players and musicians, confirm an agreement that Onnophris and his colleagues have engaged Copreus and his band to perform to the villagers of the above-mentioned village at the festival here for five days from the 10th of Phamenoth in the present 2nd year. The daily wage will be 140 drachmas; for the five days they will get 40 double-loaves, 8 cotylae of coleseed oil, one jar of wine and one of sour wine. Copreus acknowledges that he has received 20 drachmas as advance payment. Onnophris and his colleagues will send 10 asses to fetch Copreus and his band from Oxyrhynchus and escort them to the above-mentioned village.

(*c*)   In the consulship of our lords Licinius Augustus (6th time) and Licinius Caesar (2nd time). To Aurelius Eugenius, gymnasiarch and senator of Hermopolis, greetings from Aurelius Psenymis, son of Kollouthos and Melitene, a flute-player from Hermopolis. I agree that I have contracted and pledged myself to you, the squire, to present myself at the village at the vintage-time in the vineyards with the appointed grape-treaders. There I will serve, without fail, the grape-treaders and others with my flute-playing. I promise not to leave the grape-treaders till the end of the vintage in the coming prosperous 10th special fiscal year. For the flute-playing and the pleasure I give, I shall receive the agreed sum from the contracting party.

Signed, the 24th of Choiak in the above-named consulship,

Aurelius Psenymis.

I will fulfil the conditions as stated.

I, Aurelius Pinoution, his assistant, have written for Anicetus, since he is illiterate.

DEIFICATION OF SEPTIMIUS SEVERUS
A.D. 211

Emperor worship really started with Julius Caesar. His heir, Augustus, claimed to be the son of Divus Julius, no doubt largely for political reasons. Thereafter most emperors were deified, although not many followed the example of Gaius (37–41) in asking for divine honours while still alive. Septimius Severus had to deal with an invasion across Hadrian's Wall by northern tribes, and was responsible for rebuilding the wall and also the ransacked town of York. In 209 Severus led an attack against Caledonia and received its surrender. He died in Britain two years later. Herodian, a Greek, lived in Rome at the time, and must have witnessed this ceremony and the later disturbances described on page 196.

Source: Herodian, *Histories*, IV, 2.

Further Reading: Translation by E. C. Eckols. On Deification, see H. J. Rose, *Ancient Roman Religion. C.A.H.* vol. XII, ch. i.

Before doing anything else Caracalla and Geta completed the funeral honours of their father.

It is the Roman custom to give divine status to those of their emperors who die with heirs to succeed them. This ceremony is called deification. Public mourning, with a mixture of festive and religious ritual, is proclaimed throughout the city, and the body of the dead man is buried in the normal way with a costly funeral. Then they make an exact wax replica of the man, which they put on a huge ivory bed, strewn with gold-threaded coverings, raised high up in the entrance to the palace. This image, deathly pale, rests there like a sick man. Either side of the bed is attended for most of the day, the whole Senate sitting on the left, dressed in black, while on the right are all the women who can claim special honours from the position of their husbands or fathers. Not one of these can be seen wearing gold or adorned with necklaces, but they are all dressed in plain white garments, giving the appearance of mourners.

This continues for seven days, during each of which doctors come and approach the bed, take a look at the supposed invalid and announce a daily deterioration in his condition. When at last the news is given that he is dead, the bed or bier is raised on the shoulders of the noblest members of the Equestrian Order and chosen young Senators, carried along the Sacred Way, and placed in the Forum Romanum, where the Roman magistrates usually lay down their office. Tiers of seats rise up on either side, and on one flank a chorus of children from the noblest and most respected families stands facing a body of women selected on merit. Each group sings hymns and songs of thanksgiving in honour of the dead emperor, composed in a solemn and mournful key.

After this the bier is raised and carried outside the city walls to the Campus Martius, where on the widest part of the plain a square structure is erected, looking like a house, made from only the largest timbers jointed together. The whole inside is filled with firewood, and the outside is covered with golden garments, ivory decorations and rich pictures. On top of this rests another structure, similar in design and finish but smaller, with doors and open panels. Third and fourth stories, decreasing in size, are topped by a fifth, the smallest of all. The shape of the whole might be compared with a lighthouse at the entrance to a harbour which guides ships on safe courses at night by its light. (Such a lighthouse is commonly called a 'Pharos'.) When the bier has been taken to the second storey and put inside, aromatic herbs and incense of every kind produced on earth, together with flowers, grasses and juices collected for their smell, are brought and poured in in heaps. Every nation and city, every person without distinction of rank or position competes in bringing these last gifts in honour of their emperor. When the pile of aromatic material is very high and the whole space filled, a mounted display is held around the structure. The whole Equestrian Order rides round, wheeling in well-disciplined circles in the Pyrrhic style. Chariots also circle in the same formations, the charioteers dressed in purple and carrying images with the masks of famous Roman generals and emperors.

The display over, the heir to the throne takes a brand and sets it to the building. All the spectators crowd in and add to the flame. Everything is very easily and readily consumed by the fire because of the mass of firewood and incense inside. From the highest and smallest storey, as from some battlement, an eagle is released and carried up into the sky with the flames. The Romans believe that this bird bears the soul of the emperor from earth to heaven. Thereafter the dead emperor is worshipped with the rest of the gods.

A COOK'S MEAT BILL
A.D. 215 (?)

There are two surprising things about this extract. The first is that it should have survived at all. The second is the amount of meat that was consumed. We do not know whether the man was cook for a family or a club, and Egypt may have been different from Rome where meat in this quantity would have been most unusual. Other extracts (pages 72, 133) suggest that the ordinary Egyptian diet was mainly farinaceous, with a certain amount of fish, fresh or salted. The months and dates are anglicized.

Source: Select Papyri (Loeb), vol. I, p. 427; translated by A. S. Hunt and C. C. Edgar.

September 1st   4lbs. Meat, 2 Trotters, 1 Tongue, 1 Snout
       3rd   Half a head with the tongue
       8th   2lbs. Meat, 1 Tongue, 2 Kidneys
       9th   1 lb. Meat, 1 Breast
     11th   2 lbs. Meat, 1 Breast
     13th   3 lbs. Meat
     14th   2 lbs. Meat, 1 Tongue
     15th   1 Tongue
     18th   Tripe
     19th   Tripe, 2 Kidneys
     20th   2 lbs. Meat, Tripe, 2 Kidneys
     23rd   1 Tongue
     27th   1 Breast

and before this:

August 11th   2 lbs. Meat, Tripe, 2 Kidneys
     14th   1 Breast
     16th   Half a head with the tongue, 2 Kidneys
     17th   2 lbs. Meat, 2 Kidneys
     18th   2 lbs. Meat for Tryphon, 1 Ear, 1 Trotter, 2 Kidneys
     22nd   2 lbs. Meat, 2 Trotters, 1 Tongue
     25th   1 Tongue
     26th   1 Breast

HIGHER EDUCATION
c. A.D. 225

University or higher education in the Ancient World was only possible at a few places, the most famous of them being at Athens and Rhodes. In Egypt, Alexandria was the chief cultural centre, even though its famous library was severely damaged in 48 B.C. This letter is reminiscent of the early days of Oxford and Cambridge, before the establishment of colleges, when young men attached themselves to tutors by private arrangement.

Source: Select Papyri (Loeb), vol. II, p. 133.

Further Reading: There are no works specifically on Education at this time, but see page 168.

My revered Father,

Every day, before all else, I pray for you and hope by the gods of the place in which I now live that you and all the family are thriving. But please, this is my fifth letter to you, and I have only had one in reply, either about how you are or about coming to see me. You arranged with me that you would come to find out whether the tutor was right for me or not, but you have not done so. I get almost daily questions from him about you. 'Isn't he coming yet?' And I just say, 'Oh, yes'. Please, then, come quickly, so that he can teach me, for he is ready and willing to do so. If you had accompanied me in the first place, I would have had instruction long ago. When you do come, do remember what I have so often said in my letters. So come quickly before he goes up-country.

I send my greetings to all members of the family and to my friends, and greet my old masters. Be strong, good my father, and may you and all my brothers fare well, unharmed by evil, as I pray all the time.

Your obedient son,

Thonis.

P.S. Remember to feed my pigeons.

ATTEMPTED OVERTHROW OF MAXIMINUS
A.D. 235

From 222 to 235 Rome was ruled well and successfully by Alexander Severus who did much to restore public morality after the disastrous reign of Elagabulus. He was murdered by mutinous soldiers, and succeeded by Maximinus, who was possibly at the back of the conspiracy. But his position was never very secure, and in spite of the failure of this attempt to surplant him, he was finally murdered by his own troops in 237.

Source: Herodian, *Histories*, VII, 11.

Further Reading: Translation by E. C. Eckols. *C.A.H.* vol. XII, ch. ii, and Gibbon, ch. vii.

About the same time a calamitous event occurred at Rome, which owed its origin and cause to the daring and rashness of two Senators. It was the general practice for citizens to go to the Senate House to find out the news. The troops left behind by Maximinus in the Praetorian Camp, who were near the end of their period of service and had remained at home because of their age, heard of this habit, and came as far as the entrance to the Senate wishing to find out what was happening. They were standing with the rest of the crowd, unarmed and in plain clothes and cloaks. Most of them stayed at the doors, but two or three wanted especially to hear the debate, and went into the chamber just past the base of the statue of Victory. As the soldiers stood completely off their guard with their hands in the folds of their cloaks, two members of the Senate, one an ex-consul Gallinicus, Carthaginian by birth, and the other an ex-praetor called Maecenas, attacked and struck them with the swords which they carried in their garments, wounding them in the chest. All Senators went about armed in the present state of unrest and disorder, some quite blatantly, to have some means of defending themselves against sudden attacks from their opponents. The wounded soldiers were unable to hit back because of the surprise nature of the blows, and fell in front of the base of the statue. The rest of the troops were staggered to see what had happened to their comrades, and fled in fear of the size of the mob, since they were unarmed.

Gallinicus ran from the Senate into the middle of the crowd, showing his hands and sword covered in blood, and urged them to chase and kill those whom he called the enemies of the Senate and of Rome, men who were the friends and allies of Maximinus. The people were easily duped into heaping praises on Gallinicus, and followed after the soldiers as best they could, pelting them with stones. But the latter, though few in number and wounded, managed to escape into their camp, and were able to shut the gates. Seizing their arms they guarded the walls of the camp.

Gallinicus, once having ventured on such a course, did his best to stir up civil war and destruction in the city. He persuaded the mob to break into the public arsenals to get the weapons from them, which were more suitable for ceremonies than for fighting, so that each man would have something to protect himself with. He threw open the compounds and led out the gladiators with their own specialized weapons. Any pikes, swords or axes in private possession or in the shops were all seized. The people in their frenzy fashioned into weapons any tool of any battleworthy material that came to hand. Then they advanced on the camp in a body and, as if conducting a regular siege, attacked the gates and walls. But the soldiers had the advantage of long training and were protected by the battlements and their shields. They fired arrows at them and succeeded in keeping them at a distance with long spears, eventually forcing them back from the wall. As the mob tired and the wounded gladiators were keen to withdraw now that evening was coming on, the soldiers noticed them turning away and presenting their backs, walking carelessly off without a thought that a few men would dare to attack such large numbers. So, quickly opening the gates, they ran upon the crowd, and cut down the gladiators, many of the citizens dying in the crush. The soldiers only chased them for a short distance from the camp, and on their return stayed within their wall.

This failure increased the temper of the mob and of the Senate. Generals were chosen, picked from the whole of Italy; all the young men were assembled and armed with improvised weapons; then most of these were taken off by Maximus to make war on Maximinus. The rest stayed behind to guard and defend

the city. There were repeated ineffectual attacks on the walls of
the camp. The troops were fighting from higher positions, and
the attackers, frequently wounded, retired in disorder. Balbinus,
who had remained in Rome, issued a proclamation in which he
begged the people to come to terms, promised amnesty to the
soldiers and pardon for all their crimes. But neither side would
listen to him. Indeed the trouble increased, for the large crowd
thought it a disgrace to be thwarted by such a few men, while
the soldiers were furious at suffering the same sort of treatment
from the citizens of Rome as they had from the barbarians.

Finally, when all their attacks on the wall proved unavailing,
the generals decided to cut all the water-conduits that flowed into
the camp, and so overcome them by depriving them of water and
anything to drink. So they started work, and channelled off all
the camp water into other runnels, cutting or blocking up the
ones which led into the camp. When they realized their danger,
the soldiers had no alternative in this predicament but to open
the gates and to go out on attack. A fierce fight ensued, and the
mob fled pursued by the advancing soldiers for a long distance
through the city. Defeated in the hand-to-hand struggle, they
quickly climbed onto the roofs, from where they attacked the
soldiers by throwing tiles, stones and pieces of pot at them,
causing great distress because the soldiers were not daring enough
to climb up after them in their ignorance of the buildings. Houses
and shops were bolted, but the soldiers set fire to the doors and
to any wooden balconies, of which there were many in the city.
The fire consumed the greater part of the city very easily because
the houses were so close together and mostly made of wood.
Many rich citizens were impoverished, losing wonderful costly
possessions, valuable both from the incomes derived from them
and for the expensive finery contained in them. In addition a
large number of men who could not escape because their exits
were cut off by the fire perished in the flames. The rich had all
their property looted when the lawless, worthless elements among
the population joined the troops in ransacking the houses. In
this way an area of the city was destroyed equal to the whole area
of any other city in the world.

THE EDICT OF MILAN
A.D. 313

Constantine was proclaimed Emperor at York. His victory over a rival, Maxentius, at the Milvian Bridge in 312 was attributed by him to the help of God. Three subsequent actions in his life stand out. The first is the proclamation of religious toleration, known as the Edict of Milan. The second was the founding of Constantinople. And lastly there was the first General Council of the Church, held at Nicaea in 325, where an attempt was made to patch up the differences between the orthodox faith and the Arians who denied the equality and identity of Christ with God the Father. Eusebius had a large share in the success of this Council. This extract comes from a translation made by Eusebius of a letter to a governor whose duty it would be to publicize it.

Source: Eusebius, *Ecclesiastical History*, X, v, 4.

Further Reading: Loeb translation by Kirsopp Lake. See Edwyn Bevan's *Christianity* and *The Atlas of the Early Christian World* for brief treatment. *C.A.H.* vol. XII, chs. xv and xx; Gibbon, chs. xiv–xviii and xx.

When by good fortune I, Constantine Augustus, and I, Licinius Augustus, had come to Milan and had held under review everything which tended to the public advantage and good, among or rather at the very head of other things which seemed useful for most men, we decided to arrange matters concerning divine worship and honour, that is, to see how we might give to Christians and non-Christians alike the free choice of following any worship they pleased, so that whatever divine and heavenly powers that exist might be kindly disposed to us and to all those who live beneath our sway. We ordained this wish by healthy and most right judgment, so that to no one whatsoever might be denied the power of following and choosing the observances and worship of Christianity, and that each man might be given the chance of devoting his true mind to that worship as he felt fitting for himself, so that the divinity might be able to show His customary zeal and goodness to us all. It was natural to write that this was our pleasure, that with the total removal of the terms contained in our former letters about Christians to your

Holiness, things which seemed weak and out of keeping with
our clemency might also be removed; also that each of those who
shared the wish to observe the worship of Christianity might
make his observance freely and simply, without let or hindrance.
We have decided to reveal these things most fully to your attention, that you may know that we have granted to these same
Christians free and unfettered power of conducting their own
worship. And when you see that we have granted them this
unconditionally, your Holiness will notice that to others too is
granted the power, if they wish, to follow their own observance
and worship, and the power to choose and observe his worship
in whatever way they please.

THE HUNS
c. A.D. 375

The Huns were one of the peoples from Central Asia driven south
and west by some compelling force, perhaps that of climate. The
wildest of the barbarian invaders, they caused trouble and humiliation
to the Empire for nearly a century, especially under Attila. Ammianus
Marcellinus served in the Roman army, and settled in Rome shortly
after 370.

Source: Ammianus Marcellinus, XXXI, 2.

Further Reading: Loeb translation by J. C. Rolfe. R. H. C. Davis's
A History of Medieval Europe: Constantine to St. Louis has a brief account.
Various chapters in *Cambridge Medieval History*, vol. I, discuss the
Huns (see especially T. Peisker on the Asiatic Background). For
Attila, see next extract. Gibbon, ch. xxvi.

The Huns have been but lightly touched on in old records.
They live beyond the Sea of Azov, by the frozen Ocean, and their
barbarity passes all bounds. From their earliest childhood, babies'
faces are deeply scored with steel and these puckered scars slow
down the growth of hair that comes with adolescence. So they
grow up beardless, but without any charm, like eunuchs. All
have strong, well-knit limbs and sturdy necks, and are so appal-
lingly misshapen and deformed that you would take them for
animals standing on two legs, or for the posts crudely fashioned
into images which are used for the balustrades of bridges.

They may be horribly ugly as men, but they are so tough in their way of life that they have no need of fire or of good-tasting food. Their diet consists of the roots of wild plants and half-raw meat from some animal or other. They warm this meat up a little by putting it between their thighs and the backs of their horses. They never live in houses, which they avoid like tombs set apart from common use. You cannot even find among them a hut roofed over with reeds, but they wander and roam through the mountains and woods, and from their cradles have grown accustomed to bearing with frost, hunger and thirst. They never enter strangers' houses, unless forced by dire necessity, for they feel no safety in being under a roof.

They wear clothes made of linen or the skins of wood-mice, and the same dress serves them inside and outside the home. Once a tunic of some dull colour has been put over their necks, it is not taken off or changed until it is in tatters and has shredded into rags from the constant use. They cover their heads with round caps, and their hairy legs in goat-skins. Their shoes are not fashioned on lasts, and this prevents them from walking freely. This means that they are not very adept at infantry battles.

They are almost glued to their horses, which are sturdy but ugly creatures. They sometimes sit on them side-saddle to perform their usual tasks. It is on horseback that all Huns remain day and night, to buy and sell, to eat and drink, and, leaning forward on the narrow necks of their mounts, they collapse into a sleep deep enough to allow all manner of dreams. It is on horseback too that they all consult together when any discussion arises about some important matter.

They are disciplined by no king, but are content with the wild leadership of chiefs under whom they burst through any obstacle. When provoked to battle they enter the fight in wedge formation with horrible discordant yells. They are lightly armed for speed and surprise, and so they suddenly disperse on purpose for the assault. Charging in no definite ranks, they rush around dealing out widespread slaughter. You will never catch them attacking earthworks or hurling their javelins at enemy camps because of their preoccupation with speed. They easily earn the reputation thereby of being the fiercest warriors on earth. Their missiles are hurled from a distance and instead of arrow tips have sharpened bones fastened on most cleverly. Then they gallop over the intervening ground, and, reckless of their own lives, use their swords in hand-to-hand combat. While their opponents are on their guard against sword-thrusts, they lasso them with twisted nooses and by enmeshing their limbs make them totally incapable of riding or walking.

No one ever ploughs or touches a plough among them, for the whole people wanders about without fixed abode, with no homestead, no laws, no habitual diet. They always look like fugitives, as they travel with the wagons in which they live. In these wagons, their wives weave their coarse garments, have intercourse with their husbands, and give birth to their children whom they bring up to puberty. None of them, if asked, can tell you where he comes from, for he was conceived in one place, born in another far away, and brought up in a third yet more distant spot.

They are faithless and inconstant in observing truce, wafted on the faintest breeze of any new hope, and give their all to utter violence and madness. Like senseless animals, they are completely ignorant of the distinction between right and wrong, and in parleys they are ambiguous and deceitful, bound by no reverence for religion or superstition. Gold enflames their desires inordinately. They are so changeable and easily angered that they are often estranged from friends more than once on the same day, although there is no cause for annoyance, and are reconciled again, although no one brings them together.

DINNER WITH ATTILA
c. A.D. 450

Attila became king of the Huns in 445. During the brief time he led his people, until his death in 453, he rightly earned the title 'Scourge of God'. For a time, as this extract shows, the Romans hoped to make an alliance with him. But his invasion of France in 451 brought about a union between the Romans and Goths which defeated him near Châlons. Priscus, whose works only survive in fragments, went on an embassy to Attila on behalf of the Eastern Empire. His visit coincided with a party from Rome.

Source: Priscus in *Historici Graeci Minores* (ed. Dindorf), p. 315.

Further Reading: C. D. Gordon, *The Age of Attila—5th Century Byzantium and the Barbarians*, gives a general treatment. Chapters x and xii in *C.M.H.* vol. I, and Gibbon, ch. xxxiv, are also useful and entertaining.

When we had returned to our tent, Orestes' father came to say that Attila invited both parties of us to dine with him about 3 o'clock that afternoon. We waited for the time of the invitation, and then all of us, the envoys from the Western Romans as well, presented ourselves in the doorway facing Attila. In accordance with the national custom the cupbearers gave us a cup for us to make our libations before we took our seats. When that had been done and we had sipped the wine, we went to the chairs where we would sit to have dinner. All the seats were ranged down either side of the room, up against the walls. In the middle Attila was sitting on a couch with a second couch behind him. Behind that a few steps led up to his bed, which for decorative purposes was covered in ornate drapes made of fine linen, like those which Greeks and Romans prepare for marriage ceremonies. I think that the more distinguished guests were on Attila's right, and the second rank on his left, where we were with Berichos, a man of some renown among the Scythians, who was sitting in front of us. Onegesios was to the right of Attila's couch, and opposite him were two of the king's sons on chairs. The eldest son was sitting on Attila's own couch, right on the very edge, with his eyes fixed on the ground in fear of his father.

When all were sitting properly in order, a cupbearer came to offer Attila an ivy-wood bowl of wine, which he took and drank a toast to the man first in order of precedence. The man thus honoured rose to his feet and it was not right for him to sit down again until Attila had drunk some or all of the wine and had handed the goblet back to the attendant. The guests, taking their own cups, then honoured him in the same way, sipping the wine after making the toast. One attendant went round to each man in strict order after Attila's personal cupbearer had gone out.

When the second guest and then all the others in their turn had been honoured, Attila greeted us in like fashion in our order of seating.

After everyone had been toasted, the cupbearers left, and a table was put in front of Attila and other tables for groups of three or four men each. This enabled each guest to help himself to the things put on the table without leaving his proper seat. Attila's servant entered first with plates full of meat, and those waiting on all the others put bread and cooked food on the tables. A lavish meal, served on silver trenchers, was prepared for us and the other barbarians, but Attila just had some meat on a wooden platter, for this was one aspect of his self-discipline. For instance, gold or silver cups were presented to the other diners, but his own goblet was made of wood. His clothes, too, were simple, and no trouble was taken except to have them clean. The sword that hung by his side, the clasps of his barbarian shoes and the bridle of his horse were all free from gold, precious stones or other valuable decorations affected by the other Scythians. When the food in the first plates was finished we all got up, and no one, once on his feet, returned to his seat until he had, in the same order as before, drunk the full cup of wine that he was handed, with a toast for Attila's health. After this honour had been paid him, we sat down again and second plates were put on each table with other food on them. This also finished, everyone rose once more, drank another toast and resumed his seat.

As twilight came on torches were lit, and two barbarians entered before Attila to sing some songs they had composed, telling of his victories and his valour in war. The guests paid close attention to them, and some were delighted with the songs, others excited at being reminded of the wars, but others broke down and wept if their bodies were weakened by age and their warrior spirits forced to remain inactive. After the songs a Scythian entered, a crazy fellow who told a lot of strange and completely false stories, not a word of truth in them, which made everyone laugh. Following him came the moor, Zerkon, totally disorganized in appearance, clothes, voice and words. By mixing up the languages of the Italians with those of the Huns and Goths, he fascinated everyone and made them break out into uncontrollable laughter, all that is except Attila. He remained impassive, without any change of expression, and neither by word or gesture did he seem to share in the merriment except that when his youngest son, Ernas, came in and stood by him, he drew the boy towards him and looked at him with gentle eyes. I was surprised that he paid no attention to his other sons, and only had time for this one. But the barbarian at my side, who understood Italian and what I had said about the boy, warned me not to speak up, and said that the seers had told Attila that his family would be banished but would be restored by this son. After spending most of the night at the party, we left, having no wish to pursue the drinking any further.

THEODORIC II
c. A.D. 460

The Visigoths, under Alaric, had captured Rome in 410. After some years of conflict they were given lands in Gaul and accepted as allies. Careful diplomacy secured the alliance of the Visigoths for Rome in her struggle against Attila in 451, when their king, Theodoric I, lost his life. Theodoric II, after murdering his eldest brother, became king in 453. He must not be confused with Theodoric the Great, the Ostrogoth, who was responsible for many of the fine churches and mosaics at Ravenna. Apollinaris Sidonius, a poet and letter-writer, visited Theodoric's court at Toulouse about 460, and his description gives an interesting account of the mixture of Roman and barbarian culture. The game he describes must have resembled backgammon or 'Sorry', but the exact nature is unknown and so some of the terms must remain uncertain.

Source: Sidonius, *Letters*, I, 2.

Further Reading: Loeb translation by W. B. Anderson. See *C.M.H.* vol. I, ch. x, and Gibbon, ch. xxxvi. *The Churches of Ravenna* by G. Bovini contains fine reproductions of mosaics at Ravenna.

. . . At lunch, which on non-festal days is just like that of an ordinary citizen, no panting attendant heaps a mass of unpolished, tarnished silver on the sagging tables. The only thing weighty is the conversation, for serious topics alone are discussed. The furniture consists of couches draped sometimes in purple cloth and sometimes in linen. The attraction of the food lies in its skilful preparation, not in its expensive nature, and the plates are well polished but light in weight. Cups and bowls of wine are passed round at long intervals, which gives the thirsty grounds for complaint but does not make the drunk refrain. In short, you can see there the elegance of Greece, the plenty of Gaul and the directness of Italy, a mixture of public show, private care and regal control. I think that I can omit mentioning the luxury of feast days, for even unremarkable people cannot fail to remark this.

But to return to how he spends his day. After his appetite is satisfied, he sometimes takes a midday nap, but it is always short. Whenever he finds himself drawn to the gaming-board, he gathers the dice quickly, looks at them carefully, rolls them shrewdly and throws them seriously. He talks them into coming out right and watches patiently to see what they will give him. He says nothing when a throw is good, and just smiles when it is bad; neither makes him angry or lose his philosophical calm. Second throws cause him no concern, but he never makes them himself; if the chance arises, he rejects it, while he ignores it if employed against him. He is not upset if an opponent's piece escapes, and he extricates his own pieces without help from the other side. He is so intent on winning that you would think that he was touching weapons, not pieces in a game.

During a game, he relaxes his royal aloofness, and encourages free and friendly participation. If the truth were to be told, his main fear is that he causes fear in others. He is delighted when defeated opponents are annoyed, and he is only finally satisfied that a game has not been thrown when another's anger makes him sure of the genuineness of his victory. What is surprising is that the pleasure which comes from these petty amusements has a good effect on important matters of business. Requests may have been tossed aside and their supporters wrecked, but now the harbour of a quick release is reached. When I have had some request to make, I have been happy to lose a game, for the loss of a game means the gaining of my cause. . . .

THE CAREER OF BELISARIUS
A.D. 540

The name of Justinian is rightly associated in the first place with his work on Roman Law, which has become the basis of most of the European legal codes. But he was also the last Emperor who spoke Latin and the last to make a concerted effort to restore the unity of the. whole Empire, West and East. In this project he made use of Belisarius, a devoted servant and a considerable general. Belisarius conquered the Vandals in Africa and then moved to Italy where he overcame the Ostrogoths and took Ravenna, the chief town of the Ostrogoth Theodoric who had died in 526. Justinian did much to beautify Ravenna, and was the founder of Hagia Sophia in Constantinople. Procopius travelled with Belisarius on his campaigns and was well able to describe his triumphs.

Source: Procopius, *History of the Wars,* VII, 1. His *Secret History* gives a very different picture of Belisarius and the whole court, but it seems to have been written in spite.

Further Reading: Loeb translation by B. H. Dewing. *C.M.H.* vol. I, ch. xv, and vol. II, chs. i and ii. Gibbon, chs. xli and xliv (Justinian).

So Belisarius reached Byzantium with all the treasure. Vittigis, other Gothic nobles and the children of Ildibadus were with him, as well as Ildiger, Balerian, Martin and Herodian. The Emperor Justinian was delighted to see Vittigis and his wife, and the physical beauty and size of all the barbarians filled him with wonder. He received the marvellous treasure of Theodoric in the Palace, and put it on display for members of the Council to see privately, overcome with jealousy at the size of the achievement. So he did not show it in public nor did he allow Belisarius a triumph, as he had when the latter returned from the conquest of Gelimer and the Vandals. But he won the admiration of all the common citizens; he had won two victories of a nature unparalleled in any one general in history, he had brought two kings as prisoners to Byzantium, he had gained for the Romans the unexpected spoil of the family and wealth of Gizeric and Theodoric, the most famous of all barbarian kings, providing the enemy's treasure for the state. In short, in a very few years, in campaigns on land and sea, he saved for the Empire about one half of its total area. The people of Byzantium were glad to see Belisarius walking daily in the forum on his way to and from his home, and no one could have too much of the sight. His passage seemed like a mighty procession, since a crowd of Vandals, Goths and Moors always followed him. Physically, too, he was outstandingly gifted, a large man and attractive, though he made himself so affable and easy to approach by any chance acquaintance that he seemed more like a really poor, humble fellow.

Neither his troops nor the country-folk could fight against the love which they felt for his command. Towards his men, he was the most generous of leaders. He relieved the wounds of those who had met with mishap in an engagement with large sums of money, and he offered prizes of bracelets and necklaces to those who had done well, while if any of his soldiers had lost horse, bow or anything else in battle, he immediately got a replacement from Belisarius. He won his good name from the rustics because he showed such forbearance and forethought that under his command nothing was ever forced from them, and all those on whom the mass of the army was billeted found themselves unexpectedly enriched, for they received payment at their own prices for everything. When the crops were ripe, he took special steps to prevent the cavalry from harming anything as it rode by. Permission was always refused to touch any of the ripe fruit on the trees. Self-control was his particular claim. He never touched a woman except his wedded wife, and though he captured from the Vandals and Goths a great number of women of great beauty, the like of which no one had previously seen, he did not allow any of them to come into his sight or to meet him in any other way. In addition to everything else he was pre-eminently sharp of mind and capable of forming excellent plans even for impossible situations. In the dangers of war, he mixed courage and caution, boldness with reason, sharpness and care in every encounter with the enemy as occasion demanded. Apart from that he displayed a mind that was confident in trouble and rose above the chaos of the events, and in success he was not puffed up or vain at his triumph. No one ever saw Belisarius drunk.   .

For as long as he commanded the Roman armies in Libya and Italy, he went on winning and gaining everything before him.

On his recall to Byzantium, his merit was recognized even more than it had been before. Every virtue was his. He had the power that comes with great wealth and he excelled all the generals of his day in the number of his bodyguard and spearmen, all of which naturally inspired fear in officers and men alike. No one, I fancy, dared to resist an order of his, and they never refused to carry out successfully any command he gave, respecting his virtue and fearing his power. . . .

Belisarius, then, as mentioned, had a mighty reputation and outstanding mental ability; his plans were formed to benefit the Emperor's affairs and carried out with a mind of his own. Other generals, being more on a par with each other and only thinking of their personal gain in their conduct of operations, began to plunder the Romans and to subject the citizens to the will of the soldiers, never considering their duty or keeping the troops obedient to their commands. So they made many mistakes, and in a very short time the whole Roman Empire fell down in ruins about them.

GLOSSARY

Acropolis: The hill or mound on which stood the citadel of a Greek city. In this book used only of Athens, and containing the famous buildings built in the time of Pericles.

Agora: The centre of any Greek city; the equivalent of the Roman *Forum*. Public buildings and markets were grouped together in it.

Archon: The leading politician in many Greek states. In Athens, there were nine archons, but one was nominally supreme, and years were known from his name.

Capitol: One of the 'Seven Hills' of Rome. On it stood the Citadel and also the most important Temple to Juppiter.

Censor: A public figure at Rome, of whom two were appointed every five years. Their main duties were to carry out a Census and to keep a check on public morality, especially of the Senate.

Centurion: The commander of a CENTURY (*q.v.*). The equivalent of an N.C.O.

Century: A unit of the Roman army, nominally 100 strong, but usually numbering about sixty.

Circus Maximus: The largest arena in Rome, used chiefly for chariot-races.

Cohort: A unit of the Roman army, comprising six centuries.

Consul: The most important political figure in Rome. Two consuls were elected annually from 510 B.C. They were commanders-in-chief of the army and had special rights in the Senate.

Council: Word used for the Athenian *Boule*, a council of 500 members, elected annually by lot. Their duties were of an advisory and administrative nature.

Delian League: The league based on the sacred island of Delos after the defeat of the Persians in 479 B.C. The League was gradually taken over by Athens.

Dictator: A Roman official, originally appointed for a maximum of six months in times of national emergency. Later it lost this meaning, but dictators retained the wide powers previously given.

Duty Tribe: The Council at Athens was composed of 50 members of each of the 10 Tribes. Each tribe was immediately responsible for sudden decisions for one-tenth of the year. On page 59 it is called the Cabinet.

Equestrian Order: The members of this order were called the *Equites* or Knights. They were the top financial class at Rome, and were responsible for tax-collecting, etc.

Forum: The centre of any Roman city; the equivalent of the Greek *Agora*. The Forum at Rome lay beneath the Capitol and contained the law courts and the main platform for public speaking.

Helots: The serf population of Sparta. Most of the Helots originally came from Sparta's western neighbours, Messenia.

Hoplites: The heavy-armed Greek infantry.

Imperator: A Latin word meaning General. It was only used if victorious troops acclaimed their general. Later it became almost synonymous with Emperor.

Knights: See EQUESTRIAN ORDER.

Long Walls: A pair of defensive walls which connected Athens with her port at Peiraeus.

Ostrogoths: One of the two divisions of the Goths, named *Ostro-* (or Eastern) from a former territory east of the Visigoths (or Western Goths).

Patricians: A technical term at Rome for the descendants of a certain number of old families. The number of such families could only be increased by a king.

Peiraeus: The port of Athens, about five miles from the Acropolis.

Pontifex Maximus: The most important religious figure at Rome. The title was later taken over by the Popes.

Praetor: A Roman official, responsible for the administration of justice. Praetors were often appointed governors of small provinces.

Praetorian Guard: The only soldiers legally allowed south of the River Rubicon. They were stationed in the Praetorian Camp at Rome. They and their commander (Prefect) exercised considerable influence on the appointment of Emperors.

Principate: Another name for the Roman Empire. Emperors often preferred to be called *Princeps* or *First Citizen*.

Sacred Way: The road leading from the Tiber, through the Forum and up to the Capitol. The road passed under the Triumphal Arches, three of which still stand.

Satraps: The governors of provinces in the Persian Empire.

Senate: The deliberative council at Rome. Decrees of the Senate, though not legally binding unless ratified by the people, often had the force of law.

Stoa: An open colonnade.

Stoicism: A philosophy named after the meeting-place (Stoa) of its founders. Stoicism was a metaphysical philosophy maintaining that all things on earth participated in what they called *Mind*. On death, humans would be reunited with this universal *Mind* and would find it difficult if sullied by unclean lives.

Tribune: A Roman official originally elected to look after the interests of the common people. Later they became political leaders.

Trireme: The most common type of oared boat. The exact nature of the arrangement of the oars is uncertain, but they were presumably in three banks of some sort.

Triumvir: A member of a commission of three. Triumvirates might be appointed for many purposes, but the term is most famously applied to two groups (Caesar, Pompey, Crassus, and Antony, Octavian, Lepidus) whose interests were purely political.

Visigoths: One of the two divisions of the Goths, named *Visi-* (or Western) from a former territory west of the Ostrogoths (or Eastern Goths).

Date	MAIN EVENTS IN GREECE	Pages
1600 B.C. | 1200	Greek-speaking Hellenes enter Greece, overcome Crete (*c.* 1450) and Troy (*c.* 1200).	1–2
1200 | 800	Invasion of Dorians from the North. Dark Ages. Art of writing forgotten.	
800 | 600	Emergence of city-states. Colonization and trade flourish with Oriental influences. Commercial tyrants replace family despotisms.	2–5
600 | 479	Sparta and Athens rise to outshine Corinth. Sparta develops isolationist policy. Athens undergoes democratic reforms. Greece unites to repel Persian invasions (490 and 480–79).	5–10
479 | 431	Athens dominant. Creation of Athenian Empire. Golden Age of Arts and Literature.	10–16
431 | 404	So-called Peloponnesian War between Athens and Sparta. Sparta victorious.	16–44
404 | 371	Sparta dominant, but weakened by her intolerance and. an Athens-Thebes alliance.	44–54
371 | 360	Thebes dominant under Pelopidas and Epaminondas. Rise of federalisms throughout Greece.	55–58
359 | 323	Philip of Macedon overcomes Greece by diplomacy and war. His son Alexander conquers Persian Empire (334–323), and founds Alexandria in Egypt (332).	58–63
323 | 199	Successors of Alexander divide his Empire, e.g. Ptolemy in Egypt. Struggles between them and several large leagues now forming in Greece.	63–75
199 | 146	Entry of Rome by invitation into Greece. Macedonia, because of rebellion, made a Roman province in 146.	75–78 83–84
146 | 27	All Greece under Roman control after destruction of Corinth in 146. Achaia (S. Greece) made a Roman province in 27.	

Date	MAIN EVENTS IN ROME	*Pages*
753 B.C. | 510	Monarchy at Rome. History mainly mythical.	
510 | 275	Gradual expansion of Rome under increasingly democratic Republic until, by 275 B.C., she controlled all Italy south of the Po valley.	
275 | 202	Rome victorious over Carthage at sea (264–241) and on land against Hannibal (218–202). Gains Sicily, Sardinia and Corsica.	69–70
202 | 133	Expansion outside Italy by gaining Spain, Greece and Tunisia. Start of Roman literature under Greek influences.	75 78–86
133 | 31	Intermittent Civil War. Age of the big generals—Sulla *v.* Marius, Caesar *v.* Pompey, Antony *v.* Octavian. External expansion to Turkey, Syria, Egypt, Crete, Cyrenaica and France.	86–124
31 | A.D. 180	Emperors at Rome start with Augustus. The great period of the Empire. External expansion stops at Britain, Rhine, Danube and the desert. At home, wealth and luxury increase, but stability depends on who is emperor.	125–187
180 | 313	Less able emperors and more struggles for power. Persecution of Christians ends with Constantine's proclamation of religious toleration.	187–200
313 | 410	Final stages of Western Empire. More power switched to newly-founded Constantinople. Rome sacked by Alaric the Goth.	200–202
410 | 565	Eastern Empire faces invasions of Huns, and, under Justinian (died 565), recovers Italy from barbarians for the last time.	202–209

THE EARLY EMPERORS OF ROME

Augustus	27 B.C.–A.D. 14
Tiberius	14– 37
Gaius (Caligula)	37– 41
Claudius	41– 54
Nero	54– 68
Galba, Otho, Vitellius	68– 69
Vespasian	69– 79
Titus	79– 81
Domitian	81– 96
Nerva	96– 98
Trajan	98–117
Hadrian	117–138
Antoninus Pius	138–161
Marcus Aurelius	161–180
Commodus	180–193
Pertinax, Julianus, Niger	193
Septimius Severus	193–211
Caracalla, Geta	211–217
Macrinus, Diadumenianus	217
Elagabulus	218–222
Alexander Severus	222–235
Maximinus	235–237
Diocletian	284–305
Constantine the Great	306–337
(often with partners)	
Honorius (in the West)	395–424
Arcadius (in the East)	395–408

Emperors continue in both East and West until the last Western Emperor:

Romulus Augustulus	475–476
Justinian	527–565

GREECE

ITALY AND SICILY

THE

INDEX